Reader's Guide
to
JOHN KEATS

Reader's Guide to JOHN KEATS

W. Cormier

CENTRUM PRESS
NEW DELHI-110002 (INDIA)

CENTRUM PRESS
H.O.: 4360/4, Ansari Road, Daryaganj,
New Delhi-110 002 (India)
Ph.: 23278000, 23261597

B.O.: No. 1015, Ist Main Road, BSK IIIrd Stage
IIIrd Phase, IIIrd Block,
Bangalore - 560 085 (India)
Tel.: 080-41723429
Visit us at: www.centrumpress.com

Reader's Guide to John Keats

First Edition, 2009

ISBN 978-93-80106-73-1

PRINTED IN INDIA

Printed at Balaji Offset, Delhi.

Contents

Preface

John Keats, renowned poet of the English Romantic Movement, wrote some of the greatest English language poems. John Keats was born on 31 October 1795 in Moorgate, London, England, the first child born to Frances Jennings (b.1775-d.1810) and Thomas Keats (d.1804), an employee of a livery stable. He had three siblings: George (1797-1841), Thomas (1799-1818), and Frances Mary "Fanny" (1803-1889).

After leaving school in Enfield, Keats went on to apprentice with Dr. Hammond, a surgeon in Edmonton. After his father died in a riding accident, and his mother died of tuberculosis, John and his brothers moved to Hampstead. It was here that Keats met Charles Armitage Brown (1787-1842) who would become a great friend. Much grieved by his death, Brown worked for many years on his memoir and biography, *Life of John Keats* (1841). In it Brown claims that it was not until Keats read Edmund Spencer's *Faery Queen* that he realised his own gift for the poetic. Keats was an avid student in the fields of medicine and natural history, but he then turned his attentions to the literary works of such authors as William Shakespeare and Geoffrey Chaucer.

Keats had his poems published in the magazines of the day at the encouragement of many including James Henry Leigh Hunt Esq. (1784-1859), editor of the *Examiner* and to whom Keats dedicated his first collection *Poems* (1817). Having worked on it for many months, Keats finished his epic poem comprising four books, *Endymion: A Poetic Romance—"A thing of beauty is a joy for ever"*—in 1818. John Keats died on 23 February 1821 in Rome, Italy, and now rests in the Protestant Cemetery in Rome, by the pyramid of Caius Cestius, near his friend Shelley.

Author

Chapter 1

Introduction

John Keats was an English poet who became one of the principal poets of the English Romantic movement during the early nineteenth century. During his short life, his work received constant critical attacks from periodicals of the day, but his posthumous influence on poets such as Alfred Tennyson has been immense.

Elaborate word choice and sensual imagery characterize Keats's poetry, including a series of odes that were his masterpieces and which remain among the most popular poems in English literature. Keats's letters, which expound on his aesthetic theory of "negative capability", are among the most celebrated by any writer.

LIFE

John Keats was born in 1795 at 85 Moorgate in London, England, where his father, Thomas Keats, was an hostler. The pub is now called 'Keats at the Globe', only a few yards from Moorgate station. Keats was baptised at St Botolph-without-Bishopsgate and lived happily for the first seven years of his life. The beginnings of his troubles occurred in 1804, when his father died of a fractured skull after falling from his horse. A year later, in 1805, Keats' grandfather died. His mother, Frances Jennings Keats, remarried soon afterwards, but quickly left the new husband and moved herself and her four children (a son had died in infancy) to live with Keats's grandmother, Alice Jennings.

There, Keats attended a school that first instilled a love of literature in him. In 1810, however, his mother died of tuberculosis, leaving him and his siblings in the custody of their grandmother.

Keats's grandmother appointed two guardians to take care of her new "charges", and these guardians removed Keats from his old school to become a surgeon's apprentice at Thomas Hammond's apothecary shop in Edmonton (now part of the London Borough of Enfield). This continued until 1814, when, after a fight with his master, he left his apprenticeship and became a student at Guy's Hospital (now part of King's College London, University of London). During that year, he devoted more and more of his time to the study of literature. Keats traveled to the Isle of Wight in the spring of 1819, where he spent a week. Later that year he stayed in Winchester. It was here that Keats wrote Isabella, St. Agnes' Eve and Lamia. Parts of Hyperion and the five-act poetic tragedy Otho The Great were also written in Winchester.

Following the death of his grandmother, he soon found his brother, Tom Keats, entrusted to his care. Tom was suffering, as his mother had, from tuberculosis. Finishing his epic poem "Endymion", Keats left to work in Scotland and Ireland with his friend Charles Armitage Brown. However, he too began to show signs of tuberculosis infection on that trip, and returned prematurely. When he did, he found that Tom's condition had deteriorated, and that *Endymion* had, as had *Poems* before it, been the target of much abuse from the critics. On 1 December 1818, Tom Keats died of his disease, and John Keats moved again, to live in Brown's house in Hampstead, next to Hampstead Heath. There he lived next door to Fanny Brawne, who had been staying there with her mother. He then quickly fell in love with Fanny. However, it was overall an unhappy affair for the poet; Keats's ardour for her seemed to bring him more vexation than comfort. The later (posthumous) publication of their correspondence was to scandalise Victorian society. In the diary of Fanny Brawne was found only one sentence regarding the separation: "Mr. Keats has left Hampstead." Fanny's letters to Keats were, as the poet had requested, destroyed upon his death. However, in 1937, a collection of 31 letters, written by Fanny Brawne to Keats's sister, Frances, were published by Oxford University Press. While these letters revealed the depth of Brawne's feelings toward Keats and in many ways attempted to redeem her rather promiscuous reputation, it is arguable whether or not they succeeded.

This relationship was cut short when, by 1820, Keats began showing serious signs of tuberculosis, the disease that had plagued his family. On the suggestion of his doctors, he left the cold airs of London behind and moved to Italy with his friend Joseph Severn. Keats moved into a house, which is now a museum that is dedicated to his life and work, The Keats-Shelley House, on the Spanish Steps, in Rome, where despite attentive care from Severn and Dr. John Clark, the poet's health rapidly deteriorated. He died in 1821 and was buried in the Protestant Cemetery, Rome. His last request was to be buried under a tombstone reading, "Here lies One Whose Name were writ in Water." His name was not to appear on the stone. Despite these requests, however, Severn and Brown also added the epitaph: "This Grave contains all that was mortal, of a Young English Poet, who on his Death Bed, in the Bitterness of his heart, at the Malicious Power of his enemies, desired these words to be Engraven on his Tomb Stone" along with the image of a lyre with broken strings.

Shelley blamed his death on an article published shortly before in the *Quarterly Review*, with a scathing attack on Keats's *Endymion*. The offending article was long believed to have been written by William Gifford, though later shown to be the work of John Wilson Croker. Keats's death inspired Shelley to write the poem *Adonais*.'; Byron later composed a short poem on this theme using the phrase "snuffed out by an article." However Byron, far less admiring of Keats's poetry than Shelley and generally more cynical in nature, was here probably just as much poking fun at Shelley's interpretation as he was having a dig at his old fencing partners the critics. The largest collection of Keats's letters, manuscripts, and other papers is in the Houghton Library at Harvard University. Other collections of such material can be found at the British Library; Keats House, Hampstead; The Keats-Shelley House, Rome;

and the Pierpont Morgan Library in New York. Keats is also a distant relative of the Metaphysical poet, John Donne.

WORKS

- Addressed to Haydon (1816) text
- Addressed to the Same (1816) text
- After dark vapours have oppressed our plains (1817)
- As from the darkening gloom a silver dove (1814)
- Asleep! O sleep a little while, white pearl! text
- A Song About Myself
- Bards of Passion and of Mirth text
- Before he went to live with owls and bats (1817?)
- Bright star, would I were stedfast as thou art (1819)
- Calidore: A Fragment (1816)
- The Day Is Gone, And All Its Sweets Are Gone
- Dedication. To Leigh Hunt, Esq.
- A Dream, After Reading Dante's Episode Of Paolo And Francesca text
- A Draught of Sunshine
- Endymion: A Poetic Romance (1817)
- Epistle to John Hamilton Reynolds
- Epistle to My Brother George
- The Eve of Saint Mark
- The Eve of St. Agnes (1819) text
- The Fall of Hyperion: A Dream (1817)
- Fancy (poem)
- Fill for me a brimming bowl (1814) text
- Fragment of an Ode to Maia
- Give me women, wine, and snuff (1815 or 1816)
- God of the golden bow (1816 or 1817)
- The Gothic looks solemn (1817)
- Had I a man's fair form, then might my sighs (1815 or 1816)
- Hadst thou liv'd in days of old (1816)
- Happy is England! I could be content (1816)
- Harlem Blues (1817)
- Hither, hither, love (1817 or 1818)
- How many bards gild the lapses of time (1816)

- The Human Seasons
- Hymn To Apollo
- Hyperion (1818)
- I am as brisk (1816)
- I had a dove
- I stood tip-toe upon a little hill (1816)
- If By Dull Rhymes Our English Must Be Chain'd
- Imitation of Spenser (1814) text
- In Drear-Nighted December
- Isabella or The Pot of Basil (1818) text
- Keen, fitful gusts are whisp'ring here and there (1816)
- La Belle Dame sans Merci (1819) text
- Lamia (1819)
- Lines Written on 29 May, the Anniversary of Charles's Restoration, on Hearing the Bells Ringing (1814 or 1815)
- Lines on Seeing a Lock of Milton's Hair
- Lines on The Mermaid Tavern
- Meg Merrilies
- Modern Love (Keats)
- O Blush Not So!
- O come, dearest Emma! the rose is full blown (1815)
- O grant that like to Peter I (1817?)
- O Solitude! if I must with thee dwell (1815 or 1816)
- Ode (Keats)
- Ode on a Grecian Urn (1819) text
- Ode on Indolence (1819)
- Ode on Melancholy (1819) text
- Ode to a Nightingale (1819) text
- Ode to Apollo (1815)
- Ode to Fanny
- Ode to Psyche (1819)
- Oh Chatterton! how very sad thy fate (1815)
- Oh! how I love, on a fair summer's eve (1816)
- Old Meg (1818)
- On a Leander Which Miss Reynolds, My Kind Friend, Gave Me (1817)
- On Death

- On Fame text
- On First Looking into Chapman's Homer (1816) text
- On Leaving Some Friends at an Early Hour (1816)
- On Peace (1814) text
- On Receiving a Curious Shell, and a Copy of Verses, from the Same Ladies (1815)
- On Receiving a Laurel Crown from Leigh Hunt (1816 or 1817)
- On Seeing the Elgin Marbles (1817)
- On Sitting Down to Read King Lear Once Again
- On the Grasshopper and Cricket (1816)
- On the Sea (1817) text
- On The Story of Rimini (1817)
- On The Sonnet
- The Poet (a fragment)
- A Prophecy - To George Keats in America
- Robin Hood. To A Friend
- Sharing Eve's Apple
- Sleep and Poetry (1816)
- A Song of Opposites
- Specimen of an Induction to a Poem (1816)
- Staffa
- Stay, ruby breasted warbler, stay (1814)
- Stanzas
- Think not of it, sweet one, so (1817)
- This Living Hand
- This pleasant tale is like a little copse (1817)
- To a Friend Who Sent Me Some Roses (1816)
- To a Lady seen for a few Moments at Vauxhall
- To A Young Lady Who Sent Me A Laurel Crown (1816 or 1817)
- To Ailsa Rock
- To Autumn (1819) text
- To Lord Byron (1814) text
- To Charles Cowden Clarke (1816)
- To Fanny
- To G.A.W. (Georgiana Augusta Wylie) (1816)
- To George Felton Mathew (1815)

- To Georgiana Augusta Wylie
- To Haydon
- To Haydon with a Sonnet Written on Seeing the Elgin Marbles (1817)
- To Homer
- To Hope (1815)
- To John Hamilton Reynolds
- To Kosciusko (1816)
- To Leigh Hunt, Esq. (1817)
- To My Brother George (epistle) (1816)
- To My Brother George (sonnet) (1816)
- To My Brothers (1816)
- To one who has been long in city pent (1816)
- To Sleep
- To Solitude
- To Some Ladies (1815)
- To the Ladies Who Saw Me Crown'd (1816 or 1817)
- To the Nile
- Two Sonnets on Fame
- Unfelt, unheard, unseen (1817)
- When I have fears that I may cease to be (1818) text
- Where Be Ye Going, You Devon Maid?
- Where's the Poet?
- Why did I laugh tonight?
- Woman! when I behold thee flippant, vain (1815 or 1816)
- Written in Disgust of Vulgar Superstition (1816)
- Written on a Blank Space
- Written on a Summer Evening
- Written on the Day that Mr Leigh Hunt Left Prison (1815)
- Written Upon the Top of Ben Nevis
- You say you love; but with a voice (1817 or 1818)

ADDITIONAL WORKS

- *The Complete Poetical Works and Letters of John Keats*, ed. Horace Elisha Scudder, Boston: Riverside Press (1899) full text available through Google Books

- *The Complete Poetical Works of John Keats,* ed. H. Buxton Forman. Oxford University Press (1907) full text available through Google Books
- *The Letters of John Keats, 1814-1821, Volumes 1 and 2,* ed. Hyder Edward Rollins, Harvard University Press (1958)
- *The Poems of John Keats,* ed. Jack Stillinger, Harvard University Press (1978)
- *Complete Poems,* ed. Jack Stillinger, Harvard University Press (1982)
- *John Keats: Poetry Manuscripts at Harvard, a Facsimile Edition,* ed. Jack Stillinger, Harvard University Press (1990)
- *Selected Letters of John Keats,* ed. Grant F. Scott, Harvard University Press (2002)
- Poetry as Enforcement: Conquering the Muse in Keats's 'Ode to Psyche'

Often dismissed as considerably inferior to the subsequent Spring odes of 1819 and 'To Autumn', Keats's 'Ode to Psyche' has not received as much critical attention as it deserves. Yet, in order to gain a fuller insight into the astonishing advancement of Keats's poetic powers at that stage of his writing career, one cannot afford to ignore this remarkably self-revealing composition. I believe that the 'Ode to Psyche' illustrates in a pertinent way how Keats recovered his self-confidence as a poet, literally found his Muse and, what is even more important, managed to secure her constant presence.

This appropriation of the Muse, however, presupposes a virility in the poet which is traditionally not associated with Keats. Many critics indeed tend to ascribe an effeminacy of character to the 'latest born' of the Romantic poets, whilst his writings are repeatedly conceived of as abounding in a tasteless kind of affectation. The reference in the *Encyclopaedia Britannica* of 1857 to his 'style of babyish effeminacy' characterised by a 'nauseous sweetness', still reverberates in a considerable number of modern literary studies.

In this respect, Susan Wolfson has rightly pointed out that Keats's works are envisaged as a singularly gratifying study object by recent interpreters who treat the poet 'as an exception to, or anomaly within, a monolithically conceived "masculine" discourse'.

What many commentators fail to discern is the 'masculine' undercurrent in Keats's poems. By this I mean the tendencies stereotypically attributed to the male, as those inferred by Anne Mellor when she represents Keats 'in the traditionally feminine pose of passivity, indolence, waiting'. Evidently, Mellor does not regard this quality as carrying any negative imputations. Yet, it seems to me that in her attempts to revalue an aspect of Keats, she adheres to an inadequate but still widely adopted premiss.

A careful reading of Keats's oeuvre will reveal the presence of the often covert but nonetheless clearly recognisable urge, not for passivity, but for action and dominion instead, as well as a keen awareness of self-identity. The latter is again at odds with Mellor's conclusion that Keats's empathy, 'lack[ing] a strong sense of its own ego boundaries', can be defined as non-masculine. Lest there should be a misunderstanding of my argument, I hereby emphasise that I do not wish to imply that Keats is a worse or better poet because he is not that effeminate after all. I only want to rectify the still popular misconception of Keats as a pusillanimous poet exemplifying an effeminacy of character.

In this article, I will concentrate on the 'Ode to Psyche' as an example of a poem indicative of Keats's often neglected or misinterpreted (male) gender politics. More particularly, it is my intention to demonstrate that if the persona of the poet in Keats's 'Ode to Psyche' should, on the surface, appear to be rather effeminate and unmanly, this may only be a means, a very carefully constructed manoeuvre, to gain full possession of the goddess he desires. The poem shows how the poet, out of what has been called 'narcissistic similitude and involution', comes to annihilate the distinction between himself and the desired object, that is to say Psyche.

It is true that Keats attains such a unification with the goddess by feminising himself, but this empathic engagement will turn out to be no more than an intermediate stage in the process of subjecting the 'Bloomiest' (l. 36) of deities. I will argue that the poet only *temporarily* loses himself in another object so as to realise his masculine desire of self-possession and to reaffirm his identity. Indeed, the poet's fervent urge to possess Psyche also kindles his relentless and 'virile' endeavours to absorb her selfhood in a most radical manner.

This entails a complete displacement of Cupid, Psyche's 'legitimate' lover, after which the poet's own cannibalistic desire will virtually obliterate the goddess's identity. In other words, the consummation of his love results in the merciless consumption of the beloved. Through this absorption, the by then self-sufficient poet will be enabled both to beget and to give birth to a numerous offspring, i.e. his future poetic compositions. In this respect, the 'Ode to Psyche' is 'a true ode insofar as it becomes a celebration; it celebrates the authority of the poet's own voice'. This is in a nutshell, a crude paraphrase of the main argument I will try to elucidate in the next few pages. Keats, I repeat once more, was not an 'ideological transvestite' who 'positioned [himself] within the realm of the feminine gender'.

Having said this, it cannot be denied that from the onset of the ode, the poet's identity bears strong feminine connotations. The four opening lines seem to suggest that the poet has adopted the role of an ancient oracle, uttering prophesying 'numbers' (l. 1). The powerful and effective enjambment (wrung / By sweet enforcement), with its innuendo of physical rape, externalises the very process of divination and poetic frenzy. Prophesying is after all a considerably demanding task, leaving the oracle exhausted after each consultation.

Of all oracles in Antiquity, undoubtedly the most illustrious one operated in Delphi, where the sanctuary was devoted to Apollo, the god who features so dominantly in Keats's poetry. It will be remembered, however, that in this holy place the intermediary role between the divine and the mortal realm was fulfilled by priestesses. Keats may well have read in his Lemprière dictionary that at Delphi, 'the oracles were generally given in verse' (cf. 'numbers') and 'always delivered by a priestess called *Pythia* '. In line 48, the poet blatantly utters his desire to be Psyche's shrine and oracle, and, by implication, appears to assume a feminine role. One may here perhaps call to mind B. R. Haydon's description of Keats as a poet with 'an eye that had an inward look, perfectly divine, like a Delphian priestess who saw visions'. In his capacity of an obsequious soothsayer, then, the poet has been turned into a humanised version of the typically Romantic image of the aeolian harp, passively waiting for the wind to pluck its strings. But, as I will argue later on, this overtly submissive act might very well be interpreted as a highly ironic gesture.

In some degree affinitive to the mental state described as 'remembrance dear' (l. 2), the dreamlike trance during which the priestess mumbles inarticulate sounds, is carried on into the fifth line. The scene of Psyche and Cupid lying in a passionate embrace is presented as a divine revelation to the poet-gazer: 'Surely I dreamt to day; or did I see, / The winged Psyche'? The verb 'see' I believe to be of the utmost importance here. It certainly reinforces the oracular quality of Keats's *poeta vates* which, in this case, is materialised in the figure of a Delphic *Pythia* .

The poem continues with an immediate second reference to visual/visionary perception. When the poet sets eyes on the embracing couple, he faints with surprise, just like Psyche did when she discovered the true identity of her lover. In his poetry, Keats is often preoccupied with swooning, fainting, indolence, sleep, all of which are traditionally considered as predominantly feminine 'activities'. Consequently, Keats's 'Ode to Psyche' seems, so far, to be a perfect example of the feminised poet revelling in 'leafy luxury' ('To Leigh Hunt, Esq.', l. 13), overflowing himself and melting into the Other. This impression is even enhanced by the following few lines in the poem.

After the poet's apparent feminisation in the opening lines of the ode, there now occurs a meaningful merger of the poet-gazer and the goddess he desires. From a grammatical point of view, the poet's identification with Psyche is so intense that it is virtually impossible to tell whose eyes are 'awaken'd' in line six. Is it the poet who is capable of viewing the *locus amoenus*, or is it Psyche who can now safely set eyes on Cupid after he first required complete darkness for their amorous encounters? I have already alluded to the fact that the emphasis on seeing and vision is striking throughout the ode. It is actually the intricate pattern of seeing and hiding which offers the reader a crucial clue of how to interpret the real nature of the poet's self.

I grant that at this stage, the poem has far from disclosed the persona's 'virility' which I claimed to be present in its deeper semantic strata. However, from now onwards the ode contains a whole series of significant markers, related to the pattern I have just referred to, which will substantiate my claim. I believe that the complex interrelationship and calculated oscillation between seeing and hiding parallels both the poet's masculine drive to yield to his feelings of sexual lust, and his subsidiary feminine desires to see his beloved. The feminised part of his personality, which manifests itself in this 'unmanly' curiosity, can only be satisfied by a privileged vision of this beloved. Incidentally, this desire dovetails with the poet's masculine urge to exert total and unrestricted control over the goddess by hiding her away. It should be borne in mind that the possessive poet conceals Psyche *from* his male rival Cupid in a remote vale secluded by mountains where the stars have no name and are still unmapped. Yet at the same time, has the poet in the ode not once again feminised himself by adopting the role of Psyche who, too, was driven by a yearning to see her lover?

Apuleius's version of the myth, which, through Adlington's sixteenth-century translation, was Keats's primary source, strongly associates curiosity with feminine indulgence and feebleness of mind. In *The Golden Ass*, Apuleius relates how Psyche goes to the underworld as part of a series of superhuman tasks set by Venus. The latter had become increasingly jealous, both of Psyche's beauty and popularity, and now desires to see her rival destroyed once and for all.

Her wrath reaches its climax when the girl contrives to transgress a sacred taboo by literally bringing to light the true identity of her mystery lover. This is none other than Venus's son, Cupid, who feels compelled to abandon Psyche, seemingly for good, after the fatal discovery. Willing to atone for her own uncurbed curiosity, the girl descends into Hades in quest of her lover and returns in the possession of 'a mysticall secret in a boxe'. The gods of the Underworld, taking pity on her, repeatedly warn the girl not to look at its contents. As foreseen by Venus, this prohibition nonetheless proves too demanding: Apuleius's flaccid Psyche soon forsakes control again and yields to her curiosity:

When Psyches [sic] was returned from hell, to the light of the world, shee was ravished with great desire [...]. And by and by shee opened the boxe where she could perceive no beauty nor any thing else, save onely an infernal and deadly sleepe, which immediately invaded all her members as soone as the boxe was uncovered, in such sort that shee fell downe upon the ground, and lay there as a sleeping corps.

Just when she is about to expire from the consequences of her rash act, she is rescued from her deathlike swoon by a reproachful Cupid: 'O wretched Caitife, behold thou wert well-nigh perished againe, with the overmuch curiositie'. But all is quickly forgiven: Psyche is bestowed with immortality and the lovers are reunited for good. It is only this very last part of the myth which is related in Keats's ode. By leaving out the adventurous and troublesome prologue, Keats strips Psyche of all individuality she could possibly possess.

As a consequence, it is she, and not the poet, who is forced into female passivity. Her desperate but brave search for her beloved, as well as her perseverance, through which she gains her divine status, is completely ignored in the ode. In the long journal letter written to his brother George in America and containing the transcript of the 'Ode to Psyche', Keats emphatically points out that it is through hardship and misadventure that one's soul acquires its identity. He outlines this philosophy in the famous 'vale of Soul-making' passage:

There may be intelligences or sparks of the divinity in millions but they are not Souls till they acquire identities, till each one is personally itself. [...] Do you not see how necessary a World of Pains and troubles is to school an Intelligence and make it a soul? A Place where the heart must feel and suffer in a thousand diverse ways! (*Letters* , II, p. 102).

In *Hyperion* , Apollo likewise takes on his divine selfhood by painfully living through 'dire events', 'agonies' and 'destroyings' (*Hyperion* , III, ll. 114, 115, 116). The denial in Keats's poem of Psyche's catharsislike rites of passage as they occur in the original story necessarily withholds her every sense of personality. The deconstruction of her identity, marking the process of the poet's masculine domination, has now fully commenced.

The poet's possessiveness is further apparent by his act of isolating and hiding Psyche. Though Cupid and Psyche had chosen a secret bower, safely buried in the forest and 'scarce espied' (l. 12) for their *rendez-vous* , this will not suffice for the poet. Just as he stumbled accidentally on the scene, so may future potential rivals find out the sacred spot. The ultimate seclusion, therefore, must be realised through an act of internalisation. The poet will literally lock up Psyche in the 'delphic labyrinth' of his 'brain' ('On Receiving a Laurel Crown from Leigh Hunt', ll. 2-3) where she will be unreachable for others.

He opts for a place, heretofore untrodden, and unknown, where his branched thoughts will weave an impenetrable prison. Even in his early youth, Keats interiorised his ideal women in the manner described above: 'When I was a Schoolboy I though[t] a fair Woman a pure Goddess, my mind was a soft nest in which some one of them slept' (*Letters* , I, p. 341). Keats's portrayal of a passive woman meekly waiting in some hidden recesses to satisfy the male's needs appears to be a favourite fantasy of his. It is a fantasy most cynically exploited in *The Eve of St Agnes* . With regard to the 'Ode to Psyche', a faint echo of this ideal is found in the parallel image of the 'active' zephyrs lulling to sleep the inert and 'passive' Dryads (ll. 56-57).

As far as the complex pattern of vision and non-vision (or hiding) is concerned which I believe to hold the key to the poem's meaning, it is undeniably so that the poet's passionate feelings for Psyche are themselves aroused by viewing the embracing pair. The next step for the poet is to appropriate this privileged vision. Before the act of internalisation, however, the external, sensory part of reality needs must be imbued with a quality of the poet's own self. Thus it will become much easier to absorb reality within the mind itself and to capture it within the 'wide hollows of [the] brain' (*Hyperion* , III, l. 117). Rather than a complete self-dispersal in the physical world, the ode demonstrates how nature is seen as an extension of the poet's egocentric and tyrannical personality.

In this respect, everything is looked upon as possessing the same innate quality of vision: the brooklet, at last, allows itself to be visually located (l. 12); the flowers are 'fragrant eyed' (l. 13); the morning is referred to as 'eye-dawn' (l. 20); Vesper is compared to a glow-worm (l. 27), thereby resembling an eye of heaven; Psyche is seen with 'awaken'd eyes' (l. 6) and she is the 'loveliest vision far / of all Olympus' faded Hierarchy' (ll. 24-25). Obviously, here has been a poet at work who is continually 'filling some other Body' (*Letters* , I, p. 387).

Ironically enough, though, Keats used this phrase to define his much debated idea of the 'cameleon Poet'. But instead of an empathising poet, the ode shows how reality itself is adjusted in order to fit the poet's perception of the material world. In other words, the aeolian harp has turned into a tonometer to which everything else must become attuned. This may look like a rebuttal of the 'cameleon Poet' doctrine, but only because critics have overlooked similarly important statements by Keats with regard to his conception of the ideal poet.

Does Keats not explicitly state elsewhere that a proper identity is a prerequisite for creative activity? For instance, in his reply to Shelley's invitation to come to Italy, where the milder climate would be beneficial for his health, Keats writes that 'an artist' must 'have "self concentration"' (*Letters*, II, p. 322-3). His poetry also bears proof of a strong awareness of the relationship between personal independence and creativity. In *Hyperion,* Saturn, who is deprived of his previous glory and all power which made up his identity, is faced with the mortifying consequences of his loss of selfhood:

I am gone
Away from my own bosom: I have left
My strong identity, my real self,
Somewhere between the throne, and where I sit
Here on this spot of earth. [...]
Search, Thea, search! and tell me, if thou seest
A certain shape or shadow, making way
With wings or chariot fierce to repossess
A heaven he lost erewhile: [...]
But cannot I create?
Cannot I form? Cannot I fashion forth
Another world, another universe,
To overbear and crumble this to nought?
(Hyperion , I, ll. 112-6, 121-4, 141-4)

The reader cannot but answer negatively to Saturn's set of agonising questions. The deity may once have held the power to create harmony out of chaos, but these times are now gone with the annihilation of his former self. It may be meaningful that the 'Ode to Psyche' is the first poem written after the abandonment of *Hyperion* . Perhaps as a compensation for his own failure in generating a finished work, Keats needed to nerve himself for the exacting task of writing new poetry. In this respect, the Cupid-Psyche myth may have appealed to Keats because it occasioned a candid gesture of self-definition and a search for a well-developed identity.

Keats must indeed have felt it necessary to prove his mettle and to reinstate himself as a serious, independent poet after the patronising reviews of the previous month. Hence, in a suddenly regained state of inspiring reassurance, he composes a song for Psyche, his Muse, who will, as from now on, be perfectly obedient to him. The almost obsessive preoccupation with self and identity which resurfaces in the ode can thus be seen as an indispensable self-affirmation necessary for composing poetry.

If the poem emphasises the poet's independence, it is clear that in the 'Ode to Psyche' the woman/goddess is seen as a highly eroticised object which exists only by the grace of the poet's desire. Indeed, in her 'rosy sanctuary' (l. 59), reminiscent of Lamia's 'purple-lined palace of sweet sin' (*Lamia* , II, l. 31), Psyche will be pushed into the role of a deified temple-prostitute, common in Antiquity. For if Psyche allegorically stands for the poet's imagination, the poet will procreate new compositions through the consummation of his love for the goddess (cf. the 'pleasant pain' of line 52).

The poet appears here in the guise of the love god Cupid who is described in Apuleius's tale as capable of inflicting similarly oxymoronic '*sweet wounds* [by his] piercing darts, by the *pleasant heate* of his fire' (p. 100, italics mine). In return for the endurance of her imposed passivity, the poet, who is convinced of his own superior sexual prowess, will most generously gratify her with 'soft delight' (l. 64). After all, 'poetry', to quote Sandra M. Gilbert, is the creative act, the act of life, the archetypal sexual act. Sexuality is poetry. The lady is [the poet's] creation, or Pygmalion's statue. The lady is the poem.

Imprisoned in the manacles of the poet's fabrications, Psyche has become no more than a glorified reproductive organ, a divine womb delivering future compositions without respite. The 'wreath'd trellis of [his] working brain' (l. 60) will prevent her from any possible escape and so will the barrier of 'dark-cluster'd trees' (l. 54). In addition, the closely knit pattern of alliterations, assonances and rhymes in the concluding stanza audibly tightens the net around the chased Psyche.

Unperturbed by his own possessive ploys, the poet now proclaims himself Psyche's assiduous priest, safeguarding the object of his private and idiosyncratic religion in a secret 'temple of Delight' ('Ode on Melancholy', l. 25). One may be reminded here of De Quincey's famous statement in his *Confessions of an English Opium-Eater* , published two years after the completion of Keats's ode. This time it was no 'hethen [sic] Goddess' (*Letters* , II, p. 106) but ruby-red laudanum which was the highly individualised idol of worship: 'This is the doctrine of the true church on the subject of opium: of which church I acknowledge myself to be the only member the alpha and the omega'. Like the religious fanatic described in the opening of *The Fall of Hyperion* , the poet in the 'Ode to Psyche' is to weave himself a private paradise, a pleasure garden or *hortus conclusus* in which he will be the omnipotent gardener.

In order to gain an even better insight into the poet's unabating attempts to dominate Psyche, it may be worth while at this stage to examine the origin of the word 'temple'. The etymology of temple reads: 'A consecrated place, sanctuary, prob. rel. to Gr. temenos *reserved or sacred enclosure* ' [italics mine]. Thus, apart from a place of worship, a temple can be regarded as a gilded prisonhouse where mankind tries to keep the godhead under strict human control. It has, for instance, been pointed out by anthropologists that 'the Persians despised [Grecian] temples, considering it wrong', in Cicero's later words, 'to keep shut up within walls the gods whose dwelling place was the whole world'.

When Apuleius's Psyche has spent her bridal night in Cupid's 'princely Edifice' and 'place of pleasures', and wakes up the following morning to find herself abandoned, she believes 'that now shee was past all hopes of comfort, in that shee was closed within the walls of a prison deprived of humane conversation'. The real nature of the temple-like building appears to have dawned upon her in all its menacing terror. Likewise, the term sanctuary, a word as post-Augustan as Psyche herself, occurs in classical Latin only in the sense of 'the private cabinet of a prince' (*OED*). It is no surprise, then, that the poet in Keats's ode firmly pronounces his intention to build 'a Fane' (l. 50) as to keep his beloved well under his authority. C. G. Jung has also pointed out that 'the round and square enclosures' constituting 'the precincts of a temple or any isolated place' have 'the purpose of protective walls or of a *vas hermeticum* , to prevent an outburst or a disintegration'.

It is only in this protective environment that germination can take place. In Keats's *temenos* , therefore, the process of the persona's inner growth, strongly dependent on Psyche's presence, or rather, incarceration, is secured against uncontrollable seepage. The prison walls of Psyche's temple are permeable in one direction only: they allow the poet to take in as much of the outer world without having to fear any loss of his own self-consciousness and identity from within:

The mandala denotes and assists exclusive concentration on the centre, the self. [...] It is a much needed self-control for the purpose of avoiding inflation and dissociation. [...] [The temple] protects and isolates an inner content or process that should not get mixed up with things outside.

This process, needless to say, is the poet's self-realisation at the expense of Psyche's individuality. The gender shift from the oracular priestess to the male priest is the dramatic outcome of the persona's never-waning struggle to dominate and possess Psyche. On the one hand, by assuming the feminine role of a *Pythia* , the poet has become the mouthpiece of a literally dumb and acquiescent goddess, thereby capable of gross manipulation. Clad with the doctrinal authority of a high priest, on the other hand, the poet succeeds in giving vent to his masculine despotism. Taken together, both are very effective stratagems to sway the object of his lust, as I will now try to demonstrate.

Psyche's subordinate role now comes even more to the fore in the ten-line catalogue of emphatically highlighted negatives referring to the youngest of goddesses (ll. 28-37). With what seems to border on malicious delight, Keats uses almost an entire stanza to inform his audience that Psyche has no temple, altar, or virgin-choir; no lute or incense sweet and was born too late to be venerated in song along with the other Olympian deities. In sum, she is denied all the common paraphernalia of worship.

But most important of all, she has no voice and, as a consequence, no power. She can utter neither any protests nor can she even comply with the poet's desire. She is rudely silenced, incapacitated and thus deprived of all autonomy. All the poet does to enliven 'Olympus' faded hierarchy' (l. 25) is to assert his own visionary and vocal authority. [...] The poet claims to be Psyche's champion, yet his benevolence is that of the despot. Psyche remains silently subservient, while the poet usurps the privilege of discourse[.]

Parenthetically, Psyche's dumbness may be read as accentuating her status as a captive, for Freud has argued that dumbness and concealment can be equated. The contrast between the dumbness and the bold assertive claim in line 43 displays again the superiority and dominion of the poet and Psyche's submissive position in the power relationship.

This line has a pivotal role in the ode: it contains a most crucial reference to a visual/visionary experience, and it explicates the poet's superiority over the object of his concupiscence. Inspired by his tyrannical love, the poet *sees* and *sings*, thereby creating not only his but also Psyche's identity. Indeed, I have already suggested above that Psyche's existence depends exclusively on the persona's act of worship and invocation. Though referring to the unfinished 'Ode to Maia', the following comment by Martin Aske is very well applicable to Psyche's position: she is 'an object of desire who needs to be coaxed into presence through the poet's own voice'. This dependence on the poet's invocation bereaves the goddess of any free volition.

Just like Adam who acquired supremacy over all living creatures by giving them a name (Genesis 2: 19), so the poet gains full possession of the goddess by ejaculating hers. Is it not very appropriate that all tension of the first stanza is released in the final, almost aggressively short line 'His Psyche true!' (l. 23)? One may even tentatively suggest that the "naming of [Psyche as] muse is a deliberate act of aesthetic self-definition".

In response to the concatenation of negatives of non-being, the poet asserts himself Psyche's grove and shrine, which, in practice, make up the sarcophagus (literally 'flesh-eating' coffin) of her individuality. The poet indeed is about to absorb her identity completely. D. L. Hoeveler has astutely observed that the Romantic poets were very keen on 'creat[ing] female characters with whom their male heroes (often slightly veiled versions of themselves) could merge in a sort of apocalyptic union'.

Put in an even more straightforward way, Hoeveler stresses how 'The Romantics cannibalistically consumed these female characters, shaped them into their ideal alter egos, and most of the time destroyed them by the conclusion of the poem'. In the ode, the poet's ploys of conjuring Psyche into being through ritualistic invocation, only to deconstruct her afterwards, fits this scheme very well. The poet came to the sacred, 'scarce espied' bower, saw the goddess, recognised her and thus acquired absolute ascendancy. 'I see and sing' and, one may complete, conquered; or *Vene vidi vici* .

The 'Ode to Psyche' is by no means the only instance in Keats's work which contains such an all-devouring propensity in the persona. The following excerpt, taken from a sonnet addressed to Keats's beloved, Fanny Brawne, is particularly revealing:

O, let me have thee whole, all, all be mine!
That shape, that fairness, that sweet minor zest
Of love, your kiss, those hands, those eyes divine,
That warm, white, lucent, million-pleasured breast,
Yourself your soul in pity give me all,
Withhold no atom's atom or I die
('I cry your mercy', ll. 5-10)

A comparable example can be found in a letter which Keats wrote during his walking tour in Scotland to his then recently married brother George:

Notwithstand[ing] your Happiness and your recommendation I hope I shall never marry. The mighty abstract Idea I have of Beauty in all things stifles the more divided and minute domestic happiness an amiable wife and sweet Children I contemplate as part of that Beauty. [B]ut I must have a thousand beautiful particles to fill up my heart (*Letters* , I, p. 403).

Here the poet appears as an insatiable Bluebeard, devouring the objects (note how Keats writes about 'particles', not 'human beings') arousing his passion in order to shape and extend his own sense of individuality. Just like Coleridge's secondary imagination, Keats's mind 'dissolves, diffuses, dissipates, in order to re-create'. A similar oppressive attitude can be read in the concluding torch-and-casement image of the ode. Psyche (the word means both 'soul' and 'butterfly' or 'moth' in Greek) will be attracted by the light of the burning torch, an image of phallic reassurance for the poet. But her 'lucent fans' (l. 41) will be scorched by it so that escape will become entirely impossible. This is by no means a far-fetched assumption. Like many others, Keats possessed a small collection of Tassie gems which were inexpensive miniature reproductions of classical artefacts and sculptures, very fashionable at this time and used as seals.

Among these baubles are some of particular interest for my argument. On the Tassie gems dealing with the Cupid-Psyche myth, 'Psyche is invariably designated with the wings of a butterfly, and sometimes a Cupid is represented as burning her wings (those on which she should mount to heaven) with his flaming torch'. Lempriere's classical dictionary too mentions this particular attribute and its usage under the 'Cupido' entry: 'On gems, and all other pieces of antiquity, [Cupido] is represented as [...] playing with a nymph, catching a butterfly, or trying to burn [its wings] with a torch'. In *Polymetis* , another important source of classical myth for Keats, Joseph Spence reproduces several ancient Cupid-Psyche gems with the following explanatory comment:

Here are two of them [i.e. Cupids] very seriously employed about the catching of a butterfly; and there another, as intent to burn one with the torch he holds in his hands. Tho' this indeed might be brought as an instance of their power, as well of their idle tricks: for the butterfly is generally used by the Greek artists as an emblem for the human soul; and a Cupid fondling or burning a butterfly, is just the same with them as a Cupid caressing or tormenting the Goddess Psyche.

The image of the torch, of course, is widespread in ancient mythology, and Keats seems to have drawn on several interdependent meanings of the symbol. *The Pantheon* , which Keats knew through Andrew's Tooke translation of 1713, interestingly pairs Hymeneus, the god presiding over marriage, with Cupid, both of whom are carrying a torch. This concurrence justifies the reading of the poet's 'Fane' for Psyche as literally a 'marriage chamber', or a *thalamos* as the ante-chamber to a Greek temple was called. It is there that the poet and his divine, silenced 'bride of quietness' will be linked in sacred wedlock. Evidently, Cupid will be irreverently displaced in the process. My intention in the next paragraphs is to evince that Psyche's marriage in Keats's poem will actually lead to her own destruction insofar as it is the epitome of the poet's conquest. This corresponds, the reader will recall, to the final, 'cannibalistic' phase in Hoeveler's scheme of the Romanticists' gender politics.

Though the final stanza is the part most heavily discussed by commentators of the 'Ode to Psyche', strangely enough, no one seems to have detected the link between the burning torch with the 'casement ope at night' (l. 66) and the Hero and Leander myth as recorded by Musaeus. Hero, locked up in a tower (not unlike Psyche in her sanctuary) lights a torch every night as a beacon to guide her lover Leander who has to cross the Hellespont by swimming. One tempestuous night, Hero falls asleep whilst waiting and the torch is extinguished by the wind. Consequently, Leander perishes in the seething water. Keats was undoubtedly familiar with the myth as shown by his sonnet 'On a [Tassie gem portraying] Leander Which Miss Reynolds, My Kind Friend, Gave Me'.

When, in Keats's ode, Love is identified with Cupid, it seems as if the poet is longing for Cupid-Leander's imminent death. After Cupid's displacement, the poet, who has substituted himself for the rival love god, will now rekindle the torch and use it as an instrument to abject the impotent goddess. I believe it to be highly revealing that in Apuleius's tale, the people light 'blacke torches' in preparation for Psyche's marriage to a yet unknown but allegedly monstrous husband whom the oracle of Apollo had described as a 'Serpent dire and fierce as might be thought'. After the torches are lit, the family and people of the city 'went to bring this sorrowfull spowse, not to her marriage, but to her finall end and buriall'.

Thus, Cupid's blazing flare merges with the downward pointing torch of Thanatos, the god of Death and annihilation. Keats seems to have picked up the idea that Psyche's marriage will effect her imminent death. It is after all a 'rash and bold lampe', revealing her husband's true nature, which marks the start in the original tale of a whole series of calamities. In an almost perversively triumphant mood, the poet literally cries out his delight at the prospect of his pending victory. Indeed, the first three stanzas of the ode all begin with the exclamative 'O', like the repetitive and hypnotising *euoi* in the Bacchic hymns sung at sacred orgies. The allegedly explicit sexual nature of the heathen festivities during which a particular godhead was venerated in song (*wdh* in Greek, hence the word 'ode') is notorious.

Therefore, it is particularly significant that the poet in the ode refers to Psyche's 'secrets' (l. 3) for this may be interpreted as an echo of such an ancient Mystery celebration. The overall erotic and sensuous nature of the ode is obvious enough. Apart from Keats's favourite *topos* of the bower of love, the rich and lush scenery seems to celebrate the sensuousness of the couched lovers. It may be a fortuitous coincidence, but the compound 'soft-conched' (l. 4) can be interpreted as a sophisticated pun when the meaning of 'vulva' (concha) is read into it.

As a trained medical student, Keats is likely to have been familiar with the term. In analogy with the Annunciation in Christianity, then, the poet sings the secret words into Psyche's ear, thus fathering the very ode itself. I refer here, of course, to the early Scholastics who suggested that the Virgin Mary conceived Jesus at the word of the archangel Gabriel. This belief was founded on the authoritative phrase 'And the Word was made flesh, and dwelt among us' in John 1:14a. A thirteenth-century English dancing song phrases it as follows:

Glad us maiden, mother mild
Through thine ear thou wert with child
Gabriel he said it thee.

The 'casement ope at night' may, in turn, refer to the *fenestra ovalis* and *fenestra rotundum* which are parts of the ear leading into the inner region of the head behind the *ossa temporum* or temple (possibly another anatomical pun in Keats's ode). By the act of 'mak[ing] melodious moan' (l. 30) and by uttering the *logos spermatikos*, the poet will engender the subservient receptacle of his passion with future compositions, yet 'never breed[ing] the same' (l. 63). Such a tremendous output is guaranteed by the extraordinary intensity and fullness of his vision. The experience of complete sexual gratification resulting in the cannibalistic death of Psyche, will always remain a 'remembrance dear' (l. 2) for the poet.

As the case may be, this recollection will turn out to be the germ of all potential 'numbers' he is still to sing; it is the major catalyst of the essentially sexualised act of writing. Keats himself established the connexion between recollection on the one hand and writing on the other in one of his letters: 'Poetry should [...] appear almost as a Remembrance' (*Letters* , I, p. 238). Yet, do these 'tuneless numbers' sound not somehow remarkably familiar? 'This do in remembrance of me', Jesus told his disciples whilst breaking the bread and pouring the wine (Luke 22: 19b). Analogously, each new poem will perpetuate the original mystery in which the poet partook. Hence, like the convoluted shape of Psyche's auricle, the poet is about the fold back upon himself and his earlier experiences in what has now basically become, after the mental absorption of the goddess's identity, an act of shameless auto-eroticism. Could Byron possibly have realised how close he was to the truth when he declared that Keats was 'always fr—g—g his *Imagination* '?

Now it only remains for the poet to penetrate his own orgiastic 'O's', which, in a most graphic manner, constitute a series of 'casements ope at night' (l. 66), in order to engender his poetical offspring. Ergo, invocation becomes impregnation. The firm and climactic 'Yes' at the beginning of the concluding stanza proves that the persona will be thoroughly successful in his creative desires. Truly, this was not a meaningless or overconfident exclamation on Keats's part. Though the 'Ode to Psyche', in itself, would have been enough of a corroboration, the unique sequence of his subsequent odes endorses beyond any doubt how Keats had managed to appropriate fully an inspiring, and above all, personal, Muse.

Chapter 2

Hyperion John Keats

Constructed as two poems, *Hyperion* and its attempted revision as *The Fall of Hyperion* are considered important works by John Keats. Although both were unfinished, these poems are some of Keats's most ambitious and successful writings, within which he integrates his theories of aesthetics with his ideas on mortality and morality. In drawing upon mythology and earlier poets' works in the *Hyperion* poems, Keats addressed issues that were pivotal in the Romantic period, including concerns about beauty and truth, imagination, knowledge, and the connection between art and life. *Hyperion* was undertaken during what many critics consider Keats's most intense period of creative productivity, a period also marked by personal difficulties.

After embarking upon a walking tour of Scotland and the Lake District, Keats returned home creatively energized. His publication of *Endymion* in 1818 drew harsh reviews, some of which included personal attacks. More significantly, his brother Tom's tuberculosis had worsened, and Keats felt responsible for his brother's care. Letters Keats wrote to his friends during this period indicate Keats felt divided between his obligations to Tom and his obligations to his poetry. After Tom's death in December 1818, *Hyperion* remained unfinished; Keats abandoned the poem entirely by April 1819.

Late in 1819, after he had met and fallen in love with Fanny Brawne, Keats began to revise *Hyperion* extensively. By that time Keats was suffering from the advanced stages of tuberculosis, which eventually precluded him from working and left the revision, like the first version, incomplete. *The Fall of Hyperion,* as it is now titled, remained unpublished until 1856, long after Keats's death in 1821.

PLOT AND MAJOR CHARACTERS

Stylistically and thematically influenced by earlier works, the *Hyperion* poems demonstrate Keats's interest in and response to classic literature. *Hyperion* exists in two fragmented versions, with narratives drawn from Greek mythology, and the second poem attempts to revise the first. It is stylistically different from the earlier poem, adding a long prologue and altering the poem's structure and theme. Reactions to these two versions vary: some critics consider *The Fall of Hyperion* mostly a revision, others claim it is an entirely new work, and yet others see it as a continuation of the first version.

Hyperion relates the fall of the Titans, elemental energies of the world, and their replacement by newer gods. The Olympian gods, having superior knowledge and an understanding of humanity's suffering, are the natural successors to the Titans. Keats's epic begins after the battle between the Titans and the Olympian gods, with the Titans already fallen. Hyperion, the sun god, is the Titans' only hope for further resistance. The epic's narrative, divided into three sections, concentrates on the dethronement of Hyperion and the ascension to power of Apollo, god of sun and poetry. Book I presents Saturn fallen and about to be replaced and Hyperion threatened within his empire. At the council of the Titans, Book II, Oceanus advocates acceptance of their inevitable defeat, though his speech is contrasted with those of other Titans. In the unfinished Book III, Apollo undergoes his transformation into the new ruling god. He meets with Mnemosyne, or memory and the mother of the Muses, in order to assume his powers and to attain immortality.

The Fall of Hyperion is darker than *Hyperion,* with the former suggesting that beauty can only be achieved through pain, and that poetry is incomplete if it evades and leaves unexpressed the suffering of humanity. In this fragment, the poet occupies the space of the poem in a dream-vision. The Poet asks for help, and he receives the vision of the fall of

Hyperion and the ascension of Apollo, elements which structure the first *Hyperion.* The action begins in a forest, where the speaker, consciously portrayed as the Poet, consumes fruits and drinks a toast to all poets. This drink initiates a dream-vision where the Poet meets a Muse figure, Moneta, who challenges the Poet to ascend to the world of art, where fame offers a type of immortality.

Although humbled by this challenge, the speaker enters a holy shrine to poetry, where he undergoes a death and rebirth. The Muse and the Poet debate the nature of poetry, happiness, visionary experience, and the role of the poet in the modern world. Moneta distinguishes poets from dreamers, whose imaginations focus only on individual ideals. True poets have awakened their imaginations to tragic pain but attempt to redeem sorrow with compassion and visionary acceptance. Moneta permits the speaker to enter the temple of Saturn, and she reveals to him her story. The Poet then describes Moneta's vision of the decline of the Titans. The speaker empathizes with the gods, and his ability to feel pain and suffering through imagination defines him as a Poet. The remainder of the poem narrates the laments of the Titans as they are replaced by the Olympian powers and led by Apollo. It ends with the introduction of Hyperion, who attempts to lead the final fight of the Titans against the new gods.

MAJOR THEMES

The thematic differences between the two versions of *Hyperion* have been extensively addressed by a wide variety of critics. In addition to Greek mythology, both poems draw from earlier poetic works, including Milton's *Paradise Lost* which is both imitated and challenged. *Hyperion* is often considered Miltonic in style and theme, and *The Fall of Hyperion* has been compared to Dante's *The Divine Comedy,* in terms of its structure as a dream-vision and in its use of a Muse figure.

Many themes introduced in the *Hyperion* poems are identifiable as those associated with Romanticism. *Hyperion,* which marks the exchange of the old powers for the new, addresses ideas about poetry, beauty, knowledge, and experience. These ideas are also present in *The Fall of Hyperion*. *Hyperion*'s dominant themes address the nature of poetry and its relationship to humanity. The narrative suggests a thematic consideration of progress, particularly toward enlightenment and depictions of beauty, even as it evokes classical ideals found in Greek mythology.

Visual and verbal representations, in the use of language and of Greek sculptural forms, contribute to this exploration. Through his representation of gods, Keats's commentary on Romantic opposites includes the real and ideal, history versus myth, finite versus infinite. The theme of truth is also prevalent. The speech of Oceanus and the ascension of Apollo both point to *Hyperion*'s concern with truth and its relationship with beauty, knowledge, and suffering. Truth is closely associated with knowledge and both are acquired through pain, which results from the understanding and acceptance of change and impermanence. However painful, truth is pure and beautiful, and what is beautiful is eternal. It is this honorable truth that the human spirit strives to attain.

The structure of *The Fall of Hyperion,* assessed as a conscious integration of the Poet and his debates with Moneta, encourages a thematic consideration of the nature of art and beauty. In this version, the significance of the imagination is central. Here, the dream-vision structure emphasizes the Romantic tension between material representations and inner visions. The immortality offered by art, as opposed to human mortality or divine immortality, contribute to thematic issues with life and death. Like *Hyperion, The Fall of Hyperion* is concerned with both pleasure and pain as integral to life and asserts the predominance of suffering. Also expressed is the relationship between knowledge, suffering, and divine power. Perhaps the strongest theme presented by the poem is the Poet's identity and his responsibility to humankind.

Many commentators have noted that the *Hyperion* poems illustrate Keats's aesthetic theories. One dominant theme in the poems is Keats's notion of "negative capability," his assertion that the ability to entertain opposing ideas, images, and concepts without "any irritable reaching after fact and reason" is a poetic necessity. This aesthetic quality is believed to be present in those rare individuals who transcend Selfhood, leaving them able to identify with and express the experience rather than with their perception of the experience, and thus able to convey art's truth and beauty.

CRITICAL RECEPTION

The general critical reaction to Keats's *Hyperion* poems, like the reaction to much of his poetry, has focused on one of two dominant areas. Many critics examine the poems to illuminate Keats's life and aesthetic theories, while others use Keats's work to identify either characteristics of the Romantic period or to suggest possible connections between Romanticism and other influences. Keats's letters remain important to scholarship as articulations of Keats's intentions. In most assessments, Keats's *Hyperion* poems are considered as valuable for their biographical and cultural revelations as they are significant as art in their own right. The various approaches to the *Hyperion* poems reinforce that Keats's works are valued by scholars as representations of his developing aesthetic theories and as expressions of Romanticism.

Paul Sheats notes Keats's growth as a poet in the *Hyperion*'s increasingly restrained use of imagery and intensity of sensation. Marlon Ross, in examining Keats's patriarchal discourse, suggests Keats attempted to position himself as a "great poet" through the use of an obtuse language which would distinguish himself from those poets whose work he mimicked. Those who primarily concentrate on the poems as demonstrations of Keats's aesthetic concerns are especially interested in *The Fall of Hyperion.* Irene Chayers looks at Keats's focus on the composition of poetry as demonstrated within that work, particularly in the passage which juxtaposes the poet and the dreamer. Responding to the poem in a similar manner. Stuart Sperry views the poem as an allegory for poets and poetry. Other critics discuss Keats's articulations of artistic development as evidenced in the poems. Geoffrey Hartman (see Further Reading), considers both *Hyperions* as a single work that offers a divine world representing Keats's struggles with artistic identity. Similarly, Christoph Bode characterizes the *Hyperion* poems as a developing expression of Keats's poetics and of his understanding of his "negative capability."

Both *Hyperion* and *The Fall of Hyperion* also have been examined for their embodiment of Romantic ideals, particularly in terms of Keats's influences. Paul Sherwin's examination of *Hyperion* asserts the poem is a response to Milton's *Paradise Lost,* evoking the poem yet attempting to subvert its message. Johnathan Bate claims that both *Hyperion* and *The Fall of Hyperion* are attempts to create a more progressive poem that minimizes the influence of *Paradise Lost* on the works. In her analysis of Keats's use of mythology and divine speech, Anya Taylor focuses on reflection of Romantic period traits, as do Warren Ober and W. K. Thomas, whose analysis of Keats's use of Pan as an embodiment of the Romantic Imagination

In addition to the two main schools of critical analysis of *Hyperion,* commentators have offered a variety of approaches. In her examination of masculinity and homoeroticism in the *Hyperion* poems, Ellen Brinks posits that a Gothic subtext is present, while Joel Faflak looks at connections between Romanticism and psychoanalysis in *Hyperion.* Carol Bernstein illustrates connections between *Hyperion* and modernism and postmodernism. Keats's *Hyperion* poems, as unfinished fragments, continue to generate scholarly analysis of ideas, development as a poet, and position as a Romantic.

Chapter 3

Poems of John Keats

In earlier articles in this series, we have examined the lives of a number of the great poets in the English language, and to some extent we have seen the evolution of English poetry from Chaucer on. Following the romantically inclined poetry of the late16th and 17th centuries renaissance period, the 18th century became more formal, with Alexander Pope's (1688 – 1744) *An Essay on Criticism*, which was published in 1711, largely defining the direction. The majority of the poets for the next hundred years followed this path, and the large majority were from the upper classes and educated at Oxford or Cambridge.

Typically, they had a good knowledge of Latin, and often Greek as well; and they also had some knowledge of one or two more modern European languages. Of course, the major voice before that was Shakespeare, who didn't fit into any of these groups; you may remember Ben Jonson (1573 – 1637) saying in his memorial to him that he had "small Latin, and less Greek". For this reason, during the 17th century Shakespeare was sometimes dismissed as naïve. Towards the end of the 18th century the Romantic poets, notably Wordsworth (1770 – 1850), Coleridge (1772-1834) and Southey (1774 – 1843) began the change in direction, but they still were generally still in the cultural 'educated class'.

The time was ripe for a working class poet, and John Keats was the man. Even the poets in the same school as himself, notably Percy Bysshe Shelley (1792 – 1822) and James Henry Leigh Hunt (1784 – 1859), tried to portray Keats as a fragile person -- as Jonson described Shakespeare as 'nature's child'. Here is the great actor Henry Irving, in an address on *The*

Drama to the Philosophical Institution in Edinburgh, on November 8th, 1881:

"It has been too much the custom to talk of Shakespeare as nature's child—as the lad who held horses for people who came to the play—as a sort of chance phenomenon who wrote these plays by accident and unrecognized. How supremely ridiculous! How utterly irreconcilable with the grand dimensions of the man!"

I believe that the image of Keats that has come down to us, first protected by his friend Shelley, and then made acceptable to the Victorians by Tennyson and others, gives us a view 'irreconcilable with the grand dimensions of the man'. It is sad that an illness which was a family problem cut his creative life so short, but he has left us with a legacy that everyone should value.

As I was writing this column, I received a new book, *John Keats – Fugitive Poems* with a Foreword by Andrew Motion that takes a very similar view of Keats; it also has a number of poems that one does not often see, and I recommend it to anyone interested in the important changes in English poetry. John Keats was born on October 31st, 1795, at the Swan and Hoop inn and livery stables in London.

His father was Thomas Keats, who was head ostler at the stables (an ostler was a stableman, and the head ostler was essentially the stable manager). Thomas has been described as an ambitious and energetic young man. He had come up to London from Devon, and married the 'handsome and headstrong' Frances, the daughter of the stable proprietor, John Jennings. John was their first child; they had two other sons, George, who was born in 1797, and Thomas, who was born on in 1799. In 1801, they had a third son, Edward, but he died in infancy. In 1803, their daughter, Frances Mary (always called Fanny), was born. In that same year, John entered John Clarke's School at Enfield; George entered the school at the same time, and Tom joined them later.

Thomas Keats died in April, 1804, as a consequence of a fall from his horse, while he was returning from a visit to John and George at school. Just two months later, his widow married William Rawlings. This marriage led to a family row, and the children went to live with their grandparents. John Jennings, their grandfather, was an astute business man who left a respectable estate at his death in March, 1805, but the family became embroiled in financial troubles which were not finally sorted out until well after John Keats's death. Meanwhile, their mother Frances left her new husband and, after some years, returned in 1809 to the family home ill with tuberculosis. John had always been deeply attached to his mother, and he took over the responsibility for nursing her; he was heartbroken when she died in March, 1810.

As a refuge from his grief he turned to books, a passion which never left him. Before this he had been an indifferent scholar – at Enfield he had a reputation as a sportsman and a fighter – but he threw himself into his studies and "won all the school prizes in sight". (This quote is from Aileen Ward's introduction to *The Poems of John Keats*, a collection first published in 1966). On their mother's death, Richard Abbey and John Rowland Sandell were appointed the children's guardians.

The boys remained in school, and Fanny was moved to the Abbey family, where she remained for several years. In 1811 John and George left school, and John decided to follow a medical career. The biographers appear to have somewhat different views on whether this was his idea, or Richard Abbey's suggestion. There are several biographical sources, with considerable differences, both in the facts and in the interpretations.

I have used a timeline from a website, the compiler is Merilee; I have also used some of the biographical details from the site, but I could not find an author's name. I have also used my regular source, Merriam-Webster's Encyclopedia of Literature. Another site, contains this statement:

"Details of Keats's early life are scarce. During the last few years of his life, letters allow one to track him virtually week-to-week but his childhood and adolescence are another matter. Indeed, virtually all the information known is in the form of reminiscences, many taken years after Keats had died.

Understandably, one must view these memories with some skepticism.

Whether discussing Keats's physical appearance (his brother George said he resembled their mother while a family friend said it was the father) or his pastimes, these sources contradict one another." Keats became apprenticed to the apothecary Dr. Hammond of Edmonton, and apparently enjoyed the work and did well; his apprenticeship was due to be completed in mid 1815.

An apothecary was what we would now call a pharmaceutical chemist. However, in July 1815 the Apothecary Act was passed, the purpose of this being to ensure that an apothecary had adequate medical training. This meant that Keats could not simply become an apothecary by completing the apprenticeship, and as a consequence he entered Guy's Hospital. He planned to study there for a year and then apply for membership in the Royal College of Surgeons. His classes include a variety of subjects - anatomy, chemistry, dissection, physiology, botany, as well as various duties around the hospital. Contrary to later rumors, Keats did well enough to earn a 'dressership' at Guy's for the new year. (Only 12 dressers were chosen from 700 students.)

Henry Stephens, a classmate (and later the inventor of blue-black ink) described the would-be poet:

"Whilst attending lectures, he [Keats] would sit & instead of Copying out the lecture, would often scribble some doggerel rhymes, among the Notes of Lecture, particularly if he got hold of another Student's Syllabus - In my Syllabus of Chemical Lectures he scribbled many lines on the paper cover, This cover has been long torn off, except one small piece on which is the following fragment of Doggerel rhyme

Give me women, wine and snuff
Until I cry out "hold, enough!"
You may do so sans objection
Till the day of resurrection;
For, bless my beard, they aye shall be
My beloved Trinity."

While at school, Keats had formed a close friendship with

Charles Cowden Clarke, the son of the school Principal. Clarke was eight years older than Keats, and appears to have been his tutor. As Keats discovered his interest in literature, Clarke encouraged him, and Keats continued to visit the school on a regular basis after his departure.

In 1813 Clarke read Spenser's *Epithalamion* to him, and Keats was enormously impressed and excited. Clarke then lent him a copy of *The Faerie Queene* which he went through in a week, as Clarke recalled "like a young horse through a spring meadow, ramping." Later he read Shakespeare. Clarke himself was attempting to establish himself as a poet, and discussed the work of Leigh Hunt (1784 – 1859) with John. This led the young Keats in the direction of Romantic poetry, which, as I said before, had fallen out of favour in the 18th Century. 'Hunt's first collection of poetry, *Juvenilia,* showed his love for Italian literature, and later in *The Story of Rimini* he reintroduced a freedom of movement in English couplet verse lost in the 18th Century' (*Merriam-Webster*).

At this time, critical periodicals were of enormous importance, both in the publication of new poetry, and in sometimes savage criticism. Hunt and his brother John launched the reformist weekly *The Examiner* in 1808, and in 1813 the brothers were imprisoned for their attacks on the unpopular Prince Regent. After Leigh's release in 1815 he moved to Hampstead, then the home of Keats, and in 1817 introduced him to Percy Bysshe Shelley (1792 – 1822), a friend of Hunt's since 1811.

The Examiner supported the new Romantic Poets against the attacks by such journals as *Blackwood's Magazine,* who referred to them as 'the Cockney Poets'. In addition to Hunt himself, Shelley, and Keats, this group included William Hazlitt (1778 – 1830). Their principal attacker was the Scottish critic John Gibson Lockhart (1794 – 1854), who was later the biographer of Sir Walter Scott, as some of the readers of this column may remember!

In early 1814 Keats wrote what were apparently his first poems, *Imitation of Spenser* and *On Peace*; later in that year he wrote *Fill for Me a Brimming Bowl*. Here is *Imitation of Spenser*:

Now Morning from her orient chamber came,
And her first footsteps touch'd a verdant hill;
Crowning its lawny crest with amber flame,
Silv'ring the untainted gushes of its rill;
Which, pure from mossy beds, did down distill,
And after parting beds of simple flowers,
By many streams a little lake did fill,
Which round its marge reflected woven bowers,
And, in its middle space, a sky that never lowers.
There the king-fisher saw his plumage bright
Vieing with fish of brilliant dye below;
Whose silken fins, and golden scales' light
Cast upward, through the waves, a ruby glow:
There saw the swan his neck of arched snow,
And oar'd himself along with majesty;
Sparkled his jetty eyes; his feet did show
Beneath the waves like Afric's ebony,
And on his back a fay reclined voluptuously.
Ah! could I tell the wonders of an isle
That in that fairest lake had placed been,
I could e'en Dido of her grief beguile;
Or rob from aged Lear his bitter teen:
For sure so fair a place was never seen,
Of all that ever charm'd romantic eye:
It seem'd an emerald in the silver sheen
Of the bright waters; or as when on high,
Through clouds of fleecy white, laughs the coerulean sky.
And all around it dipp'd luxuriously
Slopings of verdure through the glossy tide,
Which, as it were in gentle amity,
Rippled delighted up the flowery side;
As if to glean the ruddy tears, it tried,
Which fell profusely from the rose-tree stem!
Haply it was the workings of its pride,
In strife to throw upon the shore a gem
Outvieing all the buds in Flora's diadem.

On the 3rd of March, 1816, John began work as a dresser at Guy's. He was assigned to a surgeon whose operations were 'very badly performed and accompanied by much bungling if not worse.' Keats was required to dress wounds, change bandages and hold patients down during operations. He handled emergencies during his night duties and accompanied the surgeon on rounds. He sometimes performed his own operations. On the 25th of July in Blackfriars, John sat for the four exams necessary to become a Licentiate of the Society of Apothecaries.

The exams covered the following topics: a translation of the pharmacopoeia and physicians' prescriptions; the theory and practice of medicine; pharmaceutical chemistry; and *materia medica*. Keats passed. He was 20 years old and had become an apothecary 'in the shortest time possible and at the earliest possible age.' Neither of his roommates passed the exams.

However, in the same year, his first poem is published in *The Examiner*. *O Solitude!* was a sonnet, and during his brief life Keats would write 64 sonnets, generally using the Petrarchian form (see our article on Sonnets for a discussion of sonnet forms!). Recently a collection of his sonnets has been published as *The 64 Sonnets by John Keats* with an Introduction by Edward Hirsch (Paul Dry Books, Philadelphia, 2004). Here is his first:

O Solitude! if I must with thee dwell,
Let it not be among the jumbled heap
Of murky buildings: climb with me the steep,—
Nature's observatory—whence the dell,
In flowery slopes, its river's crystal swell,
May seem a span; let me thy vigils keep
'Mongst boughs pavilioned, where the deer's swift leap
Startles the wild bee from the foxglove bell.
But though I'll gladly trace these scenes with thee,
Yet the sweet converse of an innocent mind,
Whose words are images of thoughts refined,
Is my soul's pleasure; and it sure must be
Almost the highest bliss of human-kind,
When to thy haunts two kindred spirits flee.

In late September, Keats moved to a new apartment, and

began his next year at Guy's. Clarke had moved to London, and had shown Hunt some of Keats's poetry (the sonnet above had been submitted anonymously). In mid-October, Clarke and Keats read the translation of Homer's *Iliad* by George Chapman (1559 – 1634), published in 1611; his translation of the *Odyssey* appeared in 1616. This translation had been largely forgotten; at that time, the best-known translation of Homer was that of Alexander Pope, and one can understand that two young poets exploring a new form of poetry would be excited by the more 'romantic' version of the early seventeenth century poet. Walking home from Clarke's, Keats composed a sonnet which he had delivered to Clarke by 10 a.m. the following morning. This is regarded as his first mature work, *On First Looking Into Chapman's Homer*:

Much have I travell'd in the realms of gold,
And many goodly states and kingdoms seen;
Round many western islands have I been
Which bards in fealty to Apollo hold.
Oft of one wide expanse had I been told
That deep-brow'd Homer ruled as his demesne;
Yet did I never breathe its pure serene
Till I heard Chapman speak out loud and bold:
Then felt I like some watcher of the skies
When a new planet swims into his ken;
Or like stout Cortez when with eagle eyes
He star'd at the Pacific—and all his men
Look'd at each other with a wild surmise—
Silent, upon a peak in Darien.

Tennyson pointed out (considerably later) that it wasn't Cortez, it was Balboa; but it doesn't matter. An earlier critic pointed out that 'demesne' and 'serene' don't actually rhyme, but that matters rather less today than it did then. Keats began to meet the group of friends he would keep for the rest of his life.

Among them were Leigh Hunt, James Rice, John Hamilton Reynolds, and the painter Benjamin Robert Haydon. On the 3rd of November, Keats visited Haydon's studio and wrote a sonnet praising Haydon, Hunt and William Wordsworth.

Haydon sent the sonnet to Wordsworth. John met the influential critic William Hazlitt through Haydon.

In late 1816 or early 1817 Keats met Shelley, and they went for walks on Hampstead Heath, during which Shelley tried to persuade Keats not to publish his early poems. I have not been able to find why Shelley did this, but the following may give a clue. Richard Henry Horne (1802 – 1884) in 1844 wrote New Spirit of the Age, a collection of essays on contemporary writers. Here is an extract:

"When somebody expressed his surprise to Shelley, that Keats, who was not very conversant with the Greek language, could write so finely and classically of their gods and goddesses, Shelley replied 'He was a Greek.'"

"This was the highest sort of praise from Shelley, who wrote to Leigh Hunt's wife Marianne of his desire to help Keats: 'I am aware indeed that I am nourishing a rival who will far surpass me and this is an additional motive & will be an added pleasure.'"

My belief, therefore, is that Shelley wanted to delay his publication until his work had achieved the maturity that Shelley expected; the barrage of criticism that Keats's early work received may suggest that his advise was wise.

In December of 1816, Keats informed Richard Abbey that he has decided not to continue his medical career. As one might expect, Abbey was not very happy about this, and later recalled the conversation: 'Not intend to be a Surgeon! Why what do you mean to be? I mean to rely on my Abilities as a Poet - John, you are either mad or a Fool, to talk in so absurd a Manner. My mind is made up said the youngster very quietly. I know that I possess Abilities greater than most Men, and therefore I am determined to gain my Living by exercising them.'

On the first or second of March 1817, Haydon took Keats to see the Elgin Marbles. Haydon had played a significant role in having them arranged for public exhibition and Keats (as by now you might expect) promptly wrote a couple of sonnets about them. The next day, his first collection, *Poems*, was published by C. and J. Ollier. On March 14th he lodged at

Carisbrooke on the Isle of Wight and began the writing of his first long poem, *Endymion*. This begins:

A thing of beauty is a joy for ever:
Its loveliness increases; it will never
Pass into nothingness; but still will keep
A bower quiet for us, and a sleep
Full of sweet dreams, and health, and quiet breathing.
Therefore, on every morrow, are we wreathing
A flowery band to bind us to the earth,
Spite of despondence, of the inhuman dearth
Of noble natures, of the gloomy days,
Of all the unhealthy and o'er-darkened ways
Made for our searching: yes, in spite of all,
Some shape of beauty moves away the pall
From our dark spirits. Such the sun, the moon,
Trees old and young, sprouting a shady boon
For simple sheep; and such are daffodils
With the green world they live in; and clear rills
That for themselves a cooling covert make
'Gainst the hot season; the mid forest brake,
Rich with a sprinkling of fair musk-rose blooms:
And such too is the grandeur of the dooms
We have imagined for the mighty dead;
All lovely tales that we have heard or read:
An endless fountain of immortal drink,
Pouring unto us from the heaven's brink.

Keats described this as "A Poetic Romance. 'The stretched metre of an antique song.' Inscribed to the memory of Thomas Chatterton."

On November 28th, he finished *Endymion*. A couple of weeks later, Haydon took Keats to meet William Wordsworth (1770 – 1850), and the two poets met several time afterwards.

On December 28th, 1817, Haydon held what has become famous as "The Immortal Dinner". The guests in addition to Keats were Wordsworth; the engraver John Landseer; the essayist Charles Lamb; the explorer Joseph Ritchie; Mary Wordsworth's cousin Tom Monkhouse; John Kingston, the Comptroller of Stamps, who was Wordsworth's boss; and perhaps others. The occasion was described in great detail in Haydon's autobiography, but it recently has been the subject of a delightful book by Penelope Hughes-Hallett (*The Immortal Dinner: A Famous Evening of Genius and Laughter in Literary London, 1817*).

During the evening, Keats recited a portion of *Endymion,* which he had presented to Wordsworth a few days earlier. It has been said that Wordsworth was initially critical, but since Keats repeated it at the dinner a month later, he can't have been too depressed! As one might suppose, the painter described the physical appearances of his guests: Wordsworth was the tallest, at about five foot nine inches, and Lamb the shortest, at just under five feet. Keats was also short, at a little over five feet, but he had very broad shoulders and an athletic build; he always stood in a very upright manner, leaning a little back to make himself appear taller. He was a bit sensitive about his height: he once commented on Byron's showing the benefits of being an aristocrat and six feet tall!

In August of 1818, attacks appear in two of the critical magazines on *Poems* and *Endymion*. To some extent, these attacks were more directed at Hunt than at Keats. Here is a little of John Gibson Lockhart, in *Blackwood's Edinburgh Magazine,* August 1818:

"As for Mr. Keats's 'Endymion', it has just as much to do with Greece as it has with "old Tartary the fierce;" no man, whose mind has ever been imbued with the smallest knowledge or feeling of classical poetry or classical history, could have stooped to profane and vulgarise every association in the manner which has been adopted by this "son of promise".....[We] must inform our readers that this romance is meant to be written in English heroic rhyme. To those who have read any of Hunt's poems, this hint might indeed be needless. Mr. Keats has adopted the loose, nerveless versification, and Cockney rhyme of the poet of Rimini; but in fairness to that gentleman, we must add, that the defects of the system are tenfold more conspicuous in his disciple's work than in his own. Mr. Hunt is a small poet, but he is a clever man. Mr. Keats is a still smaller poet, and he is a boy of pretty abilities, which he has done everything in his power to spoil.

And now, good-morrow to "the Muses' son of Promise;" as for "the feats he yet may do," as we do not pretend to say, like himself, "Muse of my native land am I inspired," we shall adhere to the safe old rule of pauca verba.

We venture to make one small prophecy, that his bookseller will not a second time venture 50 quid upon any thing he can write. It is a better and a wiser thing to be a starved apothecary than a starved poet; so back to the shop Mr. John, back to "plasters, pills, and ointment boxes," &c. But, for Heaven's sake, young Sangrado, be a little more sparing of extenuatives and soporifics in your practice than you have been in your poetry."

John Wilson Croker, in *The Quarterly Review*, April 1818, wrote:

"Reviewers have been sometimes accused of not reading the works which they affected to criticise. On the present occasion we shall anticipate the author's complaint, and honestly confess that we have not read [Endymion: A Poetic Romance]. Not that we have been wanting in our duty - far from it - indeed, we have made efforts almost as superhuman as the story itself appears to be, to get through it; but with the fullest stretch of our perseverance, we are forced to confess that we have not been able to struggle beyond the first of the four books of which this Poetic Romance consists. We should extremely lament this want of energy, or whatever it may be, on our parts, were it not for one consolation - namely, that we are no better acquainted with the meaning of the book through which we have so painfully toiled, than we are with that of the three which we have not looked into.

It is not that Mr. Keats, (if that be his real name, for we almost doubt that any man in his sense would put his real name to such a rhapsody,) it is not, we say, that the author has not powers of language, rays of fancy, and gleams of genius - he has all these; but he is unhappily a disciple of the new school of what has been somewhere called Cockney poetry; which may be defined to consist of the most incongruous ideas in the most uncouth language....

[Mr. Keats] is a copyist of Mr. Hunt; but he is more unintelligible, almost as rugged, twice as diffuse, and ten times more tiresome and absurd than his prototype, who, though he impudently presumed to seat himself in the chair of criticism, and to measure his own poetry by his own standard, yet generally had a meaning. But Mr. Keats had advanced no dogmas which he was bound to support by examples: his nonsense therefore is quite gratuitous; he writes it for its own sake, and, being bitten by Mr. Leigh Hunt's insane criticism, more than rivals the insanity of his poetry...."

There is considerable disagreement as to how Keats reacted to this criticism. Some of his friends believed he was bitterly disappointed; but as we have seen above, his belief in his own talent was considerable. Nevertheless, here is one of his Odes, the *Ode on Melancholy*:

No, no, go not to Lethe, neither twist
Wolf's-bane, tight-rooted, for its poisonous wine;
Nor suffer thy pale forehead to be kiss'd
By nightshade, ruby grape of Proserpine;
Make not your rosary of yew-berries,
Nor let the beetle, nor the death-moth be
Your mournful Psyche, nor the downy owl
A partner in your sorrow's mysteries;
For shade to shade will come too drowsily,
And drown the wakeful anguish of the soul.
But when the melancholy fit shall fall
Sudden from heaven like a weeping cloud,
That fosters the droop-headed flowers all,
And hides the green hill in an April shroud;
Then glut thy sorrow on a morning rose,
Or on the rainbow of the salt sand-wave,
Or on the wealth of globed peonies;
Or if thy mistress some rich anger shows,
Emprison her soft hand, and let her rave,
And feed deep, deep upon her peerless eyes.
She dwells with Beauty—Beauty that must die;
And Joy, whose hand is ever at his lips
Bidding adieu; and aching Pleasure nigh,

Turning to poison while the bee-mouth sips:
Ay, in the very temple of Delight
Veil'd Melancholy has her sovran shrine,
Though seen of none save him whose strenuous tongue
Can burst Joy's grape against his palate fine;
His soul shalt taste the sadness of her might,
And be among her cloudy trophies hung.

Over the next few months, Keats produced many of his major works. In January of 1819 he wrote *The Eve of St. Agnes,* and in February, *The Eve of St. Mark.* In late April, he wrote *La Belle Dame Sans Merci,* which has appeared in these pages before.

In this year also he wrote the *Odes* that are regarded as perhaps his major contributions, and he became unofficially engaged to Fanny Brawne. Tragically, in July and August of the same year he experienced the first signs of the tuberculosis that would eventually kill him. He was staying in the Isle of Wight again, at Shanklin, beginning *Lamia.* In October, having moved to Winchester, where he wrote *To Autumn,* and began and abandoned *The Fall of Hyperion.*

As early as January, 1818, he seems to have recognized that his lifetime might be too short to realise his promise:

When I have fears that I may cease to be
Before my pen has gleaned my teeming brain,
Before high-piled books, in charactery,
Hold like rich garners the full-ripened grain;
When I behold, upon the night's starred face,
Huge cloudy symbols of a high romance,
And think that I may never live to trace
Their shadows, with the magic hand of chance;
And when I feel, fair creature of an hour,
That I shall never look upon thee more,
Never have relish in the faery power
Of unreflecting love – then on the shore
Of the wild world I stand alone, and think
Till love and fame to nothingness do sink.

In 1820, in June, following two severe haemorrhages he moved to Leigh Hunt's home. That July, *Lamia, Isabella,* and

The Eve of St. Agnes and other poems were published and well-reviewed. Here is the opening to *St. Agnes*:

St. Agnes' Eve—Ah, bitter chill it was!
The owl, for all his feathers, was a-cold;
The hare limp'd trembling through the frozen grass,
And silent was the flock in woolly fold:
Numb were the Beadsman's fingers, while he told
His rosary, and while his frosted breath,
Like pious incense from a censer old,
Seem'd taking flight for heaven, without a death,
Past the sweet Virgin's picture, while his prayer he saith.

On the 17th of September, John sailed for Italy with his artist friend Joseph Severn, arriving in Rome in November. On the 23rd of February 1821, John Keats died at 26 Piazza di Spagna, Rome; and on the 26th of February he was buried in the Protestant Cemetery there.

Percy Bysshe Shelley, his wife Mary and Mary's stepsister Claire Clairmont were staying in a house on Lake Geneva. Keats had promised he would come in the spring but he died in February. It was April before Shelley heard of his death, which inspired one of his greatest poems, *Adonais*; we discussed this poem in our earlier piece on Shelley. Here is a brief portion from stanzas 42 and 43:

He is made one with Nature: there is heard
His voice in all her music; from the moan
Of thunder to the song of night's sweet bird;
He is a presence to be felt and known
In darkness and in light, from herb and stone,
Spreading itself where'er that Power may move
Which has withdrawn his being to its own;
Which wields the world with never wearied love,
Sustains it from beneath, and kindles it above.
He is a portion of the loveliness
Which once he made more lovely: he doth bear
His part, while the one Spirit's plastic stress
Sweeps through the dull dense world, compelling there
All new successions to the forms they wear.

By this time, of course, Shelley felt that the criticisms Keats had received contributed to his early death. He wrote to Byron to inform him of Keats's death, and received a reply, of which this is an extract:

"I am very sorry to hear what you say of Keats - is it actually true? I did not think criticism had been so killing. Though I differ from you essentially in your estimate of his performances, I so much abhor all unnecessary pain, that I would rather he had been seated on the highest peak of Parnassus than have perished in such a manner.

Poor fellow! though with such inordinate self-love he would probably have not been very happy. I read the review of "Endymion" in the Quarterly. It was severe, - but surely not so severe as many reviews in that and other journals upon others.

I recollect the effect on me of the Edinburgh on my first poem; it was rage, and resistance, and redress - but not despondency nor despair. I grant that those are not amiable feelings; but, in this world of bustle and broil, and especially in the career of writing, a man should calculate upon his powers of resistance before he goes into the arena.

"Expect not life from pain nor danger free,
Nor deem the doom of man reversed for thee."

You know my opinion of that second-hand school of poetry. You also know my high opinion of your own poetry, - because it is of no school. I read Cenci - but, besides that I think the subject essentially undramatic, I am not an admirer of our old dramatists, as models.

I deny that the English have hitherto had a drama at all. Your Cenci, however, was a work of power, and poetry. As to my drama, pray revenge yourself upon it, by being as free as I have been with yours.

I have not yet got your Prometheus, which I long to see. I have heard nothing of mine, and do not know if it is yet published. I have published a pamphlet on the Pope controversy, which you will not like. Had I known that Keats was dead - or that he was alive and so sensitive - I should have omitted some remarks upon his poetry, to which I was provoked by his attack upon Pope, and my disapprobation of his own style of writing." Little more than a year later, in July 1822, Shelley was drowned while sailing off the Coast of Viareggio. The Shelleys were then living in Lerici and the bay is still known as the Bay of the Poets.

Shelley's body was identified by a book of Keats's poems which was in his pocket. His friends Trelawney and Byron made arrangements for his body to be cremated on the sea shore, and his ashes were transported to Rome and buried in the Protestant Cemetery, the same cemetery where Keats had been laid to rest.

Shelley always believed that the critical attacks on Keats's poetry were what led to his death. But I think it is clear from the information presented above that John Keats was a much stronger personality than this view would support. In particular, I think it is clear that his death was as the result of a disease that was shared by his family, exacerbated perhaps by his life style. His confidence in his own gifts, and in the poetry he produced, seem to me clear.

Keats is now regarded as one of the English language's truly great poets. As I said at the beginning of this long series, the object of the poet is the search for the right word. In the case of Keats, it appears that he didn't have to search: it was there at the end of his pen.

It is a problem to choose the Poems of the Week, but I thought I would choose three of his great Odes, all written in 1819: the *Ode on a Grecian Urn*; the *Ode to a Nightingale*; and my final Poem of this Week, appropriately enough, *To Autumn*.

I will close with one of his last sonnets, written in 1819 and directed to his love, Fanny Brawne:

The day is gone, and all its sweets are gone!
Sweet voice, sweet lips, soft hand, and softer breast,
Warm breath, light whisper, tender semitone,
Bright eyes, accomplished shape, and lang'rous waist!
Faded the flower and all its budded charms,
Faded the sight of beauty from my eyes,
Faded the shape of beauty from my arms,
Faded the voice, warmth, whiteness, paradise—
Vanished unseasonably at shut of eve,

When the dusk holiday—or holinight
Of fragrant-curtained love begins to weave
The woof of darkness thick, for hid delight;
But, as I've read love's missal through today,
He'll let me sleep, seeing I fast and pray.

I hope you enjoy this view of one of the truly great poets of the English language.

Chapter 4

Keats's "Outlawry" in "Robin Hood"

In one of his famous formulations, Keats wrote John Hamilton Reynolds on 3 February 1818 that "poetry should be great & unobtrusive, a thing which enters into one's soul, and does not startle it or amaze it with itself but with its subject." Keats included in the letter a poem that he had written a few days earlier and that Reynolds had requested, "Lines on the Mermaid Tavern," and a new poem, "Robin Hood," written specifically for Reynolds as a response to the sonnets on Robin Hood that Reynolds had just sent him.

Given their seemingly "unobtrusive" transparency of meaning and context and their distinctively minor status in Keats's work, neither of these poems has received much attention. And yet when Keats assembled his last volume of poetry in 1820, the thirteen poems that are Lamia, Isabella, The Eve of St. Agnes, and Other Poems, he included both "Lines on the Mermaid Tavern" and "Robin Hood" among the nine nonnarrative "other poems," five of the other seven, of course, being the great odes. With the exception of Isabella, no other poems written between Endymion and Hyperion except these were included in the volume, a curiosity that Walter Jackson Bate attributes to the fact that for Keats "both poems continued ... to wear well."

Given Keats's notoriously toughminded criticism of his own work, the question then, of course, is why these poems would wear so well with Keats and not at all with the critics. What significance, in other words, may these poems have had for Keats that they have not had for generations of Keats's readers?

"Robin Hood," at the very least, challenges Jerome McGann's claim that the 1820 Lamia volume is a "(politically) reactionary book" in which Keats's purpose was "to show his readers how they might, by entering his poetic space, step aside from the conflicts and tensions which were so marked an aspect of that period." If "Robin Hood" may be said to participate in the "reactionary," it does so only in a radical sense: it appropriates the national symbol of the defiant hero of revolutionary justice in feudal England to condemn the contemporary tyranny of "rents and leases" and the power of "hard money" (lines 10, 48).

Inspired by the disintegration of the literary-artistic coterie centered on Leigh Hunt, "Robin Hood" is at once a product of the coterie's collaborative discourse and, "in the Spirit of Outlawry," an indictment of the materialist interests in large part responsible for its demise. "Robin Hood" may belie McGann's assessment of Keats's purposes in the 1820 volume, but it and "Lines on the Mermaid Tavern" thoroughly illustrate McGann's broader assertion that "the most aesthetic poetry-Keats's, say, or Rossetti's—is produced within certain social contexts, and it does not merely reflect the presence and pressure of those contexts, it carries out a positive response to them."

Of and about the interdependence of the social and the aesthetic, marked in fact by their "conflicts and tensions," "Robin Hood" and "Lines on the Mermaid Tavern" must be restored to their moment in time and in text if we are to approach an understanding of the meanings they performed for Keats, meanings they have lost as they have been alienated from the world they contain.

The most immediate context of the poems is an epistolary interchange of poems between Reynolds and Keats. "Robin Hood," subtitled "To a Friend," was written specifically for Reynolds and included in his 3 February 1818 letter to Reynolds, a textual setting that will be explored in some depth later. Signing the letter as his "sincere friend and Coscribbler,"

Keats also included "Lines on the Mermaid Tavern," a poem that he had written a few days before at the Mermaid Tavern during an evening with Horace Twiss and Horace Smith and that Reynolds had soon thereafter heard recited, probably at Charles Dilke's house. Both poems were sent as an exchange for the two Robin Hood sonnets that Reynolds had just sent him, something of a return of favors, as Keats suggests: "In return for your dish of filberts, I have gathered a few Catkins, I hope they'll look pretty."

"Lines on the Mermaid Tavern" is a high-spirited "evocation," in Bate's words, "of a healthful past." Linking four time periods—the medieval forests of the legendary Robin Hood, the Elizabethan Mermaid Tavern of "poets dead and gone," the January 1818 Mermaid Tavern of Keats, and the eternal "Mermaid in the zodiac"—the poem asks the "souls of poets dead and gone" if they have found in the afterlife a place "Choicer than the Mermaid Tavern" (lines 1, 28, 26). In a playful illustration of a "favourite Speculation" that "we shall enjoy ourselves here after by having what we called happiness on Earth repeated in a finer tone and so repeated," Keats reports he has heard that his "host's sign-board flew away" and that an astrologer has spotted the "poets dead and gone" under a new old sign Sipping beverage divine, And pledging with contented smack The Mermaid in the zodiac.

(lines 19-22)

The rumor would link the Mermaid Tavern of the past with that of the present and of the eternal, and in the process, of course, thereby establish a synchronic bond between the "souls of poets dead and gone" and Keats, both then presumably raising a glass in salute to each other. The poem ends skeptically with its beginning: the question is repeated, still unanswered.

The first of Reynolds's Robin Hood sonnets ("The trees in Sherwood forest are old and good") also begins with a question, which is recast and repeated twice, but unlike "Lines on the Mermaid Tavern" it ends in an answer. Reynolds asks if the "trees in Sherwood forest" are now "deserted," if there is nothing "to mark the revelries which there have been" of those "sweet days of merry Robin Hood" (lines 1, 3, 7, 8). In the sestet, he answers by urging his reader (Keats) to "Go there," for if he does he "shalt far amid the forest know / The archer men in green," and he shall find them "feasting on pheasant, riverfowl, and swan," still "with Robin at their head, and Marian" (lines 9, 11-14).

Here, in Reynolds's Sherwood Forest, where it is always "Summer," where the trees still stand "old and good" and the grass "dimly green," the idyllic world of natural simplicity, brotherhood, and love is eternal, to be "known" if Keats will only "wander" through the forest (lines 9, 1-2). This reading would suggest that Reynolds's poem could also be a response to the concern that Keats had expressed on 22 January 1818 in his sonnet "On Sitting Down to Read King Lear Once Again":

When through the old oak forest I am gone, Let me not wander in a barren dream.

(lines 11-12)

Reynolds's poem would suggest to Keats that the dream is not "barren" but both fulfilling and fulfilled.

If the first of Reynolds's sonnets offers the possibility of experiencing the rugged idyll of the past in the present, the second, "With coat of Lincoln green and mantle too," pushes the possibility one rhetorical step further by claiming implicitly that the past has never really been the past: Robin and Marian are still there, "in the woods of Nottingham," and Reynolds describes them in the eternally present tense, for they "Can never, never die" (lines 14, 12). Reynolds's concentration on specific detail in his description of their physical presence reinforces his claim. Interestingly, this sonnet, unlike the previous two poems in the interchange, does not include a brotherhood of "merry men"; the social world is now the isolated romantic world of Robin and Marian. And in contrast with Keats's playful transportation of the paradise of the Mermaid Tavern to the eternal "in the zodiac," Reynolds has brought the eternal to Sherwood Forest.

Within this context of the personal interchange between Keats and Reynolds, Keats's response to Reynolds's Robin Hood sonnets is striking in its abrupt change of tone. Read in sequence with the previous three poems, Keats's "Robin Hood, To a Friend" is rhetorically brutal in its insistence that the glorious past is dead and irretrievable. "No!" Keats begins, "those days are gone away." Those "hours are old and gray," and even the "minutes buried all" (lines 1-3). For the eternal "Summer" of Sherwood Forest that Reynolds evokes in his first sonnet, Keats evokes an ever-recurring winter. The "loose-slung bugle" of Reynolds's Robin and the "feasting" of his "archer men in green" on "pheasant, riverfowl, and swan" have been replaced by winter's "shears" from the "frozen north" and the "chilling east" sounding "tempests" to the death of the forest, winter's "feast" (Reynolds, lines 4, 12-13; Keats, lines 6-8).

To Reynolds's call to "Go there, with Summer, and with evening,—go," with the promise that "thou shalt far amid the forest know" those "archer men in green," Keats insists in the second stanza that:

No, the bugle sounds no more, And the twanging bow no more

(lines 11-12)

for the forest is "silent" now, "no mid-forest laugh," and the only sound "some wight" might hear would be "lone Echo" (lines 15-18). If Reynolds wants to go there, he may, but no matter when or how he goes, he "never may behold /... Never one, of all the clan" (lines 23, 25).

Keats's insistence on the death of the past reaches its rhetorical climax in the first five lines of the fourth stanza:

Gone, the merry morris din; Gone, the song of Gamelyn; Gone, the tough-belted outlaw Idling in the "grene shawe"; All are gone away and past!

(lines 33-37)

Keats concludes the stanza with the most intriguing lines in the poem. Changing rhetorical strategies, he examines the consequences of Reynolds's assertion that the past may be recovered. What would be, he asks, the reactions of Robin and Marian if they could rise from their graves and encounter the England of 1818:

She would weep, and he would craze: He would swear,

for all his oaks, Fall'n beneath the dockyard strokes, Have rotted on the briny seas; She would weep that her wild bees Sang not to her—strange! that honey Can't be got without hard money!

(lines 42-48)

The world of Sherwood Forest and of Robin and Marian and the "clan" is indeed dead, a victim of a propertied world of "rents and leases" and mercantile interests. Even the ravages of winter in this world are described in commercial terms, "winter's shears" having a "feast" on the forest's "fleeces."

Having insisted through four stanzas on the impossibility of recovering a lost past, Keats begins the fifth and final stanza as abruptly as he began the first. "So it is," he tells Reynolds (line 49). The glorious past of a communal brotherhood in the forest—feasting, drinking, and singing songs—is dead, replaced by the inglorious present of their lives, where "hard money" denudes forests of oaks and domesticates the "wild bee" in order to sell its honey. The "hunting ditty" (line 27) of Robin and his clan may now be silent, but he and Reynolds can still "sing." Keats ends the poem with a rousing call to Reynolds to join him in singing in "honour" to the memory of all that "bold Robin Hood," "tight little John," "maid Marian," and "all the Sherwood clan" stood for. "Though their days have hurried by," he asks Reynolds a second and final time to join him, to assume the "burden" of song in the painful but inescapable present: "Let us two a burden try" (lines 55-62).

Within the context of the interchange, Keats's "Robin Hood" stands as the final word in a dialogue between an idealized past and a painful present. Following a pattern he employed within his own poems, Keats rejects the promise of an exclusively imaginative world, this time one that both he and Reynolds had evoked, and embraces the "burden" of the mortal world, where, however, the "burden" of "singing" may still be "tried."

Keats's "Robin Hood" is more than just the final response in a poetic dialogue between friends; it is also a comment on their lives. By February 1818 when Keats wrote "Robin Hood," the "clan" of Keats, Reynolds, Haydon, and Hunt had, to a great extent, been disbanded. The "happy atmosphere," as Bate calls it, of the heady days of late 1816, when Keats met and became fast friends with Hunt, Reynolds, and Haydon, had begun by the autumn of 1817 to degenerate into petty bickering and jealousies.

On returning in October 1817 to London from his stay with Bailey at Oxford, after having been gone for months to work on Endymion, Keats wrote him that everyone seemed to be at "Loggerheads." Haydon had moved near Hunt, but "now they live pour ainsi dire jealous Neighbors," Hunt criticizing Haydon's stalled picture "unmercifully" and Haydon warning Keats not to show Hunt Endymion lest Hunt claim that he had "done half for you." Repelled by the pettiness, Keats wrote Bailey that he was "quite disgusted with literary Men and will never know another except Wordsworth—no, not even Byron." After Wordsworth's visit to London during December and early January, Keats would not exempt Wordsworth either.

The bickering that had shocked him in October only worsened. In November, Bailey and Haydon fell out over the project to fund a year of study under Haydon for the poor Oxford student Charles Cripps, a project for which Keats had already begun raising funds. In late December and early January, the bickering between Hunt and Haydon escalated into an open breach in their friendship when Hunt was offended by Haydon's request that Hunt's wife return silver she had borrowed. The friendship between Reynolds and Haydon also degenerated into petty bitterness when Reynolds offended Haydon by not even responding to Haydon's invitation to attend his 28 December 1817 "Immortal Dinner" with Wordsworth, Lamb, Keats, and others.

The circle of his closest friends disintegrating around him, Keats wrote to his brothers on 13 and 19 January 1818 that he hoped to "bring them all together again," and, according to biographer Robert Gittings, Keats visited all three separately between 16 and 25 January, but if he tried to "bring them all together again" during these visits, his efforts failed.

In the beginning, according to Bate, when Keats had joined

in friendship with Haydon, Hunt, and Reynolds, he had believed "that there was a brotherhood in the arts, a brotherhood in all good endeavors." By 3 February 1818, when he wrote "Robin Hood," that "brotherhood" had disintegrated, causing him, as he acknowledged, "great Perplexity." The conflicts of the autumn and early winter, like the "winter" in the poem, had killed it. Read in this context, Keats's "Robin Hood" states his bitter acceptance that the glories of "the clan" are forever past and his impatience with the false promise of Reynolds's nostalgia.

"Written in the Spirit of Outlawry," Keats's "Robin Hood" may also be read as a comment to Reynolds on his recent decision to give up full-time writing in order to practice law. In April 1816, Reynolds had quit a steady job as a clerk at the Amicable Society, an insurance firm, in order to devote his full energies to writing both his poetry and his drama and poetry reviews for the Champion. In May 1817, Keats was also to reject the security of steady employment in order to live the life of a poet. As Keats's commitment to poetry strengthened, Reynolds's began to weaken. By the autumn of 1817, Reynolds was beginning to have second thoughts.

In order to marry Eliza Drewe, he had decided that he needed greater financial security, and he was worried about the stability of his job under the new owners and the new editor of the Champion. On 3 November 1817, Reynolds signed articles to read for the law in the firm of Francis Fladgate. Though Reynolds continued to write poetry and even planned a collaboration with Keats on Boccaccio's tales, both he and Keats were concerned during this period that his legal work would vitiate his ambition and ability to be a great poet. On 14 February 1818, for instance, Reynolds wrote "A Farewell to the Muses," in which he admits that he is "self banished," that the "Romance" of his youth is "past and gone."

Stoically, he accepts that his "boat is trimmed" and that he "shall coast the$shallows of the tide of Time." Farewell or not, Reynolds continued to write, but he was obviously concerned that his legal career would eventually kill his work as a poet. On 3 May 1818, Keats wrote to Reynolds addressing this concern, trying to persuade him that all knowledge, even legal knowledge, is valuable and that his study of the law should not prevent him from continuing as a poet. Within a year, however, Keats had given up on Reynolds, writing that he "is completely limed in the law: he is not only reconcil'd to it but hobbyhorses upon it."

The "Spirit of Outlawry" in which Keats describes writing "Robin Hood" is thus, on one level, a pun for his opposition to Reynolds's recent commitment to the law. As a lawyer, Reynolds will be positioned against the Robin Hoods of the world. He will work daily with the "rents and leases" of the propertied classes and will serve the commercial interests that have cut the oaks for ship timber and domesticated the "wild bee" for its honey. And like them, he will do this for "hard money," the "hard money" that he needs to obtain his "honey," in Reynolds's case, his own Maid Marian, Eliza Drewe. "So it is," says Keats, but despite the death of their carefree days as independent poets and the distraction of his legal studies, Reynolds can still join him in singing. "Let us two," Keats urges him, "a burden try."

Within this biographical context of both his and Reynolds's immediate lives, Keats may also be seen to be commenting on more than just Reynolds's new commitment to law and "hard money." During the late autumn and early winter of 1817-1818, Keats, as well as Reynolds, worked hard to raise funds for Cripps's study under Haydon. As Gittings points out, "This task partly led Keats to cultivate a set of monied people." Keats's attitude toward these new "friends" is evident in the account that he gives in his letter written on 21 and 27 December 1817 to George and Tom of a dinner at Horace Smith's, attended by several of Smith's wealthy friends, including John Kingston, the deputy comptroller of the Stamp Office and Wordsworth's superior: "These men say things which make one start, without making one feel, they are all alike ... they all know fashionables; they have a mannerism in their very eating & drinking, in their mere handling a Decanter—They talked of Kean & his low company—Would I were with that company instead of yours said I to myself! I know such like acquaintance will never do for me." Despite his reservations, Keats worked the wealthy on Cripps's behalf, writing to Haydon on 10 January that he "will ask Kingston and Co. to cash up" and to Bailey on 23 January that he will "try my luck upon as many fat-purses as I can meet with."

While his attempts to raise money from the wealthy so that poor Cripps could study art may have heightened his cousciousness of the dependency of art on the power of monied interests and exposed him more than he would have liked to the wielders of that power—a concern that surfaced again during February 1818 as he wrote Isabella and attacked the ruthlessly exploitive power of capitalism in Isabella's brothers—more important for the context of "Robin Hood" is Keats's first-hand view of how that power could "buy" even a great poet like Wordsworth. At Haydon's "Immortal Dinner" on 28 December 1817, Keats witnessed Wordsworth's introduction to his superior in the Stamp Office, Kingston. As everyone fought to suppress laughter at Lamb's drunken ridicule of Kingston for his inane attempts to engage in literary conversation, Wordsworth, learning who Kingston was, immediately tried but failed to quiet Lamb. Haydon describes Kingston's "visible effect on Wordsworth" and his chagrin for Wordsworth:

> I felt pain at the slavery of office. In command men are despotic, and those who are dependent on others who have despotic controul must & do feel affected by their presence.... I felt pain that such a Poet as Wordsworth should be under the supervisorship of such a being as this Comptroller. The People of England have a horror of Office, an instinct against it. They are right. A man's liberty is gone the moment he becomes official.

When Kingston later invited Keats and Wordsworth to dine with him on 3 January, Keats tells his brothers in his 5 January letter, "not liking that place I sent my excuse." Wordsworth, of course, accepted. Visiting Wordsworth immediately before he was to leave for Kingston's, Keats admits that he was "surp[r]ised to find him with a stiff Collar." Months later, in his 8 April 1818 letter to Haydon, the encounter with a great poet who would dress obsequiously to impress his superior is still bothering Keats: "O that he had not fit with a Warrener that is din'd al Kingston's."

Within this context and the context of Keats's obvious preoccupation with Wordsworth's deficiencies as a poet when he wrote Reynolds the 3 February 1818 letter and "Robin Hood," Keats likely had Wordsworth's subservience to state and monied interests in mind as an exemplum of the consequences of a poet's attempt to negotiate the straits between fancy and finances, a danger that of course was immediate to Reynolds and perhaps threatening to Keats. Read in this light, "Robin Hood" serves to some extent as an indictment of Wordsworth's accommodations with power and wealth.

Wordsworth, once "wild bee," no longer "sings" to "Marian" because his "honey/Can't be got without hard money!" Wordsworth's subservience to the powers of "rents and leases" is a betrayal of Robin and Marian, who stand almost mythically in the ancient ballads for the indomitable Anglo-Saxon spirit of freedom, of resistance to the tyranny of their Norman lords, embodied, of course, in the ancient counterpart to Wordsworth's official position, the Sheriff of Nottingham, the tax collector. Writing in the "Spirit of Outlawry" himself, Keats would thus be condemning another poet-outlaw who has, so to speak, "turned himself in."

Wordsworth's poetics, of course, were clearly very much on Keats's mind during the writing of "Robin Hood." The 3 February letter containing "Robin Hood," in fact, is largely devoted to the most vociferous attack on Wordsworth and Hunt that Keats would ever mount in his ambivalent negotiation of their influences on him. The attack begins with Keats's recommendation that Reynolds delete the phrase "tender and true" from the second sonnet and "not be rattlesnaked into any more of the like" by Wordsworth's influence.

"[W]e ought to read our Contemporaries" and give "Wordsworth &c ... their due," he concedes, but he worries that the effect of their influence is "to be bullied into a certain

Philosophy engendered in the whims of an Egotist." Disturbed by his recent exposure to the vanity and subservience of Wordsworth as well as by his ambivalence toward his debt to Wordsworth's poetry, poetry that he here rejects as having a "palpable design upon us," Keats positions the Elizabethan poets as alternative influences:

Modern poets differ from the Elizabethans in this. Each of the moderns like an Elector of Hanover governs his petty state, & knows how many straws are swept daily from the Causeways in all his dominions ... the antients were Emperors of vast Provinces.... I will have no more of Wordsworth or Hunt in particular.... Why should we be owls, when we can be Eagles?... Why with Wordsworths "Matthew with a bough of wilding in his hand" when we can have Jacques "under an oak &c."

Though he retreats somewhat from his attack, saying that he does not intend "to deny Wordsworth's grandeur & Hunt's merit," only that he does not want to be "teazed with grandeur & merit," Keats stands with the Elizabethans: "Let us have the old Poets, & Robin Hood."

Read in the context of Keats's concerns about poetic influences and the tradition with which he would ally himself in his struggle to mature as a poet, "Robin Hood" represents both an indictment of the moderns, represented by Wordsworth, and an acceptance that "the old Poets," though representing an attractive alternative, are indeed irrecoverable, "gone away and past" (line 37). "Never one, of all the clan" sings "some old hunting ditty," for the "merry tale" has been left a "messenger for spicy ale," the sensationalized modern poetry of Wordsworth's "egotistical sublime" (lines 25-32). In its "unobtrusiveness" the poem itself, of course, is meant to represent the very type of poetry that a poet who allies himself with the Renaissance "clan" would write. By appropriating as its subject the most famous character in ancient English ballads, Keats also may be slyly suggesting that he most confiscate the territory that Wordsworth once held and abandoned when he turned apostate to "the Spirit of Outlawry," the territory, of course, of the lyrical ballad.

The final context in which both "Lines on the Mermaid Tavern" and "Robin Hood" may be read is that of Lamia, Isabella, The Eve of St. Agnes, and Other Poems. Divided into five sections, the volume brackets nine of the other poems in the title with the four long narrative poems: Lamia, Isabella, and The Eve of St. Agnes preceding and Hyperion following. Within this section, the five great odes bracket the four remaining poems: "Ode to a Nightingale," "Ode on a Grecian Urn," and "Ode to Psyche" preceding the four, with "To Autumn" and "Ode on Melancholy" following.

The four remaining poems are thus at the centre of the section entitled "Poems," and the entire section may be said to be the centre of the volume. The volume may be thought of as having three concentric circles, the widest containing the long poems, within it the circle containing the odes, and within the odes the central circle of the four poems "Fancy," "Bards of passion and of mirth," "Lines on the Mermaid Tavern," and "Robin Hood." As one moves from the boundaries toward the centre of the volume, the poems become (within the terms of contemporary poetic currency at least) less ambitious—moving from sustained narrative to seemingly light-hearted lyric.

The constricted central circle begins with a completely unqualified commitment to the timeless and perfecting imagination in "Fancy" and ends in antithesis with an equally strong commitment to the mortal and flawed world of "Robin Hood." Following Keats's dedication to mind and imagination in "Ode to Psyche," "Fancy" begins with the total rejection of the world outside the imaginations:

Ever let the Fancy roam, Pleasure never is at home: At a touch sweet Pleasure melteth.

Having described fancy's ability to ignore the imperfections of the world as it creates its own paradise ("She will bring, in spite of frost,/Beauties that the earth hath lost"), the poem ends where it began: "Let the winged Fancy roam" for "Pleasure never is at home" (lines 29-30, 93-94). The circle of commands ("Let the ...") suggests perhaps the futility but also the persistence of the desire to withdraw from the painful world into the paradise of the mind. If Keats's world of fancy and imagination has its heroes, those heroes are unquestionably the Renaissance bards, and in the next two poems, "Bards of passion and of mirth" and "Lines on the Mermaid Tavern," those poets are portrayed as having united not only the extremes of life in their art ("passions" and "mirth") but also the mortal and the immortal, earth and heaven, "double-lived," in their earthly art and in their divine "drinking" at the "Mermaid in the zodiac" ("Bards," line 4; "Lines," line 22). In their emphasis on the union of opposites, these two poems occupy the middle circuit of the circle between "Fancy" and "Robin Hood."

"Robin Hood" completes the circle that "Fancy" began. "Robin Hood" rejects the longing of the imagination for an idyllic world of noble and simple pleasures, of timeless beauty and brotherhood—all suggested by the legend of Robin, Marian, and the "clan" in the eternal summer of the Sherwood Forest of the English imagination and by the association of the Renaissance bards in the preceding two poems with that world. Winter is very real, very deadly in this Sherwood Forest, a winter that cannot be made beantiful by "fancy." If nature and time are merciless, man is rapacious. He destroys the oak forest to build ships, and the timbers rot "on briny seas."

"Rents and leases" and "hard money" are the order of the day, not the songs of the "merry morris din" or the idyllic brotherhood of Robin, Marian, and the "clan." They are dead. "All," Keats says, "are gone away and past!" The best that we can do, this poem suggests, is to accept this world: "So it is," we must tell ourselves. Singing, however, is still possible if we only accept "the burden" of this world in our song. The final line of the poem—"Let us two a burden try"—is an invitation to the reader to enter and accept the world of time and mortality, the world that will be at the very heart of the next three poems—"To Autumn," "Ode on Melancholy," and "Hyperion."

For Keats, accepting "the burden" of this world did not mean acquiescing to it (as he thought Reynolds and

Wordsworth had done) or escaping imaginatively from it (as he was so often tempted). It meant facing it honestly and critically.

McGann's claim, then, that the Lamia volume is a "(politically) reactionary book" encouraging its readers to adopt an escapist archaicism as a refuge from present "conflicts and tensions" can be made only by ignoring the critical spirit of "Outlawry" in both Isabella and "Robin Hood." In Isabella, written soon after "Robin Hood," Keats casts the perfidious and tyrannically possessive brothers of Isabella as "ledger-men," "moneybags," whose wealth, as he describes in emphatic detail, is based on cruel and bloody exploitation (lines 137, 142). In "Robin Hood," presented finally as a public poem shorn of its epistolary and biographical contexts, he describes to contemporary Englishmen just how "craze[d]" this national hero would be were he to return to his home, a land now both controlled and destroyed by the tyranny of "rents and leases" and the power of "hard money" (lines 42, 10, 48).

Keats could count upon his readers accepting this appropriation of the Robin Hood legend to embody the "Outlawry" of his indictment of the times, for Robin Hood had come to symbolize the defiant hero of political justice. During the charged revolutionary years of the late eighteenth and early nineteenth centuries, the subversive heroics of Robin Hood were celebrated again and again on stage and in print. But it was Joseph Ritson's influential "Life of Robin Hood" in his Robin Hood of 1795 that established explicitly and authoritatively for Keats and his age the credentials of the legendary hero for the role of precursor to contemporaneous revolutionary action.

Ritson characterizes Robin Hood as a hero who "maintained a sort of independent sovereignty, and set kings, judges, and magistrates, at defiance," who "took away the goods of rich men only ... nor ever took any thing from the poor, but charitably fed them with the wealth he drew from abbots," who, under a complicated tyranny, displayed a spirit of freedom and independence which has endeared him to the common people, whose cause he maintained, (for all opposition to tyranny is the cause of the people), and, in spite of the malicious endeavours of pitiful monks, by whom history was consecrated to the crimes and follies of titled ruffians and sainted idiots, to suppress all record of his patriotic exertions and virtuous acts.

Ritson's appropriation of Robin Hood as a revolutionary hero for a revolutionary age was well within the tradition of Robin Hood's received cultural significance. Surveying the tradition of Robin Hood ballads and legends, Maurice Keen in 1961 wrote that "the historical significance" of Robin Hood resides in his being an "enemy of the existing order," that he and the other outlaws celebrated in ballads "who put themselves outside and against the law" became "popular heroes" because "the existing order was generally regarded as tyrannical."

Keats's "Robin Hood" appropriates this cultural symbol of man's fight for economic and political justice in order to condemn its contemporary defeat. For Keats, then, "Robin Hood" was much more than just a private poem that "wore well." If it "wore well," it did so because the period between its writing and its inclusion in the 1820 volume would only reinforce for Keats the validity of his condemnation. Having abandoned the outlaw life of a fulltime poet and critic and writing only sporadically, Reynolds was by 1820 permanently "limed" in the law. And Wordsworth's submission to the powers of "rents and leases" and "hard cash" would prove to be a worse betrayal than it appeared to Keats when he wrote the poem.

Though probably unknown to Keats during early February when he wrote the poem, Wordsworth, once the self-proclaimed voice of the common man, had left London abruptly in January of 1818 in order to join in a political battle to defeat a contemporary voice of the people, the well-known liberal defender of John and Leigh Hunt and of Manchester radicals, Henry Brougham. Brougham threatened a parliamentary seat controlled by the man who had made Wordsworth a tax collector, his benefactor, Lord Lonsdale. Even as Keats wrote "Robin Hood," Wordsworth was battling this liberal threat to the established order and serving his master by spying on his friends and reporting back their political allegiances. Convinced already of Wordsworth's apostasy to the liberal principles of his early poetry, Keats was nevertheless "staggered," according to Stephen Gill, when, on attempting to visit the poet in June, he was told that Wordsworth was out canvassing for Brougham's reactionary opponent.

Written during a crisis in Keats's formulation of his role as a poet, "Robin Hood" thus came to represent for Keats both a condemnation of the invidiously seductive and deadly powers of the world of "hard cash" and a defiant determination to create a poetry that would resist that world by remaining faithful to the poetic and political spirit of "Outlawry" that Robin Hood symbolized. It would be "a burden" that he, alone if he must, "would try." By including "Robin Hood" in the 1820 volume, Keats marked the moment that he took on that "burden." And in the poems that surround it, he sings the results of his labour.

Chapter 5

The Eve of Saint Mark Criticism

English lyric poet, the archetype of the Romantic writer. While still in good health, Keats was ambitious of doing the world some good, instead of focusing on his own sensitive soul. Keats felt that the deepest meaning of life lay in the apprehension of material beauty, although his mature poems reveal his fascination with a world of death and decay. Most of his best work appeared in one year.

Darkling I listen; and for many a time
I have been half in love with easeful Death
(from 'To a Nightingale')

John Keats was born in London as the son of a successful livery-stable manager. He was the oldest of four children, who remained deeply devoted to each other. Thomas, his father, was the chief hostler at the Swan and Hoop. After their father died in 1804 in a riding accident, Keats's mother, Frances Jennings Keats, remarried but the marriage was soon broken. She moved with the children, John and his sister Fanny and brothers George and Tom, to live with her mother at Edmonton, near London. She died of tuberculosis in 1810.

At school Keats read widely. He was educated at the progressive Clarke's School in Enfield, where he began a translation of the *Aeneid*. Keats, who was barely five feet tall, was not know at school for his enthusiasm for books, but his fighting. "My mind has been the most discontented and restless one that ever was put into a body too small for it," he wrote. 1811 Keats was apprenticed to a surgeon-apothecary. While studying for the licence, he completed his translation of *Aeneid*. Edmund Spenser's *Faerie Queene* impressed him deeply and his first poem, written in 1814, was 'Lines in Imitation of Spenser.' In that year he moved to London and resumed his surgical studies in 1815 as a student at Guy's hospital. Next year he became a Licentiate of the Society of Apothecaries and was allowed to practice surgery. Before devoting himself entirely to poetry, Keats worked as a dresser and junior house surgeon. In London he had met Leigh Hunt, the editor of the leading liberal magazine of the day, *The Examiner*. He introduced Keats to other young Romantics, including Shelley, and published in the magazine Keats's sonnet, 'O Solitude'.

Keats's first book, *Poems,* was published in 1817. Sales were poor. He spent the spring with his brother Tom and friends at Shankin. It was about this time Keats started to use his letters as the vehicle of his thoughts of poetry. They mixed the everyday events of his own life with comments with his correspondence. Among others T.S. Eliot considered the letters in *The Use of Poetry and the Use of Criticism* (1933) "certainly the most notable and most important ever written by any English poet," but also said about Keats's famous *Hyperion*: "it contains great lines, but I do not know whether it is a great poem." The first of his famous letters Keats wrote to Benjamin Bailey on November 22, 1817.

"You perhaps at one time thought there was such thing as Worldly Happiness to be arrived at, at certain periods of time marked out - you have necessity from your disposition been thus led away - I scarcely remember counting upon any Happiness". *Endymion,* Keats's first long poem appeared, when he was 21. It told in 4000 lines of the love of the moon goddess Cynthia for the young shepherd Endymion. It was attacked among others by John Wilson Croker and John Gibson Lochard, who wrote in *Blackwood's Edinburgh Magazine*: '... it has just as much to do with Greece as it has with "old Tartary the fierce;" no man, whose mind has ever been imbued with the smallest knowledge or feeling of classical poetry or classical history, could have stooped to profane and vulgarize every association in the manner which has been adopted by this "son of promise."' Although the critical reaction was lukewarm,

Keats was not discouraged by it, but wrote to Richard Woodhouse: "I am ambitious of doing the world some good: if I should be spared that may be the work of mature years - in the interval I will assay to reach to as high a summit in Poetry as the nerve bestowed upon me will suffer."

Keats's greatest works were written in the late 1810s, among them *Lamia, The Eve of St. Agnes,* the great odes and two versions of *Hyperion*. He worked briefly as a theatrical critic for *The Champion,* spent summer of 1818 touring the Lakes, Scotland and Northern Ireland. During his journey, which he made with his friend Charles Brown, a businessman, he vowed: "I shall learn poetry here and shall henceforth write more than ever." After returning to London he spent the next three months attending his brother Tom, who was seriously ill with tuberculosis.

After Tom's death in December, Keats moved to Hampstead to live with Charles Brown. Soon he fell in love with Fanny Brown, the daughter of a widowed neighbour, and they were betrothed. In the winter of 1818-19 he worked mainly on *Hyperion* and *The Eve of St Agnes*. The fragmentary *Eve of St Mark* were composed during a visit to his friend Charles Wentworth Dilke's parents and relatives in Sussex. In 1819 Keats finished *Lamia,* and wrote another version of *Hyperion,* called *The Fall of Hyperion*. His famous poem 'Ode on a Grecian Urn' was inspired by a Wedgwood copy of a Roman copy of a Greek vase. Josiah Wedgwood's copy was purchased by Sir William Hamilton, who sold it to the duchess of Portland. She denoted the vase to the British Museum in 1784.

'Beauty is truth, truth beauty,' - that is all
Ye know on earth and all ye need to know.
(from 'Ode on a Grecian Urn')

In 1820 appeared the second volume of Keats poems. It gained a huge critical success. However, Keats was suffering at that time from tuberculosis. His poems were marked with sadness partly because he was too poor to marry Fanny Brawne. Keats broke off his engagement and began what he called a "posthumous existence." In a letter from 1819 he had written. "I love you more in that I believe you have liked me for my own sake and nothing else. I have met with women whom I relay think would like to be married to a Poem and given away by a Novel."

When his condition gradually worsened, he sailed for Italy in September with the painter Joseph Severn, to escape England's cold winter. Declining Shelley's invitation to join him at Pisa, Keats went to Rome, where he took up residence in rooms overlooking the Piazza di Spagna, He died in Rome at the age of 25, on February 23, 1821, and was buried in the Protestant Cemetery. Keats did not invent his own epitaph, but remembered words from the play Philaster, or Love Lies-Ableeding, written by Beaumont and Fletcher in 1611. "All your better deeds / Shall be in water writ," one of the characters says. Keats told his friend Joseph Severn that he wanted on his grave just the line, "Here lies one whose name was writ in water."

Bright star! would I were steadfast as thou art -
Not in lone splendour hung aloft the night
(from 'The Last Sonnet')

In spite of early harsh criticism, Keats's reputation grew after his death. The poet's letters were published in 1848 and 1878. Keats's works have influenced among others The Pre-Raphaelites, Oscar Wilde and Alfred Tennyson. Some later poets have attacked Keats and the Romantics: for T.S. Eliot Byron was "a disorderly mind, and an uninteresting one" and Keats and Shelley were "not nearly such great poets as they are supposed to be". Andrew Motion claims in his biography on Keats (1998) that the author was obsessed with sex and had venereal disease and these aspects of the poets life were hidden by early biographers, who underlined Keats's poverty, poor health, and misunderstanding criticism.

Chapter 6

John Keats his Life and Poetry, his Friends, Critics and After-fame

The work of Keats's two mature years (if any poet or man in his twenty-third and twenty-fourth years can be called mature) seems to divide itself naturally into two main groups or classes. One class consists of his finished achievements, things successfully carried through in accordance with his first intention; the other of his fragments and experiments, things begun and broken off either from external causes or because in the execution the poet changed his mind or his inspiration failed to sustain itself.

We shall ask the reader to consider the two classes separately, the achievements first: not because there may not be even finer work in some of the fragments, but because a thing incomplete, a torso, however splendid in power and promise, cannot be judged on the same terms or with the same approach to finality as a thing of which the whole is before us.

One finished thing only, the play of Otho the Great, I shall turn over to the second or experimental class, seeing that an experiment it essentially was, and one tried under conditions which made it impossible for Keats to be his true self.

The class of achievements will include, then, besides a score of sonnets and a few minor pieces of various form, the three completed tales in verse, *Isabella, or the Pot of Basil, The Eve of St Agnes,* and *Lamia*; with the six odes, *To Psyche, On Indolence* (not published in Keats's lifetime), *On a Grecian Um, To a Nightingale, To Melancholy,* and *To Autumn*. Beginning with the minor things,—the sonnets, being mostly occasional and autobiographical, have been sufficiently touched on in our narrative chapters, and so have several of the shorter lyrics, *In drear-nighted December*, *Meg Menilies*, and *La Belle Dame Sans Merci*.

There remains chiefly the batch of pieces in the seven-syllable couplet metre printed in the *Lamia* volume between the odes *To Psyche* and *To Autumn*. Two of these, *Lines on the Mermaid Tavern* and *Robin Hood*, were written, as we have seen, at the beginning of 1818, in the months when Keats was living alone in Well Walk and resting after his labour on *Endymion*. Both are easy, spirited, and intensely English in feeling; both, for all their gay lightness of touch, are marked with that vivid imaginative life in single phrases which almost from the first, amidst all the rawnesses of his youth, stamps Keats for a poet of the great lineage. Already two years earlier, in the valentine 'Hadst thou liv'd in days of old,' he had shown a fair command of this metre, and now we can feel that he has an ear well trained in its cadences by familiarity with the finest early models, from Fletcher (in the *Faithful Shepherdess*) and Ben Jonson (in the masque of *The Satyr*, the songs To Celia, and the Charis lyrics) down to *L'Allegro* and *Il Penseroso*.

The other two pieces in the same form, *Bards of Passion and of Mirth* and *Fancy*, date from nearly a year later, when Keats had settled under Brown's roof after Tom's death, and were copied by him for his brother in a letter dated January 2nd, 1819. In the *Mermaid Tavern* lines he had followed in fancy the poet-guests of that hostelry to the Elysian fields and asked them if they found there any finer entertainment than in their old haunt. In *Bards of Passion and of Mirth*, which he wrote on a blank page in Dilke's copy of Beaumont and Fletcher, Keats singles out this particular pair of poet-partners to follow beyond the grave, and in a strain somewhat more serious tells of the double lives they lead,—their souls left here on earth in their writings, and themselves—

> *Seated on Elysian lawns*
> *Brows'd by none but Dian's fawns ...*
> *Where the nightingale cloth sing*

Not a senseless, tranceèd thing,
But divine, melodious truth;
Philosophic numbers smooth;
Tales and golden histories
Of heaven and its mysteries.
In the affirmation with which the piece concludes,—
Bards of Passion and of Mirth,
Ye have left your souls on Earth!
Ye have souls in heaven too,
Double-liv'd in regions new!—

in this affirmation it seems, as Mr Buxton Forman has pointed out, as though Keats were gaily countering the view of Wordsworth in the well-known stanzas where., declaring how the power of Burns survives 'deep in the general heart of men,' he goes on to ask what need has the poet for any other kind of Elysian after-life.

Following an eighteenth-century practice, Keats calls this set of hepta-syllabics an ode, a form which in strictness it no way resembles. A higher place is taken in his work by the longest poem he sends his brother in the same metre, *Fancy*. He calls it a rondeau, again rather at random; but he had already called the Bacchus lyric in *Endymion* a roundelay, and seems to have thought that the name might apply to any set of verses returning upon itself at the end with a repetition of its beginning. In the present case he both opens and closes his poem with the same idea as has been condensed by a later writer in the two-line refrain—

But every poet, born to stray,
Still feeds upon the far-away.
The opening lines run,—
Ever let the Fancy roam,
Pleasure never is at home:
At a touch sweet Pleasure melteth,
Like to bubbles when rain pelteth;
Then let winged Fancy wander
Through the thought still spread beyond her:
Open wide the mind's cage-door,
She'll dart forth, and cloudward soar.

O sweet Fancy! let her loose;
Summer's joys are spout by use,
And the enjoying of the Spring
Fades as does its blossoming;
Autumn's red-lipp'd fruitage too,
Blushing through the mist and dew,
Cloys with tasting: What do then?

The answer is that the thing to do is to sit by the chimney comer while Fancy goes ranging abroad to find and bring home a harvest of incompatible and contradictory delights; and after the evocation of a number of such the poem comes round at the end to a slightly altered repetition of its opening couplet,—

Let the winged Fancy roam
Pleasure never is at home.

I like to think that Keats may have drawn his impulse to writing this poem from the fine passage in Fuller *Holy State* quoted by Lamb in his brief "'Specimens'" of that author:—

Fancy.—It is the most boundless and restless faculty of the soul.... it digs without spade, sails without ship, flies without wings, builds without charges, fights without bloodshed; in a moment striding from the centre to the circumference of the world; by a kind of omnipotency creating and annihilating things in an instant; and things divorced in Nature are married in Fancy as in a lawless place.

At any rate Keats's poem, in its best and central part, is a delightful embroidery on the ideas here expressed. The notion, or vision, of a lawless place where all manner of things divorced in nature abide together and happily jostle, was one that often haunted him, as witness his verse-epistle to Reynolds from Teignmouth, the fragment he calls *The Castle Builder*, and again the piece beginning 'Welcome joy and welcome sorrow,' to which there has been posthumously given the title A Song of Opposites.

The lines evoking such a vision in this poem, *Fancy*, are almost his happiest in his lighter vein, and are written in the true Elizabethan tradition: the predominant influence in the handling of the measure being, to my ear, that of Ben Jonson, who is wont to give it a certain weight and slowness of movement by the free use of long syllables in the unaccented places; even so Keats, in the passage quoted above, puts in such places words Eke 'sweet,' 'rain,' 'still,' 'cage,' 'dart,' 'lipp'd.'

Passing from the minor to the major achievements of the time, the earliest, and to my mind the finest, of these is *Isabella, or the Pot of Basil*. During the writing of *Endymion*, Keats had intended his next effort to be on the lofty classic and symbolic theme of the dethronement of Hyperion and the Titans and the accession of Apollo and the Olympians. But certain reading and talk in the Hunt circle having diverted him from this purpose for a while, and made him take up the idea of a volume of metrical tales from Boccaccio to be written jointly by himself and Reynolds, he chose the tale of the Pot of Basil (the fifth of the fourth day in the *Decameron*), made a sudden beginning at it before he left Hampstead at the end of February (1819), and finished it at Teignmouth in the course of April.

As an appropriate vehicle for an Italian story he took the Italian *ottava rima* or stanza of eight. Several of the earlier English poets had used this metre: Keats's main model for it was doubtless Edward Fairfax, who, following other Elizabethan translators, had in his fine version from Tasso, *Godfrey of Bulloigne*, done much more than any of his predecessors towards suppling and perfecting its treatment in English. Since then it had been little employed in our serious poetry, but had lately been brilliantly revived for flippant and satiric uses, after later Italian models, by Hookham Frere and Byron. Keats goes over the heads of these direct to Fairfax, and in certain points at least, in variety of pause and cadence and subtle adaptation of verbal music to emotional effect, by a good deal outdoes even that excellent master. Of course it is of the essence of his treatment to avoid, in the closing couplet of the stanza, the special effect of witty snap and suddenness which fits it so well for the purpose of satire.

Every one knows the story: how a maiden of Messina (Keats chooses to transfer the scene to Florence), living in the house of her merchant brothers, in secret loves one of their clerks: how her brothers, discovering her secret, take out her lover to the forest and there slay and bury him: how his ghost appearing to her in a dream reveals his fate and burial place: how she hastens thither with her nurse, digs till she finds the corpse and having found it carries home the head and sets it in a pot of basil, or sweet marjoram, which she cherishes and waters With her tears until her brothers take it from her, whereupon she pines away and dies.

Boccaccio tells this story with that admirable combination of straightforward conciseness and finished grace which characterizes his mature prose. Keats in his poem romantically amplifies and embroiders it. In his way of doing so we can trace the influence of Chaucer, with whose *Troilus and Criseyde,* that miracle of detailed, long-drawn, yet ever human and rarely tedious narrative, he was by this time familiar. Keats, while avoiding Chaucer's prolixity, diversifies his tale with invocations to Love and to the Muses, with apostrophes to the reader and ejaculatory comments on the events, entirely in Chaucer's manner: only whereas Chaucer relegates the more part of such matter to the 'proems' of his several books, Keats, having plunged into the thick of the story in his first line, finds room for his apostrophes and invocations in the course of the narrative itself.

Most critics have taken the view that this is evidence of weak or immature art. To my mind this is not so: the pauses thus introduced are never long enough to hold up the flow and interest of the narrative, while they afford welcome rests to the attention, pleasant changes from a too sustained narrative construction, with consequent beautiful and happy modulations in the movement of the verse.

One of these invocations—invocation and apology together—is to Boccaccio himself, disowning all idea of improving the tale and defining the poet's attempt as made but to honour him,—

To stead thee as a verse in English tongue,
An echo of thee in the north-wind sung.

The definition is exact. The revived spirit of English romantic poetry breathes in every line of the verse, and as in

Endymion, so here, the southern setting is conceived as though it were English. 'So the two brothers and their murder'd man' (the force of the anticipatory epithet has been celebrated by every critic since Lamb)—

So the two brothers and their murder'd man
Rode past fair Florence, to where Arno's stream
Gurgles through straiten'd banks, and still doth fan
Itself with dancing bulrush, and the bream
Keep head against the freshets.

Another such criticized 'digression' tells of the toilers yoked in all quarters of the world to the service of these avaricious merchant brothers. In calling up their sufferings Keats for a moment strikes an unexpected verbal echo from the *Annus Mirabilis* of Dryden. Dryden, telling of the monopolies of the Dutch in the East India trade, had written,—

For them alone the Heav'ns had kindly heat,
In eastern quarries ripening precious dew:
For them the Idumean balm did sweat,
And in hot Ceilon spicy forests grew.

Keats writes of Isabella's brothers,—

For them the Ceylon diver held his breath,
And went all naked to the hungry shark,
For them his ears gush'd blood—

with more in the same strain, very vividly and humanly imagined, but somewhat unevenly written. On the other hand the last of the rests or interruptions in this poem is to my thinking one of its most original and admirable beauties: I mean the invocation beginning 'O Melancholy, linger here awhile,' repeated with lovely modulations in stanzas lv, lvi, and lxi; the poet deliberately pausing to heighten his effect as it were by an accompaniment of words chosen purely for their pathetic melody and more musical than music itself.

Keats's way of imagining and telling the story is not less delicate than it is intense. Flaws and false notes there are: phrases, as in Endymion, too dulcet and cloying, like that which tells how the lover's lips grew bold, 'And poesied with hers in dewy rhyme': a flat line where it is most out of place—'And *Isabella* did not stamp or rave': a far-fetched rime, as where 'love' and 'grove' draw in after them the alien idea of Lorenzo not being embalmed in 'Indian clove.' But such flaws, abundant in Endymion, are in *Isabella* rare and need to be searched for. If we want an example of the staple tissue of the poem we shall rather find it in a stanza like this:—

Parting they seem'd to tread upon the air,
Twin roses by the zephyr blown apart
Only to meet again more close, and share
The inward fragrance of each other's heart.
She, to her chamber gone, a ditty fair
Sang of delicious love and honey'd dart;
He with light steps went up a western hill,
And bade the sun farewell, and joy'd his fill.

The image of love-happiness in the last couplet is as jocund and uplifting as some radiant symbolic drawing by Blake, and poetry has few things more perfect or easier in their perfection.

In a far more difficult kind, where Keats has to deal with the features of the story that might easily make for the repulsive or the *macabre,* he triumphs not by shirking but by sheer force of passionate imagination. 'The excellence of every art is its intensity, capable of making all disagreeables evaporate from their being in close relationship with beauty and truth.' This dictum of Keats can scarcely be better illustrated than by his own handling of the *Isabella* story. Take the vision of the murdered man appearing to the girl at night:—

Strange sound it was, when the pale shadow spake;
For there was striving, in its piteous tongue,
To speak as when on earth it was awake,
And Isabella on its music hung:
Languor there was in it, and tremulous shake,
As in a palsied Druid's harp unstrung;
And through it moan'd a ghostly under-song,
Like hoarse night-gusts sepulchral briars among.
Its eyes, though wild, were still all dewy bright
With love, and kept all phantom fear aloof
From the poor girl by magic of their light.

How wonderfully, in these touches, do we feel love prevailing over horror and purging the apparition of all its charnel ghastliness. When we come to the discovery and digging up of the body, Boccaccio turns the difficulty which must inhere in any realistic treatment of the theme by simply saying that it was uncorrupted; as though some kind of miracle had kept it fresh. Keats on the other hand confronts the difficulty and overcomes it. First he acknowledges how the imagination in dwelling on the dead is prone to call up images of corruptibility:—

Who hath not loiter'd in a green church-yard,
And let his spirit, like a demon-mole,
Work through the clayey soil and gravel hard,
To see scull, coffin'd bones, and funeral stole;
Pitying each form that hungry Death hath marr'd,
And filling it once more with human soul?
Ah! this is holiday to what was felt
When Isabella by Lorenzo knelt.

Then he compulsively leads away the mind from such images to think only of the passionate absorption with which *Isabella* flings herself upon her task:—

She gaz'd into the fresh-thrown mould, as though
One glance did fully all its secrets tell;
Clearly she saw, as other eyes would know
Pale limbs at bottom of a crystal well;
Upon the murderous spot she seem'd to grow,
Like to a native lilly of the dell:
Then with her knife, all sudden, she began
To dig more fervently than misers can.
Soon she turn'd up a soiled glove, whereon
Her silk had play'd in purple phantasies,
She kiss'd it with a lip more chill than stone,
And put it in her bosom, where it dries
And freezes utterly unto the bone
Those dainties made to still an infant's cries:
Then 'gan she work again; nor stay'd her care,
But to throw back at times her veiling hair.

Is any scene in poetry written with more piercing, more

unerring, vision? The swift despairing gaze of the girl, anticipating with too dire a certainty the realization of her dream: the simile in the third and fourth lines, emphasizing the clearness of that certainty, and at the same time relieving its terror by an image of beauty: the new simile of the lily, again striking the note of beauty, while it intensifies the impression of her rooted fixity of posture and purpose: the sudden solution of that fixity, with the final couplet, into vehement action, as she begins (with a fine implied commentary on the relative strength of passions) to dig 'more fervently than misers can':—then the first reward of her toil, in the shape of a relic not ghastly, but beautiful both in itself and for the tenderness of which it is a token: her womanly action in kissing it and putting it in her bosom, while all the woman and mother in her is in the same words revealed to us as blighted by the tragedy of her life: then the resumption and continuance of her labours, with gestures once more of vital dramatic truth as well as grace:—to imagine and to write like this is the privilege of the best poets only, and even the best have not often combined such concentrated force and beauty of conception with such a limpid and flowing ease of narrative.

Poetry had always come to Keats as naturally as leaves to a tree. So he considered it ought to come, and now that it came of a quality like this, he had fairly earned the right, which his rash youth had too soon arrogated, to look down on the fine artificers of the school of Pope. In comparison with the illuminating power of true imaginative poetry, the closest rhetorical condensations of that school seem thin, their most glittering points and aphorisms mechanical: nay, those who admire them most justly will know better than to think the two kinds of writing comparable. The final consignment by *Isabella* of her treasure to its casket is told with the same genius for turning horror into beauty: note the third and fourth lines of the following, with the magically cooling and soothing effect of their open-vowelled sonority;—

Then in a silken scarf,—sweet with the dews Of precious flowers pluck'd in Araby, And divine liquids come with odorous ooze Through the cold serpent-pipe refreshfully,-She wrapp'd it up; and for its tomb did choose A garden-pot, wherein she laid it by, And cover'd it with mould, and o'er it set Sweet Basil, which her tears kept ever wet.

And she forgot the stars, the moon, and sun, And she forgot the blue above the trees, And she forgot the dells where waters run, And she forgot the chilly autumn breeze; She had no knowledge when the day was done, And the new morn she saw not: but in peace Hung over her sweet Basil evermore, And moisten'd it with tears unto the core.

In passages like these of *Isabella* Keats, for one reader at least, reaches his high-water mark in human feeling, and in felicity both imaginative and executive. The next of his three poetic tales, *The Eve of St Agnes*, does not strike so deep, though it is more nearly faultless and lives as the most complete and enchanting English pure romance-poem of its time. Little or none of the effect is due in this case to elements of magic weirdness or supernatural terror such as counted for so much in the general romantic poetry of the day, and had been of the very essence of achievements so diverse as *The Ancient Mariner, Christabel, The Lay of the Last Minstrel,* and *Isabella* itself.

The tale hinges on the popular belief that on St Agnes's Eve (January the 20th) a maiden might win sight of her future husband in a dream by going to bed supperless, silent and without looking behind her, and sleeping on her back with her hands on the pillow above her head. This belief is mentioned by two writers at least with whom Keats was very familiar: by Ben Jonson in his masque *The Satyr* and Robert Burton in the *Anatomy of Melancholy*. An eighteenth-century book of reference which he may well have known also, Brand's Popular Antiquities, cites the superstition and adds from a current chapbook a fuller account of it, mentioning other and alternative rites. But one feature of the promised vision which in Keats's mind was evidently essential, that the lover should regale his mistress after her fasting dream with exquisite viands and music, is not noted in any of these sources: Keats must either have invented it or drawn it from some other authority which criticism has not yet recognised.

It was an obvious and easy idea for Keats to weave into

the St Agnes's Eve motive the motive of a lovepassion between the son and daughter of hostile houses, and to bring the youth to a festival in the halls of his enemies in a manner which reminds one both of Romeo and Juliet and of the young Lochinvar in Scott's ballad.

A remoter source has lately been pointed out as probable for the subsequent incidents of the lover's concealment by the old nurse in a closet next the maiden's chamber, his coming in to her while she sleeps, the melting of his real self into her dream of him, her momentary disenchantment and alarm on awakening, her re-assurance and surrender and their ensuing happy union and flight. All these circumstances, it has been shown, except the immediate flight of the lovers, are closely paralleled in Boccaccio's early novel *Il Filocolo*, and look as though they must have been derived from it. The *Filocolo* is an excessively tedious and occasionally coarse amplification in prose, made by Boccaccio when his style was still unformed, of the old French metrical romance, long popular throughout Europe, of Floire et Blancheflor. The question is, how should Keats have come to be acquainted with it?

At this time he knew very little Italian. He was accustomed to read his Decameron in a translation, and eight months later we find him with difficulty making out Ariosto at the rate of ten or a dozen stanzas a day. A French seventeenth-century version of the *Filocolo* indeed existed, but none in English. Can it be that Hunt had told Keats the story, or at least those parts of it which would serve him, in the course of talk about Boccaccio? One would not have expected even Hunt's love of Italian reading to sustain him through the tedium of this early and little known novel by the master: moreover in criticizing *The Eve of St Agnes* he gives no hint that Keats was indebted to him for any of its incidents.

But there the resemblances are, too close to be easily explained as coincidences. The part played by the old nurse Angela in Keats's poem echoes pretty closely the part played by Glorizia in the *Filocolo*; the drama, dreaming and awake, played between Madeline and Porphyro, repeats, though in a far finer strain, that between Biancofiore and Florio; so that

Keats's narrative reads truly like a magically refined and enriched quintessence distilled from the corresponding chapter in Boccaccio's tale.

But the question of sources is one for the special student, and its discussion may easily tire the lay reader. Passing to the poem and its qualities, we have to note first that, fresh from treading, in his Hyperion attempt, in the path of Milton, Keats in *The Eve of St Agnes* went back, so far as his manner is derivative at all, to the example of his first master, Spenser. He shows as perfect a command of the Spenserian stanza, with its 'sweet-slipping movement,' as Spenser himself, and as subtle a sense as his of the leisurely meditative pace imposed upon the metre by the lingering Alexandrine at the close.

Narrating at this pace and in this mood, he is able at any moment with the lightest of touches to launch the imagination to music on a voyage beyond the beyonds and to charge every line, every word almost, with a richness and fullness of far-away suggestion that yet never clogs the easy harmonious flow of the verse. At the same time he does not, in this new poem, attempt anything like the depth of human passion and pathos which he had touched in *Isabella,* and his personages appeal to us in the manner strictly defined as 'romantic,' that is to say not so much humanly and in themselves as by the circumstances, scenery, and atmosphere amidst which they move.

In handling these Keats's method is the reverse of that by which some writers vainly endeavour to rival in literature the effects of the painter and sculptor. He never writes for the eye merely, but vivifies everything he touches, telling even of dead and senseless things in terms of life, movement, and feeling. From the opening stanza, which makes us feel the chill of the season to our bones,—telling us first of its effect on the wild and tame creatures of wood and field, and next how the frozen breath of the old beadsman in the chapel aisle 'seem'd taking flight for heaven, without a death,'—from thence to the close, where the lovers disappear into the night, the poetry throbs in every line with the life of imagination and beauty. The monuments in the aisle are brought before us, not by any effort of description, but solely through our sympathy with the shivering fancy of the beadsman:—

Knights, ladies, praying in dumb orat'ries,
He passeth by; and his weak spirit fails
To think how they may ache in icy hoods and mails.

Even into the sculptured heads of the corbels supporting the banquet-hall roof the poet strikes life:—

The carved angels, ever eager-eyed,
Stared, where upon their heads the cornice rests,
With wings blown back, and hands put cross-wise on their breasts.—
As to support incumbent floor or roof,
For corbel is a figure sometimes seen
That crumples up its knees into its breast;
With the feign'd posture, stirring ruth unfeign'd
In the beholder's fancy; so I saw
These fashion'd—.

The painted panes in the chamber window, instead of trying to pick out their beauties in detail, he calls—

Innumerable of stains and splendid dyes
As are the tiger-moth's deep-damask'd wings,—

A gorgeous phrase which leaves the widest range to the colour-imagination of the reader, giving it at the same time a sufficient clue by the simile drawn from a particular specimen of nature's blazonry. In the last line of the same stanza—

A shielded scutcheon blush'd with blood of queens and kings, —the word 'blush' makes the colour seem to come and go, while the mind is at the same time sent travelling from the maiden's chamber on thoughts of her lineage and ancestral fame. Observation, I believe, shows that moonlight has not the power to transmit the separate hues of painted glass as Keats in this celebrated passage represents it, but fuses them into a kind of neutral or indiscriminate opaline shimmer.

Let us be grateful for the error, if error it is, which has led him to heighten, by these saintly splendours of colour, the sentiment of a scene wherein a voluptuous glow is so exquisitely attempered with chivalrous chastity and awe. If any reader wishes to realise how the genius of Elizabethan romantic poetry re-awoke in Keats, and how much enriched and enhanced, after two hundred years, let him compare all this scene of Madeline's unrobing with the passage from Brown *Britannia's Pastorals* which was probably in his memory when he wrote it.

When Madeline unclasps her jewels, a weaker poet would have dwelt on their lustre or other visible qualities: Keats puts those aside, and speaks straight to our spirits in an epithet breathing with the very life of the wearer,—'Her warmèd jewels.' When Porphyro spreads the feast of dainties beside his sleeping mistress, we are made to feel how those ideal and rare sweets of sense surround and minister to her, not only with their own natural richness, but with the associations and the homage of all far countries whence they have been gathered—

From silken to cedar'd Lebanon.

Concerning this sumptuous passage of the spread feast of fruits, not unequally rivalling the famous one in Milton, Leigh Hunt has some interesting things to say in his *Autobiography*:—

I remember Keats reading to me, with great relish and particularity, conscious of what he had set forth, the lines describing the supper and ending with the words,

And lucent syrups tinct with cinnamon.

Mr. Wordsworth would have said the vowels were not varied enough; but Keats knew where his vowels were not to be varied. On the occasion above alluded to, Wordsworth found fault with the repetition of the concluding sound of the participles in Shakespeare's line about bees:—

The he singing masons building roofs of gold.

This, he said, was a line which Milton would never have written. Keats thought, on the other hand, that the repetition was in harmony with the continued note of the singers, and that Shakespeare's negligence, if negligence it was, had instinctively felt the thing in the best manner.

The reader will remember how Bailey records this subject of the musical and emotional effect of vowel sounds, open and close, varied or iterated as the case might be, as one on which

Keats's talk had often run at Oxford. Whatever his theories, he was by this time showing himself as fine a master of such effects as any, even the greatest, of our poets.

This same passage, or interlude, of the feast of fruits has despite its beauty been sometimes blamed as a 'digression.' A stanza which in Keats's original draft stood near the beginning of the poem shows that in his mind it was no mere ornament and no digression at all, but an essential part of his scheme. In revision he dropped out this stanza, doubtless as being not up to the mark poetically: pity that he did not rather perfect it and let it keep its place: but even as it is the provision of the dainties made beforehand by the old nurse at Porphyro's request (stanza XX) proves the feast essential to the story.

While the unique charm of *The Eve of St Agnes* lies thus in the richness and vitality of the accessory and decorative images, the actions and emotions of the personages are not less happily conceived as far as they go. What can be better touched than the figures of the beadsman and the old nurse Angela? How admirable in particular is the debate held by Angela with Porphyro in her

little moonlight room
Pale, lattic'd, chill, and silent as a tomb.

Madeline, a figure necessarily in the main passive, is none the less exquisite, whether in her gentle dealing with the nurse on the staircase, or when closing her chamber door she pants with quenched taper in the moonlight, and most of all when awakening she finds her lover beside her, and contrasts his bodily presence with her dream:—

'Ah, Porphyro!' said she, 'but even now
Thy voice was at sweet tremble in mine ear,
Made tuneable with every sweetest vow;
And those sad eyes were spiritual and clear:
How chang'd thou art! how pallid, chill, and drear!
Give me that voice again, my Porphyro,
Those looks immortal, those complainings dear!'

In all the doings and circumstances attending the departure of the lovers for a destination left thrillingly vague in the words, 'For o'er the southern moors I have a home for thee,' —in the elfin storm sent to cover their flight (the only touch of the supernatural in the story), their darkling grope down the stairway, the hush that holds the house and guest-chambers, the windshaken arras, the porter sprawling asleep beside his empty flagon, the awakened bloodhound who recognizes his mistress and is quiet—in Keats's telling of all these things a like unflagging richness and felicity of imagination holds us spell-bound: and with the deaths of the old nurse and beadsman, once the house has lost its spirit of life and light in Madeline, the poet brings round the tale, after all its glow of passionate colour and music, of trembling anticipation and love-worship enraptured or in suspense, to a chill and wintry close in subtlest harmony with its beginning:—

They glide, like phantoms, into the wide hall;
Like phantoms, to the iron porch, they glide;
Where lay the Porter, in uneasy sprawl,
With a huge empty flaggon by his side:
The wakeful bloodhound rose, and shook his hide,
But his sagacious eye an inmate owns:
By one, and one, the bolts full easy slide:
The chains lie silent on the footworn stones;
The key turns, and the door upon its hinges groans.
And they are gone: aye, ages long ago
These lovers fled away into the storm.
That night the Baron dreamt of many a woe,
And all his warrior-guests, with shade and form
Of witch, and demon, and large coffin-worm,
Were long be-nightmar'd. Angela the old
Died palsy-twitch'd, with meagre face deform;
The Beadsman, after thousand aves told,
For aye unsought for slept among his ashes cold.

The last of the trio of Keats tales in verse, *Lamia,* owed its origin, and perhaps part of its temper, to his readings in Burton *Anatomy of Melancholy*. His own experiences under the stings of love and jealousy had led him, during those spring months of 1819 when he could write nothing, to pore much over the treatise of that prodigiously read, satiric old commentator on the maladies of the human mind and body, and especially over those sections of it which deal with the cause and cure of love-melancholy.

Entertainment in abundance, information in cartloads, Keats could draw from the matter accumulated and glossed by Burton, but little or nothing to gladden or soothe or fortify him. One story, however, he found which struck his imagination so much that he was moved to write upon it, and that was the old Greek story, quoted by Burton from Philostratus, of *Lamia* the serpent-lady, at once witch and victim of witchcraft, who loved a youth of Corinth and lived with him in a palace of delights built by her magic, until their happiness was shattered by the scrutiny of intrusive and coldblooded wisdom.

In June 1819, soon after the inspiration which produced the Odes had passed away, and before he left Hampstead for the Isle of Wight, Keats made a beginning on this new task; continued it at intervals, concurrently with his attempts in drama, at Shanklin and Winchester; and finished it by the first week in September. It happened that *Thomas Love Peacock* had published the year before a tale in verse on a nearly similar theme,—that of the beautiful Thessalian enchantress Rhododaphne: one wonders whether Keats may not have felt in Peacock's attempt a challenge and stimulus to his own. Peacock's work, now unduly neglected, is that of an accomplished scholar and craftsman sitting down to tell an old Greek tale of magic in the form of narrative verse then most fashionable, the mixed four-stressed couplet and ballad measure of Scott and Byron, and telling it, for a poet not of genius, gracefully and well.

Whether Keats *Lamia* is a work of genius there is no need to ask. No one can deny the truth of his own criticism of it when he says, 'I am certain there is that sort of fire in it which must take hold of people in some way—give them either pleasant or unpleasant sensation.' But personally I cannot agree with the opinion of the late Francis Turner Palgrave and other critics—I think they are the majority —who give it the first place among the tales. On the contrary, if an order of merit among them there must be, I should put it third and lowest, for several reasons of detail as well as for one reason affecting the whole design and composition.

As to the technical qualities of the poetry, let it be granted that Keats's handling of the heroic couplet, modelled this time on the example of Dryden and not of the Elizabethans, though retaining pleasant traces of the Elizabethan usages of the over-run or *enjambement* and the varied pause,—let it be granted that his handling of this mode of the metre is masterly. Let it be admitted also that there are passages in the narrative imagined as intensely as any in *Isabella or The Eve of St Agnes* and told quite as vividly in a style more rapid and condensed.

Such is the passage, in the introductory episode which fills so large a relative place in the poem, where Mercury woos and wins his wood-nymph after Lamia has lifted from her the spell of invisibility. Such is the gorgeous, agonized transformation act of Lamia herself from serpent to woman: such again the scene of her waylaying and ensnaring of the youth on his way to Corinth. And such above all would be the whole final scene of the banquet and its break-up, from 'Soft went the music with soft air along' to the end, but for the perplexing apostrophe, presently to be considered, which interrupts it. Still counting up the things in the poem to be most praised, here is an example where the poetry of Greek mythology is very eloquently woven into the rhetoric of love:—

Leave thee alone! Look back! Ah! goddess, see
Whether my eyes can ever turn from thee!
For pity do not this sad heart belie—
Even as thou vanishest so I shall die.
Stay! though a Naiad of the rivers, stay!
To thy far wishes will thy streams obey:
Stay I though the greenest woods be thy domain,
Alone they can drink up the morning rain:
Though a descended Pleiad, will not one
Of thine harmonious sisters keep in tune
Thy spheres, and as thy silver proxy shine?

And here a beautiful instance of power and justness in scenic imagination:—

As men talk in a dream, so Corinth all,
Throughout her palaces imperial,
And all her populous streets and temples lewd,
Mutter'd, like tempest in the distance brew'd,
To the wide-spreaded night above her towers.
Men, women, rich and poor, in the cool hours,
Shuffled their sandals o'er the pavement white,
Companion'd or alone; while many a light
Flar'd here and there, from wealthy festivals,
And threw their moving shadows on the walls,
Or found them cluster'd in the cornie'd shade
Of some arch'd temple door, or dusty colonnade.

Turning now to the other side of the account: for one thing, we find jarring and disappointing notes, such as had disappeared from Keats's works since *Endymion*, of the old tasteless manner of the Hunt-taught days: for instance the unpalatable passage in the first book beginning 'Let the mad poets say whate'er they please,' and worse still, with a new note of idle cynicism added, the lines about love which open the second book.

Misplaced archaisms also reappear, such as 'unshent' and the participle 'daft,' from the obsolete verb 'daft,' used as though it meant to puzzle or daze; with bad verbal coinages like 'piazzian,' 'psalterian.' Moreover, though many things in the poem are potently conceived, others are not so. The description of the magical palacehall is surely a failure, except for the one fine note in the lines,—

A haunting music, sole perhaps and lone
Supporters of the faery-roof, made moan
Throughout, as fearful the whole charm might fade.

The details of the structure, with its pairs of palms and plantains carved in cedar-wood, its walls lined with mirrors, its panels which change magically from plain marble to jasper, its fifty censers and 'Twelve sphered tables, by twelve seats insphered,'—all this seems feebly and even tastelessly invented in comparison with the impressive dream-architecture in some of Keats's other poems: I will even go farther, and say that it scarce holds its own against the not much dissimilar magic hall in the sixth canto of *Rhododaphne*. But the one fundamental flaw in *Lamia* concerns its moral. The word is crude: what I mean is the bewilderment in which it leaves us as to the effect intended to be made on our imaginative sympathies. Lamia is a serpent-woman, baleful and a witch, whose love for Lycius fills him with momentary happiness but must, we are made aware, be fatal to him.

Apollonius is a philosopher who sees through her and by one steadfast look withers up her magic semblance and destroys her, but in doing so fails to save his pupil, who dies the moment his illusion vanishes. Are these things a bitter parable, meaning that all love-joys are but deception, and that at the touch of wisdom and experience they melt away? If so, the tale might have been told either tragically or satirically, in either case leaving the reader impartial as between the sage and his victim. But Keats in this apostrophe, which I wish he had left out, deliberately points a moral and expressly invites us to take sides:—

What wreath for Lamia? What for Lycius?
What for the sage, old Apollonius?
Upon her aching forehead be there hung
The leaves of willow and of adder's tongue;
And for the youth, quick, let us strip for him
The thyrsus, that his watching eyes may swim
Into forgetfulness; and, for the sage,
Let spear-grass and the spiteful thistle wage
War on his temples. Do not all charms fly
At the mere touch of cold philosophy?
There was an awful rainbow once in heaven:
We know her woof, her texture; she is given
In the dull catalogue of common things.
Philosophy will clip an Angel's wings,
Conquer all mysteries by rule and line,
Empty the haunted air, and gnomed mine—
Unweave a rainbow, as it erewhile made
The tender-person'd Lamia melt into a shade.

These lines to my mind have not only the fault of breaking the story at a critical point and anticipating its issue, but challenge the mind to untimely questionings and reflections. The wreaths of ominous growth distributed to each of the three personages may symbolize the general tragedy: but why are we asked to take sides with the enchantress, ignoring everything about her except her charm, and against the sage?

If she were indeed a thing of bale under a mask of beauty, was not the friend and tutor bound to unmask her? and if the pupil could not survive the loss of his Musion,—if he could not confront the facts of life and build up for himself a new happiness on a surer foundation,—was it not better that he should be let perish?

Is there not in all this a slackening of imaginative and intellectual grasp? And especially as to the last lines, do we not feel that they are but a cheap and unilluminating repetition of a rather superficial idea, the idea phrased shortly in Campbell *Rainbow* and at length in several well-known passages of Wordsworth *Excursion*, particularly that in the fifth book beginning—

Ambitious spirits!—
Whom earth, at this late season, hath produced
To regulate the moving spheres, and weigh
The planets in the hollow of their hand;
And they who rather dive than soar, whose pains
Have solved the elements, or analysed
The thinking principle—shall they in fact
Prove a degraded Race?

Wordsworth had twenty years earlier written more wisely, 'Poetry is the impassioned expression in the eyes of all science.' The latter-day Wordsworth, and Keats after him, should have realised that the discoveries of 'philosophy,' meaning science, create new mysteries while they solve the old, and leave the world as full of poetry as they found it: poetry, it may be, with its point of view shifted, poetry of a new kind, but none the less poetical. Leigh Hunt, in his review of *Lamia* published on the appearance of the volume, has some remarks partly justifying and partly impugning Keats's treatment of the story in this respect:—

Mr Keats has departed as much from common-place in

the character and moral of this story, as he has in the poetry of it. He would see fair play to the serpent, and makes the power of the philosopher an ill-natured and disturbing thing. Lamia though liable to be turned into painful shapes had a soul of humanity; and the poet does not see why she should not have her pleasures accordingly, merely because a philosopher saw that she was not a mathematical truth. This is fine and good. It is vindicating the greater philosophy of poetry.

So far, this is a manifest piece of special pleading by Hunt on Lamia's behalf. If she is nothing worse than a being with a soul of humanity liable to be turned into painful shapes, why must Apollonius feel it his duty to wither and destroy her for the safeguarding of his pupil, even at the cost of that pupil's life? Her witchcraft must consist in something much worse than not being a mathematical truth, else why is he her so bitter enemy? Hunt proceeds, more to the purpose, to protest against the poet's implication—

that modern experiment has done a deadly thing to poetry by discovering the nature of the rainbow, the air, etc., that is to say, that the knowledge of natural history and physics, by shewing us the nature of things, does away with the imaginations that once adorned them. This is a condescension to a learned vulgarism, which so excellent a poet as Mr Keats ought not to have made. The world will always have fine poetry, so long as it has events, passions, affections, and a philosophy that sees deeper than this philosophy.

There will be a poetry of the heart, so long as there are tears and smiles: there will be a poetry of the imagination, as long as the first causes of things remain a mystery. A man who is no poet, may think he is none, as soon as he finds out the physical cause of the rainbow; but he need not alarm himself:—he was none before. The true poet will go deeper. He will ask himself what is the cause of that physical cause; whether truths to the senses are after all to be taken as truths to the imagination; and whether there is not room and mystery enough in the universe for the creation of infinite things, when the poor matter-of-fact philosopher has come to the end of his own vision. In Endymion Keats had impeded and confused his narrative by working into it much incident and imagery symbolic of the cogitations and aspirations, the upliftings and misgivings, of his own unripe spirit.

Three years later, writing to Shelley from his sickbed, he contrasts that former state of his mind with its present state, saying that it was then like a scattered pack of cards but is now sorted to a pip.

The three tales just discussed, written in the interval, show how quickly the power of sorting and controlling his imaginations had matured itself in him. In them he is already an artist standing outside of his own conceptions, certain of his own aim in dealing with them (subject perhaps to some reservation in the case of *Lamia*), and scarcely letting his personal self intrude upon his narrative at all to complicate or distract it.

For the expression of his private moods and meditations he had perfected during the same interval a new and beautiful vehicle in the ode. He had been accustomed to try his hand at odes, or what he called such, from his earliest riming days: and odes also, to all intents and purposes, are the two great lyrics in Endymion, the choral hymn to Pan and the song of the Indian maiden to Sorrow. But those which he composed in quick succession, as we have seen, in the late spring of 1819 are of a reflective and meditative type, new in his work and highly personal.

That which I have shown reason for believing to be the earliest of the group, the *Ode to Psyche* written in the last days of April, differs somewhat from the rest both in form and spirit. Its strophes are longer and more irregular: its strain less inward and brooding, with more of lyric ardour and exaltation. It tells of the poet's delight in that late, exquisitely and spiritually symbolic product of the mythologic spirit of expiring paganism, the story of Cupid and Psyche. What may have especially turned his attention to this fable at that moment we cannot tell. Possibly the mention of it in Burton *Anatomy* may have set him on to reading the original source, the *Golden Ass* of Apuleius, in Adlington translation: there are passages in

Lamia which suggest such a reading,

Farewell! I yet have visions for the night,
And for the day faint visions there is store.

and the noble, rhythmical English of that Elizabethan version, loose as it may be in point of scholarship, could not fail to charm his ear. Or possibly recent study of the plates in the *Musée Napoléon* (as to which more by and by) may have brought freshly to his memory the sculptured group in which the story is embodied. But that he had always loved the story we know from the passage 'I stood tip-toe' beginning—

So felt he, who first told how Psyche went
On the smooth wind to realms of wonderment,

as well as from his confession that in boyhood he used to admire its languid and long-drawn romantic treatment in the poem of Mrs Tighe.

Cloying touches of languor, such as often disfigure his own earlier work, are not wanting in the opening lines in which he tells how he came upon the fabled couple in a dream, but are more than compensated by the charm of the scene where he finds them reposing, 'Mid hush'd, cool-rooted flowers fragrant-eyed.' What other poet has compressed into a single line so much of the essential virtue of flowers, of their power to minister to the spirit of man through all his senses at once?

Such felicity in compound epithets is by this time habitual with Keats; and of Spenser with his 'sea-shouldering whales' he is now more than the equal. The 'azure-lidded sleep' of the maiden in *St Agnes' Eve* is matched in this ode by the 'soft-conchèd ear' of Psyche,—though the compound is perhaps a little forced and odd, like the 'cirque-couchant' snake in *Lamia.*

The invocation in the third and fourth stanzas expresses, with the fullest reach of Keats's felicity in style and a singular freshness and fire of music in the verse, both his sense of the meaning of Greek nature / religion and his delight in imagining the beauty of its shrines and ritual.

For the rest, there seems at first something strained in the turn of thought and expression whereby the poet offers himself and the homage of his own mind to the divinity he addresses, in lieu of the worship of antiquity for which she came too late;

and especially in the terms of the metaphor which opens the famous fourth stanza:—

Yes, I will be thy priest, and build a fane
In some untrodden region of my mind,
Where branched thoughts, new-blown with pleasant pain,
Instead of pines shall murmur in the wind.

But in a moment we are carried beyond criticism by that incomparable distillation of one, or many, of his impressions among the Lakes or in Scotland,—

Far, far around shall those dark-cluster'd trees
Fledge the wild-ridged mountains steep by steep.

For such a master-stroke of concentrated imaginative description no praise, much as has been showered on it by Ruskin and lesser critics, can be too great.

Keats declares to his brother that this is the first of his poems with which he has taken even moderate pains. That being so, it is remarkable that he should have let stand in it as many as three unrimed line-endings: and what the poem truly bears in upon the reader is a sense less of special care and finish than of special glow and ardour, till he is left breathless and delighted at the threshold of the sanctuary prepared by the 'gardener Fancy,' his mind enthralled by the imagery and his ear by the verse, with its swift, mounting music and rich, vehemently iterated assonances towards the close:—

A rosey sanctuary will I dress
With the wreath'd trellis of a working brain,
With buds, and bells, and stars without a name,
With all the gardener Fancy e'er could feign,
With breeding flowers, will never breed the same;
And thither will I bring all soft delights
That shadowy thought can win,
A bright torch, and a casement ope at nights,
To let the warm Love in!

The four remaining spring odes are slower-paced, as becomes their more musing tenour, and are all written in a succession of stanzas repeated uniformly or with slight variations. Throughout them all each stanza is of ten lines and five rimes, the first and second rimes arranged in a quatrain, the third, fourth and fifth in a sestet: the order of rimes in the sestet varying in the different odes, and in one, the nightingale ode, the third line from the end being shortened so as to have three stresses instead of five.

Let us take first the two in which the imagery has been suggested to the poet by works of Greek sculpture whether seen or imagined. In the *Ode on Indolence* Keats merely revives his memory of a special type of Greek marble urn where draped figures of women, Seasons, it may be, or priestesses, walk with joined hands behind a solemn Bacchus, or priest in the god's guise,—he merely evokes this memory in order to describe the way in which certain symbolic personages have seëmed in a day-dream to pass before him and re-pass and again re-pass, appearing and disappearing as the embossed figures on such an urn may be made to do by turning it round.

From the 'man and two women' of the March letter they are changed to three women, whom at first he does not recognize; but seeing presently who they are, namely Love, Ambition, and that 'maiden most unmeek,' his 'demon Poesy,' he for a moment longs for wings to follow and overtake them. The longing passes, and in his relaxed mood he feels that none of the three holds any joy for him—

so sweet as drowsy noons,
And evenings steep'd in honey'd indolence.

They come by once more, and again, barely aroused from the sweets of outdoor slumber and the spring afternoon, he will not so much as lift his head from where he lies, but bids them farewell and sees them depart without a tear.

Keats did not print this ode, thinking it perhaps not good enough or else too intimately personal. But writing to Miss Jeffrey a few weeks after it was composed, he tells her it is the thing he has most enjoyed writing this year. It is indeed a pleasant, lovingly meditated revival and casting into verse of the imagery which had come freshly into his mind when he wrote to his brother of his fit of languor in the previous March. It contains some powerful and many exquisite lines, but only one perfect stanza, the fifth: and there are slacknesses—shall we say lazinesses—in the execution, as where the need for rimes to 'noons' and 'indolence' prompts the all-too commonplace prayer—

That I may never know how change the moons,
Or hear the voice of busy common-sense;

Or where, thinking contemptuously of the old 'intercoronation' days with Leigh Hunt, he declines, in truly Cockney rime, to raise his head from the flowery *grass* in order to be fed with praise and become 'a pet-lamb in a sentimental *farce*.'

In bidding the phantoms of this day-dream adieu, Keats avows that there are others yet haunting him, and while imagery drawn from the sculptures on Greek vases was still floating through his mind, he was able to rouse himself to a stronger effort and produce a true masterpiece in his famous *Ode on a Grecian Urn*.

It is no single or actually existing specimen of Attic handicraft that he celebrates in this ode, but a composite conjured up instinctively in his mind out of several such known to him in reality or from engravings. During and after those hour-long silent reveries among the museum marbles of which Severn tells us, the creative spirit within him will have been busy almost unaware combining such images and re-combining them.

Criticism can plausibly analyse this creation into its several elements. In calling the scene a 'leaf-fringed legend' Keats will have remembered that the necks and shoulders of this kind of urn are regularly encircled by bands of leaf-pattern ornament.

The idea of a sacrifice and a Bacchic dance being figured together in one frieze, a thing scarcely elsewhere to be found, will have come to him from the well known vase of Sosibios (so called from the name of the sculptor inscribed upon it), from the print of which in the *Musée Napoléon* there actually exists a tracing by his hand.

But this is a serene and ceremonial composition: for the tumult and 'wild ecstasy' of his imagined frieze, the 'pipes and timbrels,' the 'mad pursuit,' he will have had store of visions ready in his mind, from the Bacchanal pictures of Poussin, no doubt also from Bacchic vases like that fine one in the Townley collection at the British Museum and the nearly allied Borghese vase: while for the —heifer lowing at the skies.

And all her silken flanks in garlands drest, as well as for the thought of the pious morn and the little town emptied of its folk that old deep impression received from Claude "'Sacrifice to Apollo'" will have been reinforced by others from works of sculpture easy to guess at: most of all, naturally, from the sacrificial processions in the Parthenon frieze.

In the ode we read how the sculptured forms of such an imaginary antique, visualized in full intensity before his mind's eye, have set his thoughts to work, on the one hand asking himself what living, human scenes of ancient custom and worship lay behind them, and on the other hand speculating upon the abstract relations of plastic art to life.

The opening invocation is followed by a string of questions which flash their own answer upon us—interrogatories which are at the same time pictures,—'What men or gods are these, what maidens loth?' etc. The second and third stanzas express with full felicity and insight the differences between life, which pays for its unique prerogative of reality by satiety and decay, and art, which in forfeiting reality gains in exchange permanence of beauty, and the power to charm by imagined experiences even richer than the real.

The thought thrown by Leonardo da Vinci into a single line —'*Cosa bella mortal passa e non d'arte*'—and expanded by Wordsworth in his later days into the sonnet, 'Praised be the art,' etc., finds here its most perfect utterance.

Ah, happy, happy boughs I that cannot shed
Your leaves, nor ever bid the Spring adieu;
And, happy melodist, unwearied,
For ever piping songs for ever new;
More happy love! more happy, happy love!
For ever warm and still to be enjoy'd,
For ever panting, and for ever young;
All breathing human passion far above,
That leaves a heart high-sorrowful and cloy'd,
A burning forehead, and a parching tongue.

Then the questioning begins again, and again conjures up a choice of pictures,—

What little town by river or sea shore,
Or mountain built with peaceful citadel,
Is emptied of its folk, this pious morn?

In the answering lines of the sestet—

And, little town, thy streets for evermore
Will silent be; and not a soul to tell
Why thou art desolate, can e'er return,—

In these lines we find that the poet's imagination has suddenly and lightly shifted its ground, and chooses to view the arrest of life as though it were an infliction in the sphere of reality, and not merely, like the instances of such arrest given farther back, a necessary condition in the sphere of art, having in that sphere its own compensations. Finally, dropping such airy play of the mind backward and forward between the two spheres, he consigns the work of ancient skill to the future, to remain,—

In midst of other woe
Than ours, a friend to man, to whom thou say'st,
Beauty is truth, truth beauty,—

thus re-asserting his old doctrine, 'What the imagination seizes as beauty must be truth'; a doctrine which amidst the gropings of reason and the flux of things is to the poet and artist—at least to one of Keats's temper—the one anchorage to which his soul can and needs must cleave.

Let us turn now to the second pair—for as such I regard them—of odes written in May-time, those *To a Nightingale* and *On Melancholy*. Like the *Ode on Indolence*, the nightingale ode begins with the confession of a mood of 'drowsy numbness,' but this time one deeper and nearer to pain and heartache. Then invoking the nightingale, the poet attributes his mood not to envy of her song (perhaps, as Mr Bridges has suggested, there may be here an under-reminiscence from William Browne), but to excess of happiness in it.

Just as his Grecian urn was no single specimen of antiquity that he had seen, so it is not the particular nightingale he had heard singing in the Hampstead garden that Keats thus invokes, but a type of the race imagined as singing in some fax-off scene of woodland mystery and beauty. Thither he sighs to follow her: first by aid of the spell of some southern vintage—a spell which he makes us realise in lines redolent, as are none others in our language, of the southern richness and joy which he had never known save in dreams. Then follows a contrasted vision of all his own and mankind's tribulations which he will leave behind him. Nay, he needs not the aid of Bacchus,—Poetry alone shall transport him.

For a moment he mistrusts her power, but the next moment finds himself where he would be, listening to the imagined song in the imagined woodland, and divining in the darkness all the secrets of the season and the night. While thus rapt he remembers how often the thought of death has seemed welcome to him, and feels that it would be more richly welcome now than ever. The nightingale would not cease to sing—and by this time, though he calls her 'immortal bird,' what he has truly in mind is not the song-bird at all, but the bird-song, thought of as though it were a thing self-existing and apart, imperishable through the ages.

So thinking, he contrasts its permanence with the transitoriness of human life, meaning the life of the generations of individual men and women who have listened to it. This last thought leads him off into the ages, whence he brings back those memorable touches of far-off Bible and legendary romance in the stanza closing with the words 'in faery lands forlorn': and then, catching up his own last word, 'forlorn,' with an abrupt change of mood and meaning, he returns to daily consciousness, and with the fading away of his forest dream the poem closes.

Throughout this ode Keats's genius is at its height. Imagination cannot be more rich and satisfying, felicity of phrase and cadence cannot be more absolute, than in the several contrasted stanzas calling for the draft of southern vintage, picturing the frailty and wretchedness of man's estate on earth, and conjecturing in the 'embalmèd darkness' the divers odours of spring. To praise the art of a passage like that in the fourth stanza where with a light, lingering pause the mind is carried instantaneously away from the miseries of the world into the heart of the imagined forest,—to praise or comment on a stroke of art like this is to throw doubt on the reader's power to perceive it for himself.

Let him be trusted to cherish and know the poem, as every lover of English poetry should, 'to its depths,' and let us go on to the last product, as I take it to be, of this spring month of inspiration, and that is the *Ode on Melancholy*.

The music of the word—its hundred associations derived from the early seventeenth-century poetry in which his soul was steeped—foremost among them no doubt Milton *L'Allegro* and *Il Penseroso*, with the beautiful song from Fletcher Nice Valour which inspired them-his recent familiarity with Burton *Anatomy*, including those pithy stanzas of alternate praise and repudiation which preface it—all these things will have worked together with Keats's own haunting and deepest mood throughout these days to set him composing on this theme, Melancholy. He had dallied with an idea of doing so as far back as early in March, when being kept from writing both by physical disinclination and a temporary phase of self-criticism, he had written to Haydon, 'I will not spoil my gloom by writing an ode to Darkness.'

Now that in May the springs of inspiration were again unlocked in him, such negative purpose fails to hold, and he adds this ode to the rest, throwing into it some of his most splendid imagery and diction. Its temper is nearly akin on the one hand to some of the gloomier passages in his letters to Miss Jeffrey of May 31 and June 9, and on the other to the tragic third stanza of the nightingale ode. Its main purport is to proclaim the spiritual nearness, the all but inseparableness, of joy and pain in human experience when either is present in its intensity. One of the attributes, it will be remembered, which he assigns to his enchantress *Lamia* is—

a sciential brain
To unperplex bliss from its neighbour pain.

In no nature have the sources of the two lain deeper or closer together than in his own, and it is from the fullness of impassioned experience that he writes. The real melancholy, he insists, is not that which belongs to things sad or direful in themselves. Having written two stanzas piling up gruesome images of such things, and discarded on reflection the former and more gruesome of the two, he lets the second stand, and goes on, evoking contrasted images of opulent beauty, to show how the true, the utter melancholy is that which is inextricably coupled with every joy and resides at the heart of every pleasure: ending magnificently—

Ay, in the very temple of Delight
Veiled Melancholy has her sovereign shrine,
Though seen of none save him whose strenuous tongue
Can burst Joy's grape against his palate fine;
His soul shall taste the sadness of her might,
And be among her cloudy trophies hung.

One more ode remains, written in a different key and after a lapse of some four months, during which Keats had been away in the country, quieted by absence from the object of his passion and working diligently at *Otho the Great* and *Lamia.* This is the ode *To Autumn.* He was alone at Winchester, rejoicing in perfect September weather and in a mood more serene and contented than he had known for long or was ever to know again. 'How beautiful the season is now,' he writes to Reynolds, 'how fine the air—a temperate sharpness about it.

Really, without joking, chaste weather—Dian skies. I never liked stubble fields so much as now—aye, better than the chilly green of the spring. Somehow, a stubble plain looks warm, in the same way that some pictures look warm. This struck me so much in my Sunday's walk that I composed upon it.' The vein in which he composed is one of simple objectivity, very different from the passionate and complex phases of introspective thought and feeling which inspired the spring odes. The result is the most Greek thing, except the fragment *To Maia,* which Keats ever wrote. It opens up no such far-reaching avenues to the mind and soul of the reader as the odes *To a Grecian Urn, To a Nightingale,* or *To Melancholy,* but in execution is more complete and faultless than any of them.

In the first stanza the bounty, in the last the pensiveness, of the time are expressed in words so transparent and direct that we almost forget they are words at all, and nature herself and the season seem speaking to us: while in the middle stanza the touches of literary art and Greek personification have an exquisite congruity and ease. Keats himself has hardly anywhere else written with so fine a subtlety of nature-observation.

Students of form will notice a slight deviation from that of the spring odes, by which the second member of the stanza is now a septet instead of a sestet, one of its rimes being repeated three times instead of twice.

Season of mists and mellow fruitfulness,
Close bosom-friend of the maturing sun;
Conspiring with him how to load and bless
With fruit the vines that round the thatch-eaves run;
To bend with apples the moss'd cottage trees,
And fill all fruit with ripeness to the core;
To swell the gourd, and plump the hazel shells
With a sweet kernel; to set budding more,
And still more, later flowers for the bees,
Until they think warm days will never cease,
For Summer has o'er-brimm'd their clammy cells.
Who hath not seen thee oft amid thy store?
Sometimes whoever seeks abroad may find
Thee sitting careless on a granary floor,
Thy hair soft-lifted by the winnowing wind;
Or on a half-reap'd furrow sound asleep,
Drows'd with the fume of poppies, while thy hook
Spares the next swath and all its twined flowers:
And sometimes like a gleaner thou dost keep
Steady thy laden head across a brook;
Or by a cider-press, with patient look,
Thou watchest the last oozings hours by hours.
Where are the songs of Spring? Ay, where are they?
Think not of them, thou hast thy music too,—
While barred clouds bloom the soft-dying day,
And touch the stubble-plains with rosy hue;
Then in a wailful choir the small gnats mourn

Among the river sallows, borne aloft
Or sinking as the light wind lives or dies;
And full-grown lambs loud bleat from hilly bourn;
Hedge-crickets sing; and now with treble soft
The red-breast whistles from a garden-croft;
And gathering swallows twitter in the skies.

Had Keats been destined to know health and peace of mind, who can guess how much more work in this vein and of this quality the world might have owed to him?

Chapter 7

Emigration of George Keats

From finishing Endymion at Burford Bridge Keats returned some time before mid-December to his Hampstead lodging. The exact date is uncertain; but it was in time to see Kean play Richard III at Drury Lane on the 15th—the actor's first performance after a break of some weeks due to illness. J. H. Reynolds had gone to Exeter for a Christmas holiday, and Keats, acting as his substitute, wrote four dramatic criticisms for the Champion : the first, printed on December 21, on Kean in general and his re-appearance as Richard III in particular; a second on a hash of the three parts of Shakespeare Henry VI produced under the title Richard Duke of York, with Kean in the name-part and probably Kean also as compiler; a third on a tragedy of small account by one Dillon, called Retribution , or the Chieftain's Daughter, in which the young Macready played the part of the villain; and a fourth on a pantomime of Don Giovanni.

No one, least of all oneliving in Keats's circle, could well attempt stage criticism at this time without trying to write like Hazlitt. Keats acquits himself on the whole rather youthfully and crudely. In one point he is cruder than one would have expected, and that is where, after re-reading the three parts of Henry VI for his purpose, he retracts what he had begun to say about them and declares that they are 'perfect works,' apparently without any suspicion that Shakespeare's part in them is at most that of a beginner of genius touching up the hackwork of others with a fine passage here and there.

It is only in the notice of Kean as Richard III that the genius in Keats really kindles. Here his imagination teaches him phrases beyond the reach of Hazlitt, to express (there is nothing more difficult) the specific quality and very thrill of the actor's voice and utterance. The whole passage is of special interest, both what is groping in it and what is masterly, and alike for itself and for such points as its familiar use of tags from the then recent Christabel and Siege of Corinth:—

A melodious passage in poetry is full of pleasures both sensual and spiritual. The spiritual is felt when the very letters and points of charactered language show like the hieroglyphics of beauty; the mysterious signs of our immortal free-masonry! 'A thing to dream of, not to tell'! The sensual life of verse springs warm from the lips of Kean and to one learned in Shakespearian hieroglyphics—learned in the spiritual portion of those lines to which Kean adds a sensual grandeur; his tongue must seem to have robbed the Hybla bees and left them honeyless! There is an indescribable gusto in his voice, by which we feel that the utterer is thinking of the past and future while speaking of the instant. When he says in Othello, 'Put up your bright swords, for the dew will rust them,' we feel that his throat had commanded where swords were as thick as reeds.

From eternal risk, he speaks as though his body were unassailable. Again, his exclamation of 'blood, blood, blood!' is direful and slaughterous to the deepest degree; the very words appear stained and gory. His nature hangs over them, making a prophetic repast. The voice is loosed on them, like the wild dog on the savage relics of an eastern conflict; and we can distinctly hear it 'gorging and growling o'er carease and limb.' In Richard, 'Bestirring with the lark to-morrow, gentle Norfolk I' comes from him as through the morning atmosphere towards which he yearns.... Surely this intense power of anatomizing the passions of every syllable, of taking to himself the airings of verse, is the means by which he becomes a storm with such fiery decision; and by which, with a still deeper charm, he does his spiriting gently.

Other actors are continually thinking of their sumtotal effect throughout a play. Kean delivers himself up to the instant feeling, without a shadow of a thought about anything else. He feels his being as deeply as Wordsworth, or any other of our intellectual monopolists. From all his comrades he stands alone, reminding us of him, whom Dante has so finely described in his Hell: and sole apart retir'd the Soldan fierce. Although so many times he has lost the battle of Bosworth Field, we can easily conceive him really expectant of victory, and a different termination of the piece.

Keats was by this time left alone in Well Walk, having seen his brothers off for Teignmouth, whither George carried the invalid Tom for change of climate. His regular occupation for the next two months was revising and copying out Endymion for press. Regular also was his attendance at Hazlitt's evening lectures on the English Poets at the Surrey Institution.

Of the lectures on Shakespeare which Coleridge was in the same weeks delivering in Fetter Lane Keats makes no mention, and it is clear that he made no effort to go and hear them, though the distance of the lecture-hall from his Hampstead lodging was so much less.

The reader who would fain conjure up for himself the contrasted personalities and styles in public discourse of these two master critics, the shy and saturnine, yet vigorously straight-hitting and trenchantly effective Hazlitt, and the ramblingly mellifluous, sometimes beautifully inspired and sometimes painfully drug-beclouded Coleridge, can draw but a faint and tantalized satisfaction from the diaries of Henry Crabb Robinson, that assiduous friend and satellite of men of genius, who punctually records his attendance at both courses, but lacked the touch that should have made his record live.

Keats's letters to his brothers in these winter months, with a few more to Bailey and Reynolds, give us lively glimpses of his social doings, and others, interesting in the extreme, of the inward growth and workings of his mind. He tells of a certain amount of commonplace conviviality: an absurd dance and rackety supper at one Redhall's; noisy Saturday 'concerts' at his own rooms, which means that two or three intimates came to early afternoon dinner and spent the rest of the day drinking claret and keeping up a concerted racket, each in imitation of some musical instrument (Keats himself of the bassoon); but of this pastime he soon got tired and rather ashamed.

His social relations began to extend themselves more than he much cared about, or thought consistent with proper industry. We find him dining with Shelley's friend, the genial and admirable stockbroker and man of letters Horace Smith, in company with some fashionable wits, concerning whom he reflects:—'They only served to convince me how superior humour is to wit, in respect to enjoyment. These men say things which make one start, without making one feel; they are all alike; they all know fashionables; they have all a mannerism in their eating and drinking, in their mere handling a decanter. They talked of Kean and his low company. "Would I were with that company instead of yours," said I to myself.' Sunday evenings were for a while set apart for dining with Haydon, and here, on the last Sunday of the year, Keats met Wordsworth for the first time.

Wordsworth was on one of his rare visits to London, and had been staying since the beginning of December with his brother Christopher at Lambeth rectory. According to Crabb Robinson, he seems to have been in these weeks in one of his stiffest and most domineering moods of egotism, much ruffled by the moderate strictures of Coleridge in Biographia Literaria on certain qualities in his work and not at all appeased by the splendid praise which so much out-balanced them.

One evening in conversation he went so far as to treat that great helpless genius, his old bosom-friend and inspirer, with a rudeness of contradiction which even the devoted Robinson found it hard to forgive. Near about the same time, hearing that the next Waverley novel was to be about Rob Roy, he took down his ballad so named, read it aloud, and said 'I do not know what more Mr Scott can have to say on the subject.'

Keats promptly had full experience of Wordsworth's egotism, but also saw more genial aspects of his character. Quite coolly and briefly he mentions those circumstances of their first meeting which Haydon, in a famous passage of his autobiography, thrusts before us in the insistent colour and illumination of a magic-lantern picture. 'I think,' writes Keats,

' Ritchie is going to Fezan in Africa; thence to proceed if possible like Mungo Park. Then there was Wordsworth, Lamb, Monkhouse, Landseer, and your humble servant. Lamb got tipsy and blew up Kingston—proceeding so far as to take the candle across the room, hold it to his face, and show us what a soft fellow he was.'

It should be explained that Ritchie was a young explorer whom Tom had met the summer before on his run to Paris, and Kingston a thick-witted, thickskinned, intrusive but kindly gentleman of lion-hunting proclivities, who as Comptroller of Stamps had had some correspondence with Wordsworth and on the strength of this invited himself to join Haydon's party in the poet's honour. Now for Haydon:—

On December 28th the immortal dinner came off in my paintingroom, with Jerusalem towering up behind us as a background. Wordsworth was in fine cue, and we had a glorious set-to,—on Homer, Shakespeare, Milton and Virgil. Lamb got exceedingly merry and exquisitely witty; and his fun in the midst of Wordsworth's solemn intonations of oratory was like the sarcasm and wit of the fool in the intervals of Lear's passion. He made a speech and voted me absent, and made them drink my health. 'Now,' said Lamb, 'you old lake poet, you rascally poet, why do you call Voltaire dull?' We all defended Wordsworth, and affirmed there was a state of mind when Voltaire would be dull. 'Well,' said Lamb, 'here's to Voltaire—the Messiah of the French nation, and a very proper one too.'

He then, in a strain of humour beyond description, abused me for putting Newton's head into my picture,—'a fellow,' said he, 'who believed nothing unless it was as clear as the three sides of a triangle.' And then he and Keats agreed he had destroyed all the poetry of the rainbow by reducing it to the prismatic colours. It was impossible to resist him, and we all drank ' Newton's health, and confusion to mathematics.' It was delightful to see the good-humour of Wordsworth in giving in to all our frolics without affectation and laughing as heartily as the best of us.

By this time other friends joined, amongst them poor

Ritchie who was going to penetrate by Fezzan to Timbuctoo. I introduced him to all as 'a gentleman going to Africa.' Lamb seemed to take no notice; but all of a sudden he roared out, 'Which is the gentleman we are going to lose?' We then drank the victim's health, in which Ritchie joined.

In the morning of this delightful day, a gentleman, a perfect stranger, had called on me. He said he knew my friends, had an enthusiasm for Wordsworth and begged I would procure him the happiness of an introduction. He told me he was a comptroller of stamps, and often had correspondence with the poet. I thought it a liberty; but still, as he seemed a gentleman, I told him he might come.

When we retired to tea we found the comptroller. In introducing him to Wordsworth I forgot to say who he was. After a little time the comptroller looked down, looked up and said to Wordsworth, 'Don't you think, sir, Milton was a great genius?' Keats looked at me, Wordsworth looked at the comptroller. Lamb who was dozing by the fire turned round and said, 'Pray, sir, did you say Milton was a great genius?' 'No, sir; I asked Mr Wordsworth if he were not.' 'Oh,' said Lamb, 'then you are a silly fellow.' 'Charles! my dear Charles!' said Wordsworth; but Lamb, perfectly innocent of the confusion he had created, was off again by the fire.

After an awful pause the comptroller said, 'Don't you think Newton a great genius?' I could not stand it any longer; Keats put his head into my books. Ritchie squeezed in a laugh. Wordsworth seemed asking himself, 'Who is this?' Lamb got up, and taking a candle, said, 'Sir, will you allow me to look at your phrenological development?' He then turned his back on the poor man, and at every question of the comptroller he chaunted—

Diddle diddle dumpling, my son John Went to bed with his breeches on.

The man in office, finding Wordsworth did not know who he was, said in a spasmodic and half-chuckling anticipation of assured victory, 'I have had the honour of some correspondence with you, Mr Wordsworth.' 'With me, sir?' said Wordsworth, 'not that I remember.' 'Don't you, sir? I am a comptroller of stamps.' There was a dead silence;—the comptroller evidently thinking that was enough. While we were waiting for Wordsworth's reply, Lamb sung out Hey diddle diddle, The cat and the fiddle.

'My dear Charles!' said Wordsworth,-Diddle diddle dumpling, my son John, chaunted Lamb, and then rising, exclaimed, 'Do let me have another look at that gentleman's organs.' Keats and I hurried Lamb into the painting-room, shut the door and gave way to inextinguishable laughter. Monkhouse followed and tried to get Lamb away. We went back but the comptroller was irreconcilable. We soothed and smiled and asked him to supper. He stayed though his dignity was sorely affected. However, being a good-natured man, we parted all in good humour, and no ill effects followed.

All the while, until Monkhouse succeeded, we could hear Lamb struggling in the painting-room and calling at intervals, 'Who is that fellow? Allow me to see his organs once more.'

It was indeed an immortal evening. Wordsworth's fine intonation as he quoted Milton and Virgil, Keats's eager inspired look, Lamb's quaint sparkle of lambent humour, so speeded the stream of conversation, that in my life I never passed a more delightful time. All our fun was within bounds. Not a word passed that an apostle might not have listened to. It was a night worthy of the Elizabethan age, and my solemn Jerusalem flashing up by the flame of the fire, with Christ hanging over us like a vision, all made up a picture which will long glow upon-that inward eye Which is the bliss of solitude.

Keats made Ritchie promise he would carry his Endymion to the great desert of Sahara and fling it in the midst.

To complete our impression of Wordsworth at this time of his winter visit to London in his forty-eighth year, let us turn for a moment to Leigh Hunt's recollections of his looks and ways about the same time.

Certainly I never beheld eyes that looked so inspired or supernatural. They were like fires half burning, half smouldering, with a sort of acrid fixture of regard, and seated at the end of two caverns. One might imagine Ezekiel or Isaiah to have had such eyes.... He had a dignified manner, with a deep roughish but not unpleasing voice, and an exalted mode of speaking. He had a habit of keeping his left hand in the bosom of his waistcoat; and in this attitude, except when he turned round to take one of the subjects of his criticism from the shelves, he was dealing forth his eloquent but hardly catholic judgments.

Hazlitt, in words written a few years later, gives a nearly similar portrait:—

He is above the middle size, with marked features, and an air somewhat stately and Quixotic. He reminds one of some of Holbein's heads, grave, saturnine, with a slight indication of sly humour. He has a peculiar sweetness in his smile, and great depth and manliness and a rugged harmony in the tones of his voice. His manner of reading his own poetry is particularly imposing, and in his favourite passages his eye beams with preternatural lustre, and the meaning labours slowly up from his swelling breast.

Although the great man could praise or care for no contemporary poetry save his own, and had none of the sympathetic or encouraging criticism to bestow on Keats which to that ardent young spirit would have meant so much, he nevertheless showed him no little personal kindness, receiving him when he called and inviting him several times to dine or sup. On his first visit Keats was kept waiting till the poet bustled in, full dressed in stiff stock and knee breeches, in haste to keep a dinner appointment with one of his official chiefs. This experience proved no check to their acquaintance: neither did Wordsworth's chilling comment when Keats was induced to read to him the hymn to Pan from Endymion.

'A very pretty piece of Paganism,' he remarked and that was all. Severn was present at the gathering in Haydon's studio where this reading took place. The evening's talk, he relates, ran much on the virtues of a vegetable diet, which was for the moment, through the vehement advocacy of Shelley, so much in vogue in Leigh Hunt's circle that even the ruddy and robust Haydon gave himself out for a proselyte like the rest, until friends one day caught him coming privily smacking his lips out of a chophouse. Wordsworth was in a jocular mood, and asked his herbivorous friends whether they did not welcome such a succulent morsel of animal food as a chance caterpillar in their cabbage.

Was it on the same occasion that the sage and seer condescended to a pun, telling Haydon that if he ever took the name of another artist, as some of the old masters used to do, it should be Teniers, seeing that he had been ten years working on his great picture, still unfinished, of Christ's Entry into Jerusalem, in which Wordsworth and other leading personages of the time were to figure among the crowd of lookers on?

A fortnight after their first meeting Keats re-affirms to his brother the view he had formerly expressed to Haydon that 'If there were three things superior in the modern world they were The Excursion, Haydon's Pictures, and Hazlitt's depth of Taste.' About the same time, that is in the course of January, he writes of having 'seen Wordsworth frequently': and again 'I have seen a good deal of Wordsworth.' A later allusion implies that he has seen him 'with his beautiful wife and his enchanting sister.'

At one meeting Keats must have heard talk or reading that delighted him, for Severn tells how while he was toiling late one night over his miniature painting, Keats burst into his lodging fresh from Wordsworth's company and in a state of eager elation over his experience. It is hard to refrain from conjecture as to what had happened. What one would like to think is that Wordsworth had been reading Keats some of those great passages in the Prelude without which the master cannot truly be more than half known and which remained unpublished until the year of his death. Or may we possibly trace a clue to the evening's enjoyment in this further note of Hazlitt's on a phase of Wordsworth's conversation?

It is fine to hear him talk of the way in which certain subjects should have been treated by eminent poets, according to his notions of the art. Thus he finds fault with Dryden's description of Bacchus in the Alexander's Feast, as if he were a mere goodlooking youth, or boon companion

Flushed with a purple grace,

He shows his honest face—

Instead of representing the god returning from the conquest of India, crowned with vine-leaves, and drawn by panthers, and followed by troops of satyrs, of wild men and animals that he had tamed. You would think, in hearing him speak on this subject, that you saw Titian's picture of the meeting of Bacchus and Ariadne—so classic were his conceptions, so glowing his style.

It is tempting to seek some kind of connexion between Keats in his great Bacchic ode in Endymion and Wordsworth in this vein of talk. Had we not known that Endymion was finished before the elder and the younger poet met, we might have been inclined to attribute to Wordsworth's eloquence some part of Keats's inspiration. And even as it is such possibility remains open, for it must be remembered that Keats carefully re-copied the several cantos of his poem during the spring, the fourth canto not until March, at Teignmouth, and it is conceivable, though unlikely, that the triumph of Bacchus might have been an addition made in re-copying.

It was most likely a result of the interest taken by Wordsworth in Keats that the young poet received at this time a friendly call, of which he makes passing mention, from Crabb Robinson.

But the more Keats saw of Wordsworth himself, the more critically, as his letters show, he came gradually to look upon him. He disliked the idea of a man so revered dining with the foolish Kingston, and refused to dine and meet him there. He regrets, after Wordsworth has gone, that he has 'left a bad impression wherever he has visited in town by his egotism, Vanity, and bigotry;' adding, 'yet he is a great poet if not a philosopher.' The fullest expression of this critical attitude occurs in a letter written to Reynolds at the beginning of February.

Keats is for the moment out of conceit with the poets of his own time; particularly with Wordsworth, whom he had always devoutly reverenced from a distance, and with Hunt, next to Cowden Clarke his earliest encourager and sympathiser, whom to his disappointment he had lately found more ready to carp than praise when he read him the early books of Endymion. It seems Hunt would have liked the talk of Endymion and Peona to come nearer his own key of simpering triviality in Rimini.

'He says,' writes Keats, 'the conversation is unnatural and too high-flown for Brother and Sister—says it should be simple, forgetting do ye mind that they are both overshadowed by a supernatural Power and perforce could not talk like Francesca in the Rimini. He must first prove that Caliban's poetry is unnatural. This with me completely overturns his objections.' In revising Endymion for press Keats proved his wise adherence to his own point of view by cutting out some of the passages most infected with the taint of Hunt's familiar tea-party manner. The words in which he expresses his impatience of the several dogmatisms of Wordsworth and Hunt are vital in relation to his own conception of poetry and of its right aim and working:—

It may be said that we ought to read our contemporaries, that Wordsworth etc., should have their due from us. But, for the sake of a few fine imaginative or domestic passages, are we to be bullied into a certain Philosophy engendered in the whims of an Egotist? Every man has his speculations, but every man does not brood and peacock over them till he makes a false coinage and deceives himself. Many a man can travel to the very bourne of Heaven, and yet want confidence to put down his half-seeing. Sancho will invent a Journey heavenward as well as anybody.

We hate poetry that has a palpable design upon us, and, if we do not agree, seems to put its hand into its breeches pocket. Poetry should be great and unobtrusive, a thing which enters into one's soul, and does not startle or amaze it with itself, but with its subject. How beautiful are the retired flowers! how would they lose their beauty were they to throng into the highway crying out, 'Admire me, I am a violet! Dote upon me, I am a primrose!' Modern poets differ from the Elizabethans in this: each of the moderns like an Elector of Hanover governs his petty state, and knows how many straws are swept daily from the Causeways in all his dominions, and has a continual itching that all the Housewives should have their coppers well scoured.

The ancients were Emperors of vast Provinces, they had only heard of the remote ones and scarcely cared to visit them. I will cut all this—I will have no more of Wordsworth or Hunt in particular.... I don't mean to deny Wordsworth's grandeur and Hunt's merit, but I mean to say we need not be teazed with grandeur and merit when we can have them uncontaminated and unobtrusive.

These winter letters of Keats am full of similar first fruits of young reflection, thoughts forming or halfforming themselves in absolute sincerity as he writes, intuitions of his first-endeavouring mind on the search for vital truths of art and nature and humanity. Imperfect, half-wrought phrases often come from him which prove, when you have lived with them, to be more sufficient as well as more suggestive than if they had been chiselled into precision by longer study and a more confident mind.

For instance: 'the excellence of every art is its intensity, capable of making all disagreeables evaporate from their being in close relationship with Beauty and Truth': a sentence worth whole treatises and fit, sketchy as it is, to serve as text to all that can justly be discoursed concerning problems of art in its relation to nature,—of realism, romance, and the rest. Or this:—

Brown and Dilke walked with me and back to the Christmas pantomime. I had not a dispute, but a disquisition, with Dilke upon various subjects; several things dove-tailed in my mind, and at once it struck me what quality went to form a man of achievement, especially in literature, and which Shakespeare possessed so enormously—I mean Negative Capability, that is, when a man is capable of being in uncertainties, mysteries, doubts, without any irritable reaching after fact and reason. Coleridge, for instance, would let go by a fine isolated verisimilitude caught from the Penetralium of mystery, from being incapable of remaining content with half-knowledge.

This pursued through volumes would perhaps take us no

further than this, that with a great poet the sense of Beauty overcomes every other consideration, or rather obliterates all consideration.

Or this:—

In poetry I have a few axioms, and you will see how far I am from their centre.

1st. I think poetry should surprise by a fine excess, and not by singularity; it should strike the reader as a wording of his own highest thoughts, and appear almost a remembrance.

2nd. Its touches of beauty should never be half-way, thereby making the reader breathless, instead of content. The rise, the progress, the setting of Imagery should, like the sun, come natural to him, shine over him, and set soberly, although in magnificence, leaving him in the luxury of twilight.

But it is easier to think what poetry should be, than to write it. And this leads me to another axiom—That if poetry comes not as naturally as the leaves to a tree, it had better not come at all. However it may be with me, I cannot help looking into new countries with 'O for a muse of Fire to ascend!' If Endymion serves me as a pioneer, perhaps I ought to be content. I have great reason to be content, for thank God I can read, and perhaps understand Shakespeare to his depths; and I have I am sure many friends, who, if I fail will attribute any change in my life and temper to humbleness rather than pride—to a cowering under the wings of great poets, rather than to a bitterness that I am not appreciated.

Cogitations of this cast, not less fresh than deep, and often throwing a clear retrospective light on the moods and aims which governed him in writing Endymion, are interspersed at the beginning of the year with regrets at dissensions rife among his friends. The strain between Haydon and Hunt had increased since the autumn, and now, over a sordid matter of money borrowed by Mrs Hunt—by all accounts the most unabashed of petty spongers—and not repaid, grew into an active quarrel.

Another still fiercer quarrel broke out between Haydon and Reynolds, who with all his fine qualities seems to have been quick and touchy, and whom we find later in open breach with his admirable brother-in-law Thomas Hood. Keats was not involved. With his distinguished good sense and good heart in matters of friendship, he knew how to keep in close and affectionate touch with what was loveable or likeable in each of the disputants severally. His comments are the best key to the best part of himself, and show him as the true great spirit, by character not less than by gift, among the group.

Things have happened lately of great perplexity—you must have heard of them—Reynolds and Haydon retorting and recriminating, and parting for ever—the same thing has happened between Haydon and Hunt. It is unfortunate—Men should bear with each other: there lives not the Man who may not be cut up, aye lashed to pieces on his weakest side. The best of men have but a portion of good in them—a kind of spiritual yeast in their frames, which creates the ferment of existenceby which a Man is propelled to act, and strive, and buffet with Circumstance. The sure way, Bailey, is first to know a Man's and then be passive—if after that he insensibly draws you towards him then you have no power to break the link.

Before I felt interested in either Reynolds or Haydon, I was well read in their faults; yet, knowing them, I have been cementing gradually with both. I have an affection for them both, for reasons almost opposite—and to both must I of necessity cling, supported always by the hope that, when a little time, a few years, shall have tried me more fully in their esteem, I may be able to bring them together. The time must come, because they have both hearts and they will recollect the best parts of each other, when this gust is overblown.

Of Haydon himself and of his powers as a painter Keats continued to think as highly as ever, seeing in his pictures, as the friends and companions of every ardent and persuasive worker in the arts are apt to see, not so much the actual performance as the idea he had pre-conceived of it in the light of his friend's enthusiastic ambition and eloquence. Severn repeatedly insists on Keats's remarkably keen natural instinct for and understanding of the arts both of music and painting. Cowden Clarke's piano-playing had been one of the chief pleasures of his school-days: as to the capacity he felt in himself for judging the works of painting, here is his own scrupulously modest and sincere estimate expressed to Haydon a little later:

Believe me Haydon your picture is part of myself—I have ever been too sensible of the labyrinthian path to eminence in Art (Judging from Poetry) ever to think I understood the emphasis of painting. The innumerable compositions and decompositions which take place between the intellect and its thousand materials before it arrives at that trembling delicate and snail-horn perception of beauty.

I know not your many havens of intenseness—nor ever can know them: but for this I hope nought you achieve is lost upon me: for when a Schoolboy the abstract idea I had of an heroic painting—was what I cannot describe. I saw it somewhat sideways, large, prominent, round, and colour'd with magnificence—somewhat like the feel I have of Anthony and Cleopatra. Or of Alcibiades leaning on his Crimson Couch in his Galley, his broad shoulders imperceptibly heaving with the Sea. With Hunt also, in spite of the momentary causes of annoyance we have seen, Keats's intercourse continued frequent, while with Reynolds his intimacy grew daily closer. At Hunt's he again saw something of Shelley. 'The Wednesday before last Shelley, Hunt, and I, wrote each a sonnet on the river Nile,' he tells his brothers on the 16th of February, 1818.

The sonnets are preserved. They were to be written, it was agreed, in a quarter of an hour. Shelley and Keats were up to time, but Hunt had to sit up half the night to finish his. It was worth the pains, and with it for once the small poet outdid the two great.

'I have been writing,' continues Keats, 'at intervals, many songs and sonnets, and I long to be at Teignmouth to read them over to you.' With the help of his manuscripts or of the transcripts made from them by his friends, it is possible to retrace the actual order of many of these fugitive pieces. On the 16th of January was written the sonnet on Mrs Reynolds's cat, perhaps Keats's best thing in the humorous vein; on the 21st, after seeing in Leigh Hunt's possession a lock of hair reputed to be Milton's, the address to that poet beginning 'Chief of organic numbers!' which he sends to the prime Milton enthusiast among his friends, Benjamin Bailey, with the comment, 'This I did at Hunt's, at his request,—perhaps I should have done something better alone and at home.' The first two lines,—

Chief of organic numbers,
Old scholar of the spheres!

Read like an anticipation in the rough of the first stanza of Tennyson's masterly set of alcaics already referred to, beginning 'O mighty-mouthed inventor of harmonies.' To the 22nd belongs the sonnet, 'O golden tongued Romance with serene lute,' in which Keats bids himself lay aside (apparently) his Spenser, in order to read again the more rousing and human-passionate pages of Lear. This is one of the last of his sonnets written in the Petrarchan form as followed by Milton and Wordsworth, and from henceforth he follows the Shakespearean form almost exclusively. On the 31st he writes to Reynolds in a rollicking mood, and sends him the lines to Apollo beginning 'Hence Burgundy, Claret, and Port,' part rant (the word is his own) pure and simple, part rant touched with genius, and giving words to a very frequent and intense phase of feeling in himself:—

Aye, when the soul is fled
Too high above our head,
Affrighted do we gaze
After its airy maze,
As doth a mother wild,
When her young infant child
Is in an eagle's claws—
And is not this the cause
Of madness?—God of Song,
Thou bearest me along
Through sights I scarce can bear:
O let me, let me share
With the hot lyre and thee,
The staid Philosophy.
Temper my lonely hours,
And let me see thy bowers
More unalarm'd!

By way of a sobre conclusion to the same letter, he adds the very fine and profoundly felt sonnet in the Shakespearean form beginning 'When I have fears that I may cease to be,' which he calls his last.

On the 3rd of February he sends two spirited sets of verses in the favourite four-beat measure, heptasyllable varied with octosyllable, of the later Elizabethans and the youthful Milton, namely those to Robin Hood (suggested by a set of sonnets by Reynolds on Sherwood Forest) and those on the Mermaid Tavern. On the 4th comes another Shakespearean sonnet, that beginning 'Time's sea has been five years at its slow ebb,' in which he recalls the memory of an old, persistent, haunting love-fancy. The two sonnets of January 31 and February 4 should be read strictly together:—

When I have fears that I may cease to be
Before my pen has glean'd my teeming brain,
Before high-piled books, in charact'ry,
Hold like full garners the full-ripen'd grain;
When I behold, upon the night's starr'd face,
Huge cloudy symbols of a high romance,
And think that I may never live to trace
Their shadows, with the magic hand of chance;
And when I feel, fair creature of an hour!
That I shall never look upon thee more,
Never have relish in the faery power
Of unreflecting love!—then on the shore
Of the wide world I stand alone, and think,
Till Love and Fame to nothingness do sink.
Time's sea hath been five years at its slow ebb;
Long hours have to and fro let creep the sand;
Since I was tangled in thy beauty's web,
And snared by the ungloving of thine hand.
And yet I never look on midnight sky,
But I behold thine eyes' well memoried light;
I cannot look upon the rose's dye,
But to thy cheek my soul doth take its flight;
I cannot look on any budding flower,
But my fond ear, in fancy at thy lips,

And hearkening for a love-sound, doth devour
Its sweets in the wrong sense:—Thou dost eclipse
Every delight with sweet remembering,
And grief unto my darling joys dost bring.

The former is far the richer in contents, and in the light of the tragedy to come its two first quatrains now seem to thrill with prophetic meaning. But what is singular is that in the third quatrain should be recalled, in the same high strain of emotion, the vision of a beauty seen but not even accosted three-and-a-half years earlier (not really five) in the public gardens at Vauxhall, and then (August, 1814) addressed in what are almost the earliest of Keats's dated verses, those in which he calls for a 'brimming bowl,'—

From my despairing heart to charm
The Image of the fairest form
That e'er my reveling eyes beheld,
That e'er my wandering fancy spell'd....

Such, Woodhouse assures us, is the case, and the same memory fills the second sonnet: but this it might be possible to take father as a fine Shakespearean exercise than as an expression of profound feeling. On the 5th, Keats sends another sonnet postponing compliance for the present with an invitation of Leigh Hunt's to compose something in honour, or in emulation, of Spenser; and on the 8th, the sonnet in praise of the colour blue composed by way of protest against one of Reynolds preferring black, at least in the colouring of feminine eyes.

About the same time he agreed with Reynolds that they should each write some metrical tales from Boccaccio, and publish them in a joint volume; and began at once for his own part with the first few stanzas of Isabella; or, the Pot of Basil. A little later in this so prolific month of February we find him rejoicing in the song of the thrush and blackbird, and melted into feelings of indolent pleasure and receptivity under the influence of spring winds and dissolving rain. He theorizes pleasantly in a letter to Reynolds on the virtues and benefits of this state of mind, translating the thrush's music into some blank-verse lines of subtle and haunting cadence, in which, disowning for the nonce his habitual doctrine of the poet's paramount need of knowledge, he makes the thrush say,

O fret not after knowledge—I have none,
And yet my song comes native with the warmth,
O fret not after knowledge—I have none,
And yet the evening listens.

In the course of the next fortnight we find him in correspondence with Taylor about the corrections to Endymion; and soon afterwards making a clearance of borrowed books, and otherwise preparing to flit. His brother George, who had been taking care of Tom at Teignmouth since December, was now obliged to come to town, bent on a scheme of marriage and emigration; and Tom's health having made a momentary rally, Keats was unwilling that he should leave Teignmouth, and determined to join him there.

He started in the second week of March, and stayed almost two months. It was an unlucky season for weather,—the soft-buffeting sheets and misty drifts of Devonshire rain renewing themselves wave on wave, in the inexhaustible way all lovers of that country know, throughout almost the whole spring, and preventing him from getting more than occasional tantalizing snatches of enjoyment in the beauty of the scenery, the walks, and flowers. His letters are full of whimsical objurgations not only against the climate, but against the male inhabitants, whose fibre he chooses to conceive relaxed by it:—

You may say what you will of Devonshire: the truth is, it is a splashy, rainy, misty, snowy, foggy, haily, floody, muddy, slipshod county. The hills are very beautiful, when you get a sight of 'em—the primroses are out, but then you are in—the Cliffs are of a fine deep colour, but then the Clouds are continually vieing with them—the women like your London people in a sort of negative way—because the native men are the poorest creatures in England—because Government never have thought it worth while to send a recruiting party among them.

When I think of Wordsworth's Sonnet, 'Vanguard of Liberty! ye men of Kent!' the degenerated race about me are Pulvis ipecac. simplex—a strong dose. Were I a corsair, I'd make a descent on the south coast of Devon; if I did not run the chance of having Cowardice imputed to me. As for the men, they'd run away into the Methodist meeting-houses, and the women would be glad of it.... Such a quelling Power have these thoughts over me that I fancy the very air of a deteriorating quality.

I fancy the flowers, all precocious, have an Acrasian spell about them-I feel able to beat off the Devonshire waves like soap-froth. I think it well for the honour of Britain that Julius Cæsar did not first land in this County. A Devonshirer standing on his native hills is not a distinct object—he does not show against the light—a wolf or two would dispossess him.

A man of west-country descent should have known better. Why did not the ghost of William Browne of Tavistock arise and check Keats's hand, and recite for his rebuke the burst in praise of Devon from Britannia's Pastorals, with its happy echo of the Virgilian Salve magna parens and Haec genus acre virum?—

Hail thou my native soil: thou blessed plot
Whose equal all the world affordeth not I
Shew me who can so many christall rills,
Such sweet-clothed vallies, or aspiring hills,
Such wood-ground, pastures, quarries, wealthy mines,
Such rocks in whom the diamond fairly shines:
And if the earth can shew the like again;
Yet will she fail in her sea-ruling men.
Time never can produce men to o'er-take
The fames of Grenville, Davies, Gilbert, Drake,
Or worthy Hawkins or of thousands more
That by their power made the Devonian shore
Mock the proud Tagus.

Of the Devonshire girls Keats thought better than of their menkind, and writes and rimes on them with a certain skittishness of admiration. With one local family, a Mrs Jeffrey and her daughters, he and his brothers were on terms of warm friendship, as is shown by his correspondence with them a year later. One of the daughters married afterwards a Mr Prowse, and published two volumes of very tolerable sentimental verse: some of their contents, as interpreted (says Mr Buxton Forman) by Teignmouth tradition, would indicate that her heart had been very deeply touched by the young poet during his stay: but of responsive feelings on his own part his letters give no hint, and it was only a few weeks later that he wrote how his love for his brothers had hitherto stifled any impression that a woman might have made on him.

Besides his constant occupation in watching and cheering the invalid Tom, who had a relapse just after he came down, Keats was busy during these Devonshire days seeing through the press the last sheets of Endymion. He also composed, with the exception of the few verses he had begun at Hampstead, the whole of Isabella; or, the Pot of Basil, the first of his longer poems written with real maturity of art and certainty of touch. At the same time, no doubt with his great intended effort, Hyperion, in mind, he was studying and appreciating Milton as he had never done before.

He had been steeped since boyhood in the charm of the minor poems, from the Vacation Exercise to Lycidas, and had read but not greatly cared for Paradise Lost, until first Severn, and then more energetically Bailey, had insisted that this was a reproach to him: and he now threw himself upon that poem, and penetrated with the grasp and swiftness of genius, as his marginal criticisms show, into the very essence of its power and beauty. His correspondence with his friends, particularly Bailey and Reynolds, is during this same time unusually sustained and full. Sometimes his vein is light and titterly (to use a word of his own) as I have indicated, and sometimes he masks an anxious heart beneath a lively manner, as thus:—

But ah Coward! to talk at this rate to a sick man, or, I hope, to one that was sick—for I hope by this you stand on your right foot. If you are not—that's all,—I intend to cut all sick people if they do not make up their minds to cut Sickness—a fellow to whom I have a complete aversion, and who strange to say is harboured and countenanced in several houses where I visit-he is sitting now quite impudent between me and Tom—he insults me at poor Jem Rice's—and you have seated him before now between us at the Theatre, when I thought he looked with a longing eye at poor Kean. I shall say, once for all, to my friends, generally and severally, cut that fellow, or I cut you.

On another day he recurs to the mood of half real half mock impatience against those who rub the bloom off things of beauty by over-commenting and over-interpreting them, a mood natural to a spirit dwelling so habitually and intuitively at the heart of beauty as his:—

It has as yet been a Mystery to me how and where Wordsworth went. I can't help thinking he has returned to his Shell—with his beautiful Wife and his enchanting Sister. It is a great Pity that People should by associating themselves with the finest things, spoil them. Hunt has damned Hampstead and masks and sonnets and Italian tales. Wordsworth has damned the lakes. Milman has damned the old drama—West has damned wholesale. Peacock has damned satire—Ollier has damn'd Music—Hazlitt has damned the bigoted and the blue-stockinged; how durst the Man? he is your only good damner, and if ever I am damn'd—damn me if I shouldn't like him to damn me.

Once, writing to Reynolds, he resumes his habit of a year and a half earlier, and casts his fancies and reflections into rime. Beginning playfully, he tells of an odd jumble of incongruous images that had crossed his brain, a kind of experience expressed by him elsewhere in various strains of verse, e.g. the finished poem Fancy and the careless lines beginning 'Welcome Joy, and welcome Sorrow.' He supposes that some people are not subject to such freaks of the mind's eye, but have it consistently haunted by fine things such as he next proceeds to conjure up from memory—

Some Titian colours touch'd into real life,—
The sacrifice goes on; the pontiff knife
Gleams in the Sun, the milk-white heifer lows,
The pipes go shrilly, the libation flows;
A white sail shows above the green-head cliff,
Moves round the point, and throws her anchor stiff;
The mariners join hymn with those on land.

There exists no such picture of a sacrifice by Titian, and what Keats was thinking of, I feel sure, was the noble 'Sacrifice to Apollo' by Claude from the Leigh Court collection, which he had seen at the British Institution in 1816 (hung, as it happened, next to Titian's Europa from Cobham Hall), and which evidently worked deeply on his mind.

To memory of it is probably due that magic vision of a little town emptied of its folk on a morning of sacrifice, which he evoked a year later in the ode on a Grecian Urn. It shows to the right an altar in front of a temple of Apollo, and about the altar a group including king and priest and a young man holding down a victim ox by the horns; people with baskets and offerings coming up from behind the temple; and to the left tall trees with a priest leading in another victim by the horns, and a woman with a jar bringing in libation; a little back, two herdsmen with their goats; a river spanned by a bridge and winding towards a sea-bay partly encircled by mountains which close the view, and on the edge of the bay the tower and roofs of a little town indistinctly seen.

Recollection of this Claude leads Keats on quickly to that of another, the famous 'Enchanted Castle,' which he partly mixes up with it, and partly transforms by fantasy into something quite different from what it really is. He forgets the one human figure in the foreground, describes figures and features of the landscape which are not there, and remembering that the architecture combines ancient Roman with mediæval castellated and later Palladian elements, invents for it far-fetched origins and associations which in a more careless fashion almost remind one of those invented by Pope for his Temple of Fame. A year later, all this effervescence of the imagination about the picture had subsided, and the distilled and concentrated essence of its romance was expressed—so at least I conceive—in the famous 'magic casement' phrase at the end of the Nightingale ode.

From this play of fancy about two half-remembered pictures Keats turns suddenly to reflections, which he would like to banish but cannot, on the 'eternal fierce destruction' which is part of nature's law:—

But I saw too distinct into the core
Of an eternal fierce destruction,
And so from happiness I far was gone.
Still am I sick of it, and tho', to-day,
I've gathered young spring-leaves, and flowers gay

Of periwinkle and wild strawberry, Still do I that most fierce destruction see,

The Shark at savage prey,—the Hawk at pounce,—
The gentle Robin, like a Pard or Ounce,
Ravening a worm.—Away, ye horrid moods!
Moods of one's mind!

The letters of this date should be read and re-read by all who want to get to the centre of Keats's mind or to hold a key to the understanding of his deepest poetry. The richest of them all is that in which he sends the fragments of an ode to Maia written on May day with the (alas! unfulfilled) promise to finish it 'in good time.' The same letter contains the re-assertion of a purpose declared in a letter of a week before to Mr Taylor in the phrases, 'I find I can have no enjoyment in the world but the continual drinking of knowledge.

I find there is no worthy pursuit but the idea of doing some good to the world.... There is but one way for me. The road lies through application, study and thought. I will pursue it.' The mood of the verses interpreting the song of the thrush a few weeks earlier has passed, the reader will note, clean out of the poet's mind. To Reynolds his words are:—

An extensive knowledge is needful to thinking people—it takes away the heat and fever; and helps, by widening speculation, to ease the Burden of the Mystery, a thing which I begin to understand a little, and which weighed upon you in the most gloomy and true sentence in your letter. The difference of high Sensations with and without knowledge appears to me this: in the latter case we are falling continually ten thousand fathoms deep and being blown up again, without wings, and with all [the] horror of a bare-shouldered creature—in the former case, our shoulders are fledged, and we go through the same air and space without fear.

Let it never be forgotten that 'sensations' contrasted with

'thoughts' mean for Keats not pleasures and experiences of the senses as opposed to those of the mind, but direct intuitions of the imagination as opposed to deliberate processes of the understanding; and that by 'philosophy' he does not mean metaphysics but knowledge and the fruits of reading generally.

The same letter, again, contains an interesting meditation on the relative qualities of genius in Milton and Wordsworth as affected by the relative stages of history at which they lived, and on the further question whether Wordsworth was a greater or less poet than Milton by virtue of being more taken up with human passions and problems. This speculation leads on to one of Keats's finest passages of life-wisdom:—

And here I have nothing but surmises, from an uncertainty whether Milton's apparently less anxiety for Humanity proceeds from his seeing further or not than Wordsworth: And whether Wordsworth has in truth epic passion, and martyrs himself to the human heart, the main region of his song. In regard to his genius alone—we find what he says true as far as we have experienced and we can judge no further but by larger experience —for axioms in philosophy are not axioms until they are proved upon our pulses.

We read fine things, but never feel them to the full until we have gone the same steps as the author.—I know this is not plain; you will know exactly my meaning when I say that now I shall relish Hamlet more than I have ever done —Or, better—you are sensible no man can set down Venery as a bestial or joyless thing until he is sick of it, and therefore all philosophising on it would be mere wording. Until we are sick, we understand not; in fine, as Byron says, 'Knowledge is sorrow'; and I go on to say that 'Sorrow is wisdom'—and further for aught we can know for certainty 'Wisdom is folly.'

Presently follows the famous chain of images by which Keats, searching and probing for himself along pathways of the spirit parallel to those followed by Wordsworth in the Lines composed a few miles above Tintern Abbey, renders account to himself of the stage of development to which his mind has now reached:—

Well, I compare human life to a large Mansion of many

apartments, two of which I can only describe, the doors of the rest being as yet shut upon me. The first we step into we call the Infant, or Thoughtless Chamber, in which we remain as long as we do not think.

We remain there a long while, and notwithstanding the doors of the second Chamber remain wide open, showing a bright appearance, we care not to hasten to it; but are at length imperceptibly impelled by the awakening of the thinking principle within us—we no sooner get into the second Chamber, which I shall call the Chamber of Maiden Thought, than we become intoxicated with the light and the atmosphere, we see nothing but pleasant wonders, and think of delaying there for ever in delight.

However among the effects this breathing is father of is that tremendous one of sharpening one's vision into the heart and nature of Man—of convincing one's nerves that the world is full of Misery and Heartbreak, Pain, Sickness, and oppression—whereby this Chamber of Maiden Thought becomes gradually darkened, and at the same time, on all sides of it, many doors are set open—but all dark—all leading to dark passages. We see not the balance of good and evil; we are in a mist, we are now in that state, we feel the 'Burden of the Mystery.' To this point was Wordsworth come, as far as I can conceive, when he wrote Tintern Abbey, and it seems to me that his genius is explorative of those dark Passages. Now if we live, and go on thinking, we too shall explore them.

Here is a typical case of the method of evocation as against the method of exposition. Wordsworth's lines are written with a high, almost an inspired, power of describing and putting into direct words the successive moods of a spirit gradually ripening and deepening in the power of communion with nature, and through nature, with all life. But Keats, fully as he has pondered them, cannot be satisfied that they fit his own case until he has called up the history of his similar experiences in the form natural to him, the form, that is, of concrete similitudes or visions of the imagination-the Thoughtless Chamber, the Chamber of Maiden Thought with its gradual darkening and its many outlets standing open to be explored.

It is significant that such visions should still be of architecture, of halls and chambers in an imagined mysterious building.

Apart from his growing sense of the darker sides of human existence and of the mysteries of good and evil, Keats was suffering at this time from the pain of a family break-up now imminent. George Keats had made up his mind to emigrate to America, and embark his capital, or as much of it as he could get possession of, in business there. Besides the wish to push his own fortunes, a main motive of this resolve on George's part was the desire to be in a position as quickly as possible to help or if need be support, his poet-brother.

He persuaded the girl to whom he had long been attached, Miss Georgiana Wylie, to share his fortunes, and it was settled that they were to be married and sail early in the summer. Some of Keats's letters during the last weeks of his stay at Teignmouth are taken up with his plans for the time immediately following this change. He wavered for a while between two incompatible purposes. One was to go for a summer's walking tour through Scotland with Charles Brown. 'I have many reasons,' he writes to Reynolds, 'for going wonderways; to make my winter chair free from spleen; to enlarge my vision; to escape disquisitions on poetry, and Kingston-criticism; to promote digestion and economize shoe-leather.' (How 'economize,' one wonders?) 'I'll have leather buttons and belt, and if Brown hold his mind, "over the hills we go."

If my books will keep me to it, then will I take all Europe in turn, and see the kingdoms of the earth and the glory of them.' Here we find Keats in his turn caught by the romance of wild lands and of travel which had in various ways been so much of an inspiration to Byron and Shelley before him. A fortnight later we find him inclining to give up this purpose under an overmastering sense of the inadequacy of his own attainments, and of the necessity of acquiring knowledge, and ever more knowledge, to sustain the flight of poetry.

The habit of close self-observation and self-criticism is in most natures that possess it allied with vanity and egoism; but it was not so in Keats, who without a shadow of affectation judges himself, both in his strength and weakness, as the most clear-sighted and disinterested friend might judge. He is inclined, when not on the defensive against what he felt to be foolish criticism, to underrate rather than to overrate his own work, and in his correspondence of the previous year we have found him perfectly aware that in writing Endymion he has rather been working off a youthful ferment of the mind than producing a sound or satisfying work of poetry.

And when the time comes to write a preface to the poem, he in a first draft makes confession to the public of his 'non-opinion of himself' in terms both a little too intimate and too fidgeting and uneasy. Reynolds seeing the draft at once recognised that it would not do, and in criticizing it to Keats seems to have told him that it was too much in the manner of Leigh Hunt. In deference to his judgment Keats at once abandoned it, and a second attempt says briefly, with perfect dignity and taste, all that can justly be said in dispraise of his work. He warns the reader to expect 'great inexperience, immaturity, and every error denoting a feverish attempt, rather than a deed accomplished,' and adds most unboastfully:—'it is just that this youngster should die away: a sad thought for me, if I had not some hope that while it is dwindling I may be plotting, and fitting myself for verses fit to live.'

Keats and Tom, the latter for the moment easier in health, were back at Hampstead in the last week of May, in time for the marriage of their brother George with Miss Georgiana Wylie. This was the young lady to whom Keats had rimed a valentine for his brother two years earlier (the lines beginning 'Hadst thou liv'd in days of old') and to whom he had also on his own account addressed the charming sonnet, 'Nymph of the downward smile and sidelong glance.' With no other woman or girl friend was he ever on such easy and cordial terms of intimacy.

The wedding took place 'a week ago,' writes Keats on June 4, and about the same date, in order that he may not miss seeing as much of the young couple as possible before their departure, he declines a warm invitation from Bailey to visit him again at Oxford. Writing, as usual to this correspondent, with absolute openness, Keats shows that he is suffering from one of his moods of overmastering depression. First it takes the form of apathy. Bailey had written eagerly and judiciously in praise of Endymion in the Oxford Herald. Keats replies on June 1:–

My intellect must be in a 'degenerating state—it must be-for when I should be writing about—God knows what—I am troubling you with moods of my own mind, or rather body, for mind there is none. I am in that temper that if I were under water I would scarcely kick to come up to the top—I know very well 'tis all nonsense. In a short time I hope I shall be in a temper to feel sensibly your mention of my book.

In vain have I waited till Monday to have my Interest in that, or anything else. I feel no spur at my Brother's going to America, and am almost stony-hearted about his wedding. All this will blow over. All I am sorry for is having to write to you in such a time—but I cannot force my letters in a hotbed. I could not feel comfortable in making sentences for you.

Nine days later the mood has deepened to one of positive despondency, but it is the despondency of a great and generous spirit:—

Were it in my choice, I would reject a Petrarchal coronation —on account of my dying day, and because women have cancers. I should not by right speak in this tone to you for it is an incendiary spirit that would do so. Yet I am not old enough or magnanimous enough to annihilate self—and it would perhaps be paying you an ill compliment. I was in hopes some little time back to be able to relieve your dulness by my spirits—to point out things in the world worth your enjoyment—and now I am never alone without rejoicing that there is such a thing as death —without placing my ultimate in the glory of dying for a great human purpose. Perhaps if my affairs were in a different state, I should not have written the above—you shall judge: I have two brothers; one is driven, by The 'burden of Society,' to America; the other, with an exquisite love of life, is in a lingering state.

My love for my Brothers, from the early loss of our

parents, and even from earlier misfortunes, has grown into an affection 'passing the love of women.' I have been ill-tempered with them—I have vexed them—but the thought of them has always stifled the impression that any woman might otherwise have made upon me. I have a sister too, and may not follow them either to America or to the grave. Life must be undergone, and I certainly derive some consolation from the thought of writing one or two more poems before it ceases.

Meanwhile his fluctuations of purpose between a plunge into a life of solitude and study and an excursion in Brown's company to Scotland had been decided in favour of the Scottish tour. George and his bride having to set out for Liverpool on June 22, it was arranged that Keats and Brown should accompany them so far on their way to the north. The coach started from the Swan and two Necks in Lad Lane, and on the first day stopped for dinner at Redbourne near St Albans, where Keats's friend of medical student days, Mr Stephens, was in practice.

He came to shake hands with the travelling party at the poet's request, and many years afterwards wrote an account of the interview, the chief point of which is a description of Mrs George Keats. 'Rather short, not what might be called strictly handsome, but looked like a being whom any man of moderate sensibility might easily love. She had the imaginative poetical cast. Somewhat singular and girlish in her attire.... There was something original about her, and John seemed to regard her as a being whom he delighted to honour, and introduced her with evident satisfaction.'

Chapter 8

John Keats and Leigh Hunt

The history of the friendship between John Keats and Leigh Hunt is the story of Keat's development as a poet. Between the years 1816 and 1821, Keats became a mature poet, moving from the uneven workmanship of his youth to the mastery evidenced in his odes, in *La Belle Dame sans Merci,* in *Lamia,* in *The Fall of Hyperion,* and so on.

These were the years also of his friendship with Leigh Hunt. Their relationship centered around poetry from the start, and poetry was responsible for many of the sufferings which it involved. It is the reason also for the special importance of that friendship. This paper will look at three aspects of the relationship between Keats and Hunt: 1) the progress and character of the friendship, 2) Hunt's criticism of Keats's work and 3) Hunt's influence on Keats.

PROGRESS AND CHARACTER OF THE FRIENDSHIP

Along with his brothers John and Robert, Leigh Hunt edited and published the *Examiner,* a liberal weekly that did much to improve the literary quality of English journalism and did more to rile the conservative government of his time. Indeed, John and Leigh Hunt spent two years in prison, from January 1813 to January 1815, after being convicted of libel because they had called the Prince of Wales, among other things, ... a violator of his word, a libertine over head and cars in debt and disgrace, a despiser of domestic ties (he companion of gamblers and demireps, a man who has just closed half a century without one single claim on the gratitude of his country or (he respect of posterity! The concerns of Hunt and the *Examiner* extended the censoring of the new Regent's antics. Barnette Miller, in her book about Hunt and his friendships, has enumerated the issues about which he was especially concerned:

... Catholic Emancipation; reform of Parliamentary representation; liberty of the press; reduction and equalization of taxes; greater discretion in increasing the public debt; education of the poor and amelioration of (heir sufferings: abolition of child-labour and of the slave trade; reform of military discipline, of prison conditions, and of the criminal and civil laws, particularly those governing debtors.

I Hunt's responsibilities with the *Examiner* were many and varied political essays about the above issues, literary essays and theatrical reviews — but he maintained also an active interest in poetry. He also published his own poetic works in the *Examiner.*

Hunt became quite familiar to Keats through his publication. Around 1810 Keats, then aged fifteen or so, began reading and studying with an unanticipated diligence. The *Examiner* was among his regular readings at that time. Charles C. Clarke, then Keat's former teacher and close friend, wrote that "the first proof (he) had received of his having committed himself in verse" was a sonnet titled "Written on the Day that Mr. Leigh Hunt left Prison." In 1816 in a letter to his brother George, the young poet referred to Hunt as *Libertas;* the the context of the reference shows an appreciation of Hunt as both reformer and literary critic.

It was through his friend Clarke that Keats first met the much admired Hunt. Clarke brought Hunt a few of Keats's poems. He relates Hunt's reaction in his *Recollections of Keats*:

I could not but anticipate that Hunt would speak encouragingly and indeed approvingly, of the compositions - written, too. by a youth under age; but my partial spirit was not prepared for the unhesitating and prompt admiration which broke forth before he had read twenty lines of the first poem.

Clarke introduced Keats to Hunt during the spring of

1816. After a first meeting, "which stretched into three 'morning calls',... Keats was suddenly made a familiar of the household, and was always welcomed."

The first year of the friendship was the most intimate and the most harmonious. Indeed, Hunt seems to have had an extraordinary capacity for forming friendships. He also tended to idealize them. Thus, years later, writing about their relationship in his *Autobiography,* Hunt says that except for one circumstance "(for I have no reserve myself with those whom I love)... Keats and I might have been taken for friends of the old stamp, between whom there is no such thing even as obligation, except the pleasure of it."

Perhaps such would not have been an unrealistic assessment of their friendship during the year following the spring of 1816. During that time Keats was a frequent visitor of the Hunts' cottage. He and Hunt would read together and compete in poetry writing contests. The sonnets *To the Nile* and *On the Grasshopper and the Cricket* are products of those contests. To his first book, *Poems by John Keats,* published in the spring of 1817, Keats added a dedicatory sonnet to Hunt. Its last lines are as follows:

And I shall ever bless my destiny,
That in a time, when under pleasant trees
Pan is no longer sought, I feel a free,
A leafy luxury, seeing I could please
With these poor offerings, a man like thee.

Hunt printed some of Keats's poetry; and on December 1, 1816, he published the notice "Young Poets," in which he numbered Keats among three "young aspirants ... who promise[d] to help the new school [of poetry] to revive Nature and [t]o put a new spirit of youth into every thing."

Things began to take a turn for the worse, however. It is clear from Keats's letters that by May of 1817 he had become suspicious of Hunt. He was encouraged or led along in this attitude by Benjamin R. Haydon, a painter of modest abilities but of great pretensions. In a letter to Keats dated May 10, 1817, he wrote, "I love you like my own Brother, beware for God's sake of the delusions and sophistications that is (sic) ripping up the talent and respectability of our Friend (Hunt).... The following day Keats returned a letter, in which he wrote,

Perhaps it is a self-delusion to say so — but I think I could not be (sic) deceived in the Manner that Hunt is — may I die tomorrow if I am to be. There is no greater Sin after the 7 deadly than to flatter oneself into an idea or being a great Poet...

Haydon not only suspected Hunt of self-delusions; he also distrusted his motives. Later Haydon advised Keats not to show *Endymion* to Hunt. In October 1817 Keats wrote, "Haydon says to me(,) Keats(,) dont (sic) show your Lines to Hunt on any account or he will have done half for you — so it appears Hunt wishes it to be thought." The nervousness and depression which was made evident in his letters was probably one reason for his willingness to doubt the motives of one who had recently been a close friend.

There was, however, probably more to the conflict than Keats's unbalanced temper. Keats's poetic pursuits and ambitions complicated the situation. In this respect, three different problems seem to have been weakening the friendship between 1817 and 1820: 1) Keats's dislike for Hunt's style of poetry and Hunt's disapproval of *Endymion,* the epic poem which Keats wrote during the summer and fall of 1817, 2) his desire not to be considered a follower of Hunt, and 3) the idea that Hunt somehow harmed his aesthetic sense.

Keats's letters give evidence of these concerns. With respect to the first, he wrote to a friend about a proposed preface to *Endymion,* "Since you all agree that the thing is bad, it must be so — though I am not aware there is anything like Hunt in it, (and if there is, it is my natural way, and I have something in common with Hunt"); and about Hunt's criticism of *Endymion,* he wrote earlier to his brother,

... he allows it not much merit as a whole; says it is unnatural and made ten objections to it in the mere skimming over. He says the conversation is unnatural and too high-flown.... The fact is he and Shelley are hut 1, and perhaps justly, at my not having showed them the affair officiously — and ... they appear much disposed to dissect and anatomize, any trip or slip I may have made — But whose (sic) afraid? Evidence of Keat's desire not to be seen as a follower of Hunt is shown in his correspondence with Benjamin Bailey, and the desire seems to have been related to Haydon's notion that Hunt "will have done half." Keats wrote to Bailey in October of 1817,

You see Bailey how independent my writing has been ... and after all I shall have the Reputation of Hunt's eleve. His corrections and amputations will by the Knowing ones be traced in this Poem. This is to be sure the vexation of a day ...

Keats preferred being an "Eagle" with Shakespeare and Milton to being an "owl" with Hunt and Wordsworth. Finally, in a lengthy journal letter, composed during December 1818 and early January 1819 to his brother George and his wife, Keats wrote, "Hunt does one harm by making fine things petty and beautiful things hateful...." The winter of 1818-1819 seems to have marked the low point in Keats's esteem for Hunt.

The result of this reaction and disillusionment was that Keats no longer enjoyed Hunt's company — there is no indication, however, that Hunt was dissatisfied with Keats. The young poet repeated in his letters that he was "tired" of it all. He no longer valued conversations with Hunt:

... men and tin kettles are much the same in these days.... Conversation is not a search for knowledge, but an endeavor at effect. In this respect two most opposite men, Wordsworth and Hunt, are the same...

Nor did he show his former admiration for Hunt's liberal principles.

The summer of 1820 revived the friendship. Keats was very ill with tuberculosis and, during his illness, had been sharing a house with his friend Charles Brown. When Brown left on his annual summer hike through the Hebrides, Keats moved to a house near Hunt's residence in Kentish Town. On June 23rd he moved in with the Hunts.

His letters bespeak his appreciation of Hunt's kindness toward him. The renewed friendship was temporarily dampened when one of Hunt's servants opened a letter to Keats from Fanny Brawne. Keats was very upset by this and left Hunt's house. lie recognized his overreaction, however, and wrote to Hunt, "I hope to see you whenever you call get time(,) for I feel really attached to you for your many sympathies with me, and patience at my lunes."

Not long after these events, Keats left for Italy. The *Indicator,* a supplement to the *Examiner,* marked his departure with an "Adieu to Keats," saying he would "soon be back." Such was not the case; Keats died in Rome on February 23, 1821.

HUNT'S LITERARY CRITICISM

Keats had published three volumes of poetry: *Poems by John Keats* 1817; *Endymion,* 1818; and *Lamia, Isabella, The Eve of St. Agnes and Other Poems,* 1820. Hunt's criticism of each of these volumes will be considered.

Edmund Blundell in his book on the *Examiner* praises Hunt's farsighted review of *Poems.* He is "not blind to faults, but he discerns excellences with prophetic quickness." As for faults, he reveals two kinds: an indiscriminate notice of details, and variety in versification without proper "consideration of its principles." Hunt is kind in his praises of Keat's early poetry:

We come now however to the beauties; and the reader will easily perceive that they not only outnumber the faults hundred fold, but they are of a nature decidedly opposed to what is false and inharmonious. Their characteristics indeed are a fine ear, a fancy and imaginations at will, and an intense feeling of external beauty in its most natural and least expressible simplicity.

Keats's second volume, *Endymion,* was attacked in the press by *Blackwood's Magazine* and the *Quarterly Review* and was attacked in a series of articles directed primarily at Hunt; his circle was labeled the "Cockney School" and Keats was considered to be a member of that group. Hunt did not write a response defending *Endymion* against those very negative reviews. He merely published a retort by John H. Reynolds. Hunt was criticized for this and it seems that Keats expected some defence of his work by Hunt. Miller has pointed out the correctness of Hunt's response. He could not adequately defend that of which he disapproved, and, moreover, his reply would probably only have resulted in greater injury to Keats.

In a review of Keats's third volume, Hunt refers to *Endymion*. He writes,

Endymion with all its extraordinary powers, partook of the faults of youth, though the best ones; but tire reader of *Hyperion* and these other stories would never guess that they were written at twenty. [They weren't!]

The emphasis which Hunt places on Keats' maturity of genius and on his mastery of imagery and versification as shown in the third volume is striking. It was the absence of these characteristics which troubled him before. In *The Eve of St. Agnes,* he finds a passage which "affords a striking specimen of the sudden and strong maturity of tile author's genius." Hunt attempts to describe Keats's genius:

The character of his genius is that of energy and voluptuousness, each able at will to take leave of the other, and possessing in their union, a high feeling of humanity not common in the best authors who can combine them. Mr. Keats undoubtedly takes his seat with the eldest and best of our living poets. Whatever the changes in their friendship, Hunt continued to see great promise and poetic genius in Keats.

HUNT'S INFLUENCE ON KEATS

Hunt's influence on the public's opinion of Keats in his time was unfavorable. Indeed, Keats was ignored at first and later attacked largely because of his affiliation with Hunt. Clarke tells of the reception which his early work received, blaming its failure to be well received on Hunt's reputation:

The whole community, as if by compact seemed determined to know nothing about it [the first volume]....[H]e might have had a better chance of success had he been an anti-Jacobin. Keats had not made the slightest demonstration of political opinion; but ... he had dedicated his book to Leigh Hunt, a Radical and a dubbed partisan of the first Napoleon; because, when alluding to him, Hunt did not always subjoin the fashionable Cognomen of "Corsican Monster."

As was mentioned earlier, the damaging review of

Endymion from *Blackwood's Magazine* and the *Quarterly Review* were part of a general attack on the "Cockney School."

Hunt also had an influence on Keats' poetry. His effect on Keats' early poetry was considerable. Keats moved away from Hunt's influence, however, and his later works show little that could have been taken from Hunt. According to Miller, "What influence lingers is seen in the general theory of versification and in the diction, with some trace in matters of taste."

Probably the clearest movement in the friendship between John Keats and Leigh Hunt, after its having been established, was Keats' movement away from dependence upon Hunt and away from close association with him. It is not surprising, considering Keats' preoccupation with poetry, that it figured in their coming together and in the suspicions and attitudes of Keats.

Indeed, Keats's progress through the relationship was steadily toward greater independence he refused Hunt's recommendations and Shelley's invitations to him to depend on Shelley, because he cherished his independence. During the summer of 1820, Keats was forced into dependence by his illness. By then, however, the relationship was very different from what it had been at the start. Keats' poetry follows the same route, from an early dependence upon Hunt's example to a conscious independence.

Chapter 9

Using Ode to Autumn, John Keats

When you are asked to analyse a poem, paying attention to such items as rhyme, meter, voice, enjambment, imagery and all the thousands of literary terms that leave you reeling, or retching, depending on your current state of mind - do not panic. Because if you like words and love music, you have all the necessary skills and equipment in place already, I assure you. How do I know this, and how can I make such a huge generalization? Well, unless you are a plank of wood or a big rock that somebody brought into the classroom and forgot about, you can do it.

This is because you are a unique, thinking, feeling human being, equipped with senses. Now you may not have all five, but I guarantee that if you start your analysis by using those you have, then you are well on the way to understanding and appreciating poetry. After I go through how I believe this works for everybody, I will give you some good web sites and a few tips to clarify the technicalities. My initial approach, though, is to ignore these in favour of just using your brain, imagination and those senses. Get physical with the poem, become the poet.

To demonstrate how this works, take a look at Keats' 'Ode to Autumn'. Do not worry about word that you find unfamiliar, you can look them up later, or read the interpretation most books provide. No, just read it aloud to yourself, (or if you have a completely trustworthy friend or lover or whatever, who is not going to use this as evidence of insanity or lack of cool),or to an appreciative audience.

You have got to try to see what Keats is seeing, mist, fruit, apples, harvested goodness, granary bread, Indian Summer type sun and buzzing bees. He gives you images of what he looks upon, straight away. So already, you can identify visual imagery - but don't go there yet. Everybody can relate to Fall, how we see misty mornings, see a less bright, but sometimes warming sun, see drowsy insects, see birds preparing to leave for Winter in warmer places. So now you have spoken the words, seen the pictures and heard yourself.

Now, let us really listen to the sounds. "Nah", you say "it's words on a page," but don't forget you have said those words aloud, now say them or read them again, silently. As you have guessed, you have no need for an audience this time. Read it again, and hear in your mind, the words that recall sounds for you. The only word that might grab you could be "songs", or maybe it could be "music" - ok, that's good enough, because when you relate it to the sounds of nature that Keats expresses, such as lambs bleating, crickets singing, swallows twittering, and so on, you have hit the auditory image nail on the head.

Next, it is entirely your choice whether you read it aloud or savor it quietly, because you are going to touch, or at any rate, share a tactile moment with John. Call to mind what you understand by "plump" or "swell" or "stubble" or "close-bosomed" - OK behave yourself! But you will have experienced three dimensional, or physical imagery. The whole thing is building into something sensual, alive and tangible.

Next, I would ask you to put taste and smell together because I think they are almost inseparable. I mean, think about how boring and unappetizing food becomes when you have a cold. Who wants to eat something chewy, slimy and crunchy? I speak of steak, fried onions and french fries, without the aromas that tickle the taste buds, because of a blocked nose. So with that as my justification, smell and taste go together. Again, I leave it to you as to whether you read aloud or silently - I personally would declaim the poem with meaning and feeling, savoring scent and flavour. You have "sweet kernel" "cyder presses", with the nutty, appley smells making your mouth water, not to mention "fruit with ripeness to the core," and the flowers for the bees, suggesting sweet golden honey to eat, scents to savor.

OK, you have read the poem four times and I really hope terminal boredom has not taken away the will to live. What I hope is, you have found something to connect with, that links to your own experience, that has touched you sensually, lit up your imagination. That you feel Mr. Keats to be somebody you would not mind talking with, because he tells it like it is and you know now where he is coming from.

But teacher needs more, you have got to get into the technical detail, the analysis that seems to take the soul out of a poem. Which is why I am leaving this part to the end? But first let us apply these ideas to every poem you will read, dissect, enjoy, analyse or even throw in the waste-bin! The poet is portraying his or her experiences, encapsulating emotions that are so universal to the human condition, that they say it for the rest of us, better than we can ourselves. They are word-smiths, painters, dream-catchers, so immerse yourself in what they are sharing first - then let us address the technicalities, the literary labels.

For this, I suggest you read the Foreword to the book in which you find your poem. This will give you background to your poet, and a time-line you can relate to the genre. Some versions may even define linguistic terms, and if not, use your dictionary or encyclopedia.

Next, get out the Norton Poetry Anthology, the Introduction is brilliant for explanations on poetic construction, so will help you to put the labels on the literary contexts. It also contains footnotes that clarify old meanings, but hey, you have already worked them out for yourself. After all, you have used the best and most effective analytical tools at your disposal - your mind, imagination and senses.

We must remember the Internet, a marvelous source, but more important, a sort of affirmation of your interpretations, but leave that till after you have drawn your own conclusions. After nearly 50 years of reading, teaching analyzing and just plain enjoying all forms of literature, to find that there are very clever people out there with tons of letters after their names (I've got ounces), who think the same, is very comforting. So you can always go to Google and put in the poet's name, the poem and the word 'themes and tons of helpful stuff will appear. But be picky, use your own voice always. I beg you, do not do this until you have reached your own conclusions, via your unique qualities and senses.

Chapter 10

Critical Analysis of "Ode to a Nightingale" by John Keats

John Keats poems "Ode to a Nightingale" and "Ode on a Grecian Urn" exist for the purpose of describing a moment in life, such as a brief song of a nightingale and scene depicted on an urn; within each moment there exists a multitude of emotions, and changing from one to another indefinably. Keats' "Ode on a Grecian Urn" deals with the perplexing and indefinable relationship between life and art. Paradoxically, it is the life of the urn that would normally associate with stillness, melancholy and bereavement that is shown to be representative of life.

In "Ode to a Nightingale" a visionary happiness is communing with the nightingale as its song is contrasted with the dead weight of human grief and sicknesses, and the transience of youth and beauty. The odes are similar in many ways as in both Keats depicts the symbols of immortality and escapism, and grief to joy. However, the symbol of nightingale is a reality dealing with the nature and the urn is a fantasy, a piece of art. Both require different senses for admiring. By comparing the elements of poems, it is evident that all aspects relate directly to the human spirit and emotions.

The nightingale and urn are symbols of immortality, a symbol of continuity of nature and art respectively. In the "Ode to a Nightingale" Keats contrasts the birds' immortality with the mortality of human beings as he states "Here where men sit and hear each other groan, where Palsy shakes a few, sad, last gray hairs, where youth grows pale, and specter-thin, and dies,"(III, 25) but the nightingale, entertaining generations after generations has become an immortal species, so much so that the sound that poet has heard was heard in ancient days by emperor and clown, by Ruth (a virtuous Moabite widow who according to Old Testament Book of Ruth, left her own country to accompany her mother-in-law Naomi, back to Naomi's native land), where she was amidst the corn, remembering her home town; and also by fairies.

The urn in the "Ode on a Grecian Urn" is a large sculpted vessel with Greek figures is an "unravished bride"(I, 1), an immortal perfect object unmarked by the passage of time. As a "Sylvan historian" (I, 3), it provides a record of a distant culture. Although, the urn exists in the real world, which is mutable or subject to changes, yet the life it's depicting is unchanging.

Next, the poet has beautifully fused pain with imaginary relief or the unconscious joyous things of nature and art. To escape from pain of reality, he begins to move into the world of imagination. When he hears the nightingale, he yearns for fine wine from south France, not to get drunk but to achieve a state of mind, which will give him the pleasure of the company of the beautiful nightingale, "that I might drink, and leave the world unseen, And with thee fade away into the forest dim:"(II, 19-20) However, the poet realizes that he does not require wine for being with the bird, so chooses the route of flying to her through his poetry.

"Away! Away! for I will fly to thee, Not charioted by Bacchus and his pards, But on the viewless wings of Poesy... And haply the Queen-Moon is on her throne, Cluster'd around by all her starry Fays"(IV, 36,37). In "Ode on a Grecian Urn," the poet experiences the life depicted on the urn and ambiguously comments that the urn "dost tease us out of thought/As doth eternity"(V, 45). By teasing him "out of thought" (V stanza) urn draws him from the real world to an ideal, fantasy world. In lines "What mad pursuit? What struggle to escape?

What pipes and timbrels? What wild ecstasy?"(I, 5,6,7,8) poet is caught up in excitement, activities and from a keen observer becomes a participant in the life on the urn. He gets emotionally involved in the apparent activities going on including the religious sacrifice of the cow, "Who are these coming to the sacrifice? To what green altar, O mysterious priest, Lead'st thou heifer lowing at the skies, And all her silken flanks with garlands drest?"(IV, 31,32,33,34) Thus, in both the odes, Keats tried to free himself from the painful world by identifying with the nightingale, representing nature, or the urn, representing art.

The inner pain and grief engulfing the poet is revealed in a very subtle manner in both the odes of discussion. Even when the speaker is in the imaginative world with the nightingale, he is thinking of death in "embalmed darkness." Gradually the feeling of being embalmed becomes a wish for death. He also realizes that death means he could no longer hear the bird song and will be non-existent. Suddenly the beautiful bird song seems to him more like "requiem" (VI, 60), a song of death. As the reality is painful, poet realizes that, "fancy" (VIII, 73), has cheated him. The bird is not a symbol anymore but an actual bird that poet had heard in the beginning.

The nightingale flies away and its song seems a "plaintive anthem" (VIII, 75), very faint. Its voice is "buried deep" (VIII, 77) refers to its physical distance. As the music goes from his life, the poet wonders whether his end is close. In "Ode on a Grecian Urn" the poet realizes as the figures are frozen, they will never change. Keats emphasizes the feeling of permanence by repeating the words "never, never."(II, 17) The repetition implies that man will never be able to kiss the maiden because his position will never change, and the space between both of them will never decrease. Poet also realizes when he is no more in this world, the urn would still be there and it will say, "Beauty is Truth and truth beauty.... (V, 49).

In the "Ode to Nightingale" and "Ode on a Grecian Urn" the symbols contrast. The nightingale is a living creature and a part of nature. In contrast the urn is stationary and a manmade object. Although both symbols signify immortality, and continuity, the symbols contrast in that the nightingale is reality, and the life on the urn is a fantasy with the portrayal of frozen images depicting dynamic life. Both symbols require different senses for admiring. The sense of hearing allows Keats to hear the nightingale's enchanting music. By listening to the nightingale Keats other senses are mesmerized. In contrast Keats sense of sight allows him to become captivated with the urn.

By observing the urn, Keats other senses are awakened. John Keats presented in his poetry many issues, such as nature, existence and the soul. All of these aspects relate directly to the human spirit. The spiritual nature of Keats poetry concerns itself with exploring human emotions and understanding nature. He wrote the "Ode to a Nightingale" and the "Ode on a Grecian Urn" at a difficult time in his life. As a result there are many similarities and few differences. Together both the similarities and differences, illustrate the human spirit, and a multitude of emotions.

Chapter 11

Literary Analysis on John Keats' Poetry

At first glance one might perceive John Keats's two poems "Ode on Melancholy" and "To Autumn" to be polar opposites. "Ode on Melancholy" initially appears to lament the ephemeral condition of beauty and wallow in misery because it "must die;" (Melancholy line 21). This is a sharp contrast to the feeling of elation that permeates "To Autumn," which also treats temporality but glories in the cycles of nature instead of grieving over them.

"To Autumn" clearly illustrates the usual practice of the romantic ode by taking two contrary concepts, life and death, and linking them. Examining the "Ode on Melancholy" in this light, it becomes clear that it is not advising us to weep for the ephemeral, but to rejoice in the existence of such beauty because one can only know true joy through melancholy. Like "To Autumn," "Ode on Melancholy" unites two opposing ideas in the minds of the readers.

It is quite understandable to come away from a first reading of the "Ode on Melancholy" thinking that it is truly about desolation and despair. Although the speaker advises against it, the first stanza lists many macabre methods of suicide, from the obliviate Lethe, to a poisonous wine of wolf's bane, the kiss of nightshade, the fruit of the queen of the underworld, and a rosary of yew-berries symbolizing death. Then we are warned that these methods would "come too drowsily,/ and drown the wakeful anguish of the soul" (lines 9-10). This sounds as though death would end it all too quickly and that one who would truly experience anguish and self-torture should need only to read on to discover what is even worse than these self-inflicted mutilations.

The second stanza seems to imply that the short span of life given to beauty is more horrific than the previously contemplated suicide. It counsels one to

glut thy sorrow on a morning rose,
Or on the rainbow of the salt sand-wave,
Or on the wealth of globed peonies;
Or if thy mistress some rich anger shows,
Emprison her soft hand, and let her rave,
And feed deep, deep upon her peerless eyes.
(lines 15-20)

The pain one can inflict on oneself seems to fall short next to the sharp agony of the knowledge that these beauteous wonders such as roses and rainbows are so momentary, to say nothing of the knowledge that the "peerless eyes" of "thy mistress" are only hers for her brief span upon this earth.

The ode concludes by telling us that
beauty
must die;
And Joy, whose hand is ever at his lips
Bidding adieu; and aching Pleasure nigh,
Turning to poison (lines 21-24)

Taken at face value, these outwardly pessimistic words seem to make a fitting end to an ode on melancholythey inform us once again of the inevitable death of beauty, remind us that joy is fleeting, and tell us that pleasure turns to poison.

This somewhat shallow and slapdash reading of the "Ode on Melancholy" would make it appear to run counter to Keats's "To Autumn" in which temporality is celebrated as opposed to mourned. For a season most often associated with endings and the coming of winter, this poem is remarkable in its luscious and lively imagery. Autumn is personified in the first stanza as an active and benevolent entity who blesses vines with fruit, bends the trees with apples, swells the gourds, plumps the hazel shells, and sets to "budding more,/ And still more, later flowers for the bees,/ until they think warm days will never cease," (lines 8-10). This benevolence is, of course, lightly overshadowed by the knowledge that winter is drawing nigh to bring it all to an end. The overabundance of fruitfulness calms in the second stanza as Autumn rests a bit, "sitting careless on a granary floor,/ [Her] hair soft-lifted by the winnowing wind;/ Or on a half-reap'd furrow sound asleep," (lines 14-16).

Here we see the first concrete hints of awareness that Autumn does indeed herald the end of the season in the appearance of the hook, or scythe, traditionally wielded by a reaper and by The Reaper, better known as the incarnation of Death. Yet Death's emergence is gentle, indeed, the hook "spares the next swath and all its twined flowers" (line 18).

It is in the third stanza that Keats truly revels in the cycles of nature. He reminds us that Autumn's music is as fair as the songs of spring, the season of birth. We are then treated to an inspired series of images that play on the concepts of life and death and emphasize the cyclic nature of life.

Wile barred clouds bloom the soft-dying day,
And touch the stubble-plains with rosy hue;
Then in a wailful choir the small gnats mourn
Among the river sallows, borne aloft
Or sinking as the light wind lives or dies;
(lines 25-29)

In line 25 "clouds bloom" or flourish and grow as the day is "soft-dying." The "stubble-plains" of harvested corn or wheat that usually

symbolize barrenness and death are "rosy," a hue associated with warmth and liveliness. In the next lines the gnats may "mourn" as one might at a funeral, but they are then "borne" aloft as Keats plays on the word "born" and stresses the birth/death cycle. This sequence is subtly accented by the movements of the gnats as they are borne "aloft/ Or sinking" and again as "the light wind lives or dies." Keats is showing us that the difference is not that great between being borne aloft or sinking because the pendulum will eventually swing the other way and the cycle will begin again. Whether the wind lives or dies, the wind will come again.

Even the last few lines of this poem are indicative of the successive character of nature. "The red-breast whistles from a garden-croft;/ And gathering swallows twitter in the skies" (lines 32-33). These lines do not neatly close the poem but gently fade away, illustrating once again that Autumn is not an ending; in other words, dying is not an ending. He is showing us how intricately bound life and death are. These two opposed concepts are inseparable. With this reading in mind, a second look at "Ode on Melancholy" proves much more fruitful.

As previously noted, the first stanza does offer a list of lethal substances, but it is actually quite adamant to not use these things. Keats begins the poem with "No, no," in the first line, creating a spondee that insists on being heard. He is telling us not to avoid melancholy through these painful methods. Lines nine and ten warn us that these methods of creating death would "drown the wakeful anguish of the soul." In other words they would keep one from truly experiencing melancholy. This is similar to the paradox demonstrated in the first stanza of "To Autumn," when we are shown a profusion of growth and vivacity that precedes and heralds decay and death.

Like "To Autumn," this second stanza contains very little action, giving us time to slow down and observe. We note that melancholy has fallen "from heaven like a weeping cloud, / That fosters the droop-headed flowers all," (lines 12-13). Melancholy came from heaven, which is not a place noted for spreading misery, so one can only assume that there may be some merit in this cloud. Additionally, the cloud fosters, or encourages, the droopy flowers that need rain to grow. The "rainbow of the salt-sand wave" (line 16) is likely to reappear because that wave will wash up again without fail.

The angry lover's symbolize barrenness and death are "rosy," a hue associated with warmth and liveliness. In the next lines the gnats may "mourn" as one might at a funeral, but they are then "borne" aloft as Keats plays on the word "born" and stresses the birth/death cycle. This sequence is subtly accented by the movements of the gnats as they are borne "aloft/ Or sinking" and again as "the light wind lives or dies." Keats is showing us that the difference is not that great between being borne aloft or sinking because the pendulum will eventually swing the other way and the cycle will begin again. Whether the wind lives or dies, the wind will come again.

Even the last few lines of this poem are indicative of the successive character of nature. "The red-breast whistles from a garden-croft;/ And gathering swallows twitter in the skies" (lines 32-33). These lines do not neatly close the poem but gently fade away, illustrating once again that Autumn is not an ending; in other words, dying is not an ending. He is showing us how intricately bound life and death are. These two opposed concepts are inseparable. With this reading in mind, a second look at "Ode on Melancholy" proves much more fruitful.

As previously noted, the first stanza does offer a list of lethal substances, but it is actually quite adamant to not use these things. Keats begins the poem with "No, no," in the first line, creating a spondee that insists on being heard. He is telling us not to avoid melancholy through these painful methods. Lines nine and ten warn us that these methods of creating death would "drown the wakeful anguish of the soul." In other words they would keep one from truly experiencing melancholy. This is similar to the paradox demonstrated in the first stanza of "To Autumn," when we are shown a profusion of growth and vivacity that precedes and heralds decay and death.

Like "To Autumn," this second stanza contains very little action, giving us time to slow down and observe. We note that melancholy has fallen "from heaven like a weeping cloud, / That fosters the droop-headed flowers all," (lines 12-13). Melancholy came from heaven, which is not a place noted for spreading misery, so one can only assume that there may be some merit in this cloud. Additionally, the cloud fosters, or encourages, the droopy flowers that need rain to grow. The "rainbow of the salt-sand wave" (line 16) is likely to reappear because that wave will wash up again without fail.

Chapter 12

King Lear and the Christian Mystics

In the second part of his *Four Quartets* (1943), T. S. Eliot writes, "Do not let me hear / Of the wisdom of old men, but rather of their folly". Doubtless, such foolishness applies to old women as well. Perhaps my own late middle-aged folly tempts me to once more "burn through" old man King Lear's "fierce dispute / Betwixt damnation and impassion'd clay... [to] once more humbly assay / The bitter-sweet of this Shakespearean fruit" (Keats).

My hesitancy to do so arises from recognizing that Lear, as Kenneth J. E. Graham recently wrote in the journal *Modern Philology*, stands for Literature with a capital L, so that "what we write about it stands for Criticism" with a capital C. The hugeness of Lear does tend to magnify the weight of anything we can say about it. Even so sophisticated a critic as Northrop Frye expresses awe in the face of such a masterpiece.

Yet, some of the most violent philosophical arguments I have had with teachers, friends, and colleagues over the years have centered on conflicting interpretations of this tragic play. During my Duke undergraduate days, expressing my opinion about *King Lear* engendered a disturbing chastisement from Professor Helen Bevington. "What do you mean, a 'vision of transcendence'?" she all but shrieked at me. "This play has no hope, no justice, no redemption. Cordelia's dead, Gloucester's dead, Lear's Fool is dead; nothing will save them."

"But he dies believing her alive," I timidly responded.

"That's because he's crazy, insane—a nutty old man

howling at the universe! It's all absolutely meaningless!" Mrs. Bevington concluded, glaring at me, basilisk-like, through coke-bottle lenses.

And, indeed, despite a decades-old tradition that Christianizes this play about a pre-Christian Celtic king of Britain, twentieth-century materialists and current postmodernists have all but derisively discarded attempts to view it in a religious context. As Rene Fortin puts it, "Attempts to redeem *King Lear* by appealing to intimation of Christian transcendence have been summarily, if not vehemently, dismissed by secular critics". Not even critics of such stature as A. C. Bradley, G. Wilson Knight, Reuben Arthur Brower, J. A. Bryant, Robert H. West, Roy W. Battenhouse, and Northrop Frye receive much respect from postmodernists on this subject.

The pessimistic view of Shakespeare's tragic play has gathered momentum ever since Jan Kott envisioned "*King Lear* as Endgame" (1964). In *King Lear and the Gods* (1966), William R. Elton asserted that the Christians are simply wrong about the play because, in "seeking to escape the dire significance of the tragic vision, they are, in effect, guilty of wishful thinking." Elton found "the Christian optimist interpretation" invalid for two reasons: no evidence exists of Lear's salvation, and nothing in the play supports the idea of benevolent Providence.

Most recent critics think that Shakespeare's play leads only "to the edge of religious insight" (Danby 299) or opt for terms such as "ambiguity" (N. Joseph Calarco and William Empson), "paradox" (Albert Cook and Helen Gardner,), "contrariety" (Norman Rabkin and Robert Grudin,), and "complementarity" (Derek Traversi).

Nevertheless, personal predilection and cultural moment—America's own national "dark night of the soul" after 9/11—compel me to cast caution to the winds and defend mystical experience from detractors who equate the soul's dark journey with some kind of naïve idealism. Throughout its rending confrontation with pain and folly, the action of King Lear echoes the recorded experiences of mystics at the highest level of spiritual development.

Passages from T. S. Eliot's *The Waste Land, Ash Wednesday,* and *Four Quartets* offer a convenient frame on which to hang the steps of the journey. Those passages reflect Eliot's thorough knowledge of medieval and Renaissance Christian mystics, both British and European, such as Julian of Norwich and St. John of the Cross.

The journey usually begins with awareness of discomfort with old structures and proceeds through several stages: setting out on a lonely quest or dark journey that alienates one from all other companions; entering a desert, wilderness, pit, waste land, or ash heap; enduring fire, flood, storms, or roaring lions; coming to a place of nothingness, hopelessness, helplessness, of utter humility and submission; losing all reason and knowledge; and finally falling into a symbolic sleep or seeming death-like trance that represents the relinquishment of the ego.

To borrow Eliot's words, we might call them the six d's: dis-ease/disaffection, descent, darkness, deluge, destitution, and death. The seventh stage may well be delight of the soul in God, but no mystic would claim assurance of that while living in a fallen world. True, some of the heroes of faith in the book of Hebrews walked through fire and water or had their dead restored to them, but many others were exiled, cold and hungry, tortured, sawn asunder. Thus, Cordelia's hanging and King Lear's devastating final scene do not disqualify the play as Christian. Although Jews and Christians refuse to accept their own faith's prophecies that the world will become increasingly worse, few intellectual Christians who have experienced the World Wars, the Holocaust, the Vietnam War, or 9/11 could hold optimistic expectations about either this planet or their own lives upon it.

In her critically acclaimed work *Mysticism: Study in the Nature and Development of Spiritual Consciousness* (1911; republished 1990), the English poet and mystic Evelyn Underhill describes the initial impetus for spiritual development as psychic fatigue and "disease". In "Burnt Norton," the first part of *Four Quartets,* T. S. Eliot puts it this way: "Here is a place of disaffection.... Eructation of unhealthy souls". The disease in *King Lear* involves seeing with (*not* through) the eyes. The Earl of Gloucester voices the supreme irony of the play when he declares, "Come, if it be nothing, I shall not 'need spectacles'". He, Lear, and many other characters at first lack spiritual vision and desperately need "spectacles" of compassion and selflessness.

A kind of inner blindness disables most of the principal characters in *King Lear*. They pursue what is correct, what is reasonable, or what is clever; they display immense concern about proper rewards and punishments. At first, nearly all fail to recognize the unpredictable, irrational quality of the human spirit. Lear and others attempt to buy and sell love; a man's dignity is bargained over and counted out. Revenge obsesses the minds of some—they wish to give their antagonists what they deserve. Humility and mercy seldom temper their reactions. No one but Cordelia can accept love freely given without remuneration or cause—unless it is finally forced upon him.

At the beginning of the play, Lear asks: "Which of you shall we say doth love us most, / That we our largest bounty may extend / Where nature doth with merit challenge" (I.i.51-53). He believes that love is some sort of salable commodity, either paid for or won by deeds and gifts. This petty attitude is also evidenced by his references to Cordelia's suitors. He proclaims them rivals for her love, when actually all but France are rivals for her dowry. Lear's exacting standard requires gratitude as the natural return for everything he has done for his children. Other instances indicate his inflexibility. For example, when the disguised Kent supports him out of friendly devotion, Lear insists on giving him money. "Now, my friendly knave, I thank thee. There's earnest of thy service," he explains condescendingly (I.iv.88).

Lear is not the only character troubled by this flaw. When Edmund offers his services, Kent replies in terms of duty: "Then I must love you". Kent's defence of Cordelia likewise appeals to merit: he lauds her for honesty and morality. He expresses his gratitude to Gloucester with "The gods *reward* your kindness" (III.vi.5; italics mine). Regan restates this prevalent attitude more boldly. She openly describes her counterfeit affection for Lear in monetary terms: "I am made of that self mettle as my sister." Here she declares with a probable pun on "mettle" and "metal."

"And prize me at her worth," she continues, adding that Goneril yet "comes too short" in her regard (I.i.69-70, 72). Every phrase relates to coinage or trade. Later, the daughters callously measure their father's need for respect in numbers of servants and the luxury and price of his accommodations. Edmund declares himself bound to the goddess Nature—antipodal to human and heaven-ordained law—and demands in recompense her aid with his illegal, illegitimate projects. Regarding the Duke of Burgundy, Cordelia says that "respects of fortune are his love".

Indeed, only a few characters display any real insight. The King of France says, "Love's not love / When it is mingled with regards that stands / Aloof from th' entire point". He recognizes that Cordelia is "most rich being poor," for she has no payment to give for love but herself, and, therefore, must accept it freely. Though Cordelia has little according to the world's materialistic standards, she represents intangible values that have worth beyond price.

Lear does not understand intangibles; they are meaningless to him. He declares, "Nothing will come of nothing", which implies that no reward will be given without service and that no love can exist without gratitude. It also belies the orthodox doctrine of creation *ex nihilo*, or creation from nothing. Lear clutches the idea of merit tenaciously because it contains the essence of his stern retributional creed. Yet his words may well reveal a secret anxiety: the mighty ruler may fear that he has never done anything of worth to deserve affection and respect as a man and a father.

Even his desire to give up his kingdom illustrates his need to prove his worth. He cannot accept that his generosity could possibly be rewarded with nothing—that bad outcomes happen to good people. When the fool gives him advice on temperate living, Lear repeats a second time, "Why, no, boy. Nothing can be made out of nothing". Not abstractions but concrete objects and physical deeds hold significance for him.

Even the least noble speeches of the least important characters echo and reiterate such a philosophy. Much discussion concerns the bribing of servants, buying of allegiance, and paying whores for sex. Lear demands loyalty and gratitude as though they were palpable things. Without material possessions—money, land, position—a human being is considered worthless.

Except for Cordelia, none—least of all Lear—can forgive. Lear demands justice; his anger and pain clamor for revenge. Thus, he is unbending when Cordelia disappoints him. "Peace, Kent! / Come not between the dragon and his wrath," he storms as he disinherits her (I.i.121-22). Then, he sends Kent away for merely questioning his actions. For her misuse of him, Lear curses Goneril with sterility and a life of trouble.

Upon Regan he invokes lameness. Inflamed against his son, Gloucester cries, "The wingèd vengeance overtake such children" (III.vii.66). Believing that Gloucester has plotted against him, Cornwall boasts, "I will have my revenge ere I depart his house". All the hatred festers and intensifies until the audience wonders with Lear, "Is man no more than this?" It seems to the watcher that "humanity must perforce prey upon itself / As monsters of the deep," and the spectator can scarce but applaud when Lear calls down the judgment of the gods upon a wicked earth:

Blow, winds, and crack your cheeks. Rage, blow.
You cataracts and hurricanes, spout
Till you have drenched our steeples, drowned the cocks.
You sulph'rous and thought-executing fires,
Vaunt-couriers of oak-cleaving thunderbolts,
Singe my white head. And thou, all-shaking thunder,
Strike flat the thick rotundity o' th' world,
Crack Nature's moulds, all germains spill at once,
That makes ingrateful man. (III.ii.1-9).

In order to move beyond this polarized state of disaffection, the spiritual acolyte must descend lower; in order to heal the dis-ease, our sickness must grow worse. Indeed, it must become what the Danish philosopher Søren Kierkegaard calls sickness unto death. The English and continental mystics available to Shakespeare in the sixteenth century typically differentiate between the visions and imagination of their earliest illuminations and the onset of another "final stage," which often begins in what appears to be disintegration and disharmony between the self and the world. Their health often suffers, and their friends forsake them.

In *King Lear,* Gloucester seeks to blame his suffering on the stars:

These late eclipses in the sun and moon portend no good to us.... Love cools, friendship falls off, brothers divide. In cities, mutinies; in countries, discord; in palaces, treason; and the bond cracked 'twixt son and father.... [T]he King falls from bias of nature.... [A]ll ruinous disorders follow us disquietly to our graves. (I.ii.101-12).

Gloucester 's account of conditions in ancient Britain sounds mightily contemporary for Shakespeare's time as well as our own. He laments that Kent has been banished for goodness and honesty. And Lear leaves his daughter Regan's house by night, in "to-and-fro-conflicting wind and rain" (III.i.11).

Lear's experience on the heath reflects the imagery described by religious writers in all generations. In his *The Idea of the Holy* (1931), Rudolph Otto says that the experience of the dark night is represented in two ways: first, by darkness, silence, and empty distance—the *kenoma* or emptiness of the mystic journey; and second, by tumult and suffering (12-18). Both visions obviously appear in the blasted heath, the storm, and tempest of Shakespeare's play. "Here's a night pities / neither wise men nor fools," comments Lear's fool as they set out with nothing on the dark heath (III.ii.12-13).

Lear tears off his kingly robes and dresses himself, like Edgar, in the rags and weeds of a mad beggar, crying, "[U]naccommodated man is no more but such a poor, bare, forked animal as thou art. Off, off, you lendings!" (III.iv.101-03). He has already voluntarily given up his kingdom, and been divested by force of his retinue of soldiers. Out on the heath, he confronts both his guilt and his helplessness: "Tremble thou wretch, / That has within thee undivulgèd crimes" (III.ii.51-52). With these words, Lear denounces the evil done by others, but of himself he claims, "I am a man / More sinned against than sinning" (III.ii.59-60). His inability to accept his own guilt forms one major tension of the play. Without repentance, he cannot be redeemed, and he will not repent unless he recognizes his faults.

Lear begins to learn about hurt and weakness when his daughters strip him of his retinue. But he must reach beyond himself— assent to his relationship with mankind. As he himself explains, people told me he was everything. When he remarks to Gloucester that his hand smells of mortality, he admits his physicality and humanity. He tells his blinded, equally fragile, old friend that he is not "ague-proof" (IV.vi.103-04). That is, a king remains as vulnerable to chance and fate as any ordinary citizen.

But the dark night ultimately brings extraordinary sensitivity to faults and sins, sometimes "to the point of morbidity" (Underhill 415). As the play unfolds, Lear gradually realizes that he has made many grave mistakes. In the middle of a conversation, he rasps suddenly, half to himself, that he did Cordelia wrong. That single comment indicates just how wild and constant the tempest in his mind is. In the howling storm, watching other homeless people attempt to gather firewood, Lear discovers some of his own failings as king. "O, I have ta'en / Too little care of this! Take physic, pomp; / Exposed thyself to feel what wretches feel," he exclaims (III.iv.32-34). Lear's eyes are opened at last to human suffering, to the depth and complexity of human emotion.

Experience changes Lear's stern view of justice: "None does offend, none—I say none!" he cries and means that offenses, including his own, are immeasurable (IV.vi.165). Though necessary, acknowledgment of his errors is both difficult and destructive for so proud a man. Lear fights tears and shuns verbal admission. His inward burning shame, however, torments him into madness. It seems for a time that Lear has been right—that he must receive exact retribution for his deeds.

Take your own medicine, king, Lear tells himself. He cast off one daughter, and the other daughters cast him off. He failed to see that the poor and hungry were cared for, and now he must experience the same misery. He defied "nature," loving fatherhood, and nothing solid or natural remains: sin has made earth turbulent; guilt has agitated individuals and nations. People can no longer communicate coherently, for they are false and superficial. They have no words to express emotions, no form, and no order.

But Lear must be taught to discern the elusive quality of nothing. He has to learn that real love cannot be bought and that it can exist devoid of any worldly reason. According to Lear's requital scheme, Cordelia should hate him. She has good cause. By her reply, "No cause, no cause" (IV.vii.76), however, she wipes out the barrier between them and forgives him completely of her own free will. As many have pointed out, Shakespeare relates this magnanimous pardon to Christian salvation by consequence and allusion.

The storm that echoes and intensifies Lear's insanity, for example, Shakespeare describes using Judeo-Christian symbolic motifs. Both "tempests" suggest chaos, the theoretical formlessness and confusion before God's ordered creation. Pouring rain recalls the Great Flood and the ancient threat of a "Great Deluge" that would destroy the earth. Albany even introduces the image of Leviathan, the sea-monster—a truth that applies in the play both to factionalism in society and to the aberrations in individual minds. Loss of language, too, reminds us of the confounding of tongues at the Tower of Babel. When Lear enters dressed in weeds, he wears the outward signs of his inner discord, weeds being a biblical symbol of rebellion and worthlessness. 6 The desolate heath resembles the abyss, while Lear's own guilt and the elements provide his torture.

Cordelia becomes a Christ-like redeemer for Lear. Paraphrasing the words of Jesus, she whispers to him, "O dear father, / It is thy business I go about" (IV.iv.23-24). Cordelia returns only good for evil, gives something for nothing. She and the doctor array Lear in white robes. When Lear sleeps in white garments, he appears dead. The weary man awakes to a heaven of redemption and reconciliation, but he cannot accept it at first. "Thou art a soul in bliss," he says to Cordelia, "but I am bound / Upon a wheel of fire, that mine own tears / Do scald like molten lead" (IV.vii.46-48). When he finally comprehends fully, Lear cries out to Cordelia in an attitude of worshipful prayer, "You must bear with me. / Pray you now, forget and forgive. I am old and foolish" (IV.84-85).

The death of Cordelia herself displays deliberate parallels with the Crucifixion of Christ, noticed by many, perhaps most convincingly by G. Wilson Knight (*The Shakespearean Tempest* 303). Not only is she hanged, but Lear mutters, "I am old now, / And these same crosses spoil me" (V.iii.278-79), as he carries her body in a pieta-like tableau of the Lamentation. When he first realizes that she is dead, he sobs: "And my poor fool is hanged: no, no, no life? / Why should a dog, a horse, a rat, have life, / And thou no breath at all? Thou'lt come no more, Never, never, never, never, never" (V.iii.306-09).

But *King Lear*'s glorious paradox echoes that of the New Testament: Lear discovers Cordelia's living spirit at the moment of her death, so he dies believing her alive. "Do you see this? Look her lips / Look there, look there—," he gasps (V.iii.311-12). Lear also says, "This feather stirs; she lives! If it be so, / It is a chance which does *redeem* all sorrows / That ever I have felt" (V.iii.266-68; italics mine). Not only does Cordelia embody St. John of the Cross's *anima,* or little soul depicted as the feminine Bride of Christ by alchemists and mystics, but also Lear's words convey the quality of insight beyond the grave.

We do not have to rewrite *King Lear* à la Nahum Tate in order to call it Christian. The play draws us with it through perhaps the most intense vision of loss ever put on the stage. Lear's death reminds us that the ultimate union with God will "cost us not less than everything." All we can say is, "Give me an old man's frenzy"—let me seek spiritual truth with King Lear. Overwhelmed and arrested by the conspirators, he speaks submissively but with a kind of transcendent freedom:

Come, let's away to prison.

We two alone will sing like birds i' th' cage....
So we'll live,
And pray, and sing, and tell old tales, and laugh
At gilded butterflies, and hear poor rogues
Talk of court news; and we'll talk with them too—
Who loses and who wins; who's in, who's out—
And take upon 's the mystery of things
As if we were God's spies; and we'll wear out,
In a walled prison, packs and sects of great ones
That ebb and flow by th' moon....
Upon such sacrifices, my Cordelia,
The gods themselves throw incense. (V.i.8-21; italics mine)

If the maturing Shakespeare rejected court power, espionage, and political intrigue to turn toward the realm of the spirit, this passage makes a powerful statement of that change. 8 King Lear the character may never come to that place T. S. Eliot alludes to—the place in which the fire of worldly suffering becomes comprehended by Dante's multifoliate rose of Paradise. But if Lear never gets that far, I believe his creator did and displayed his transformation in *King Henry VIII* and the final comedies of forgiveness. *King Lear* marks the pivotal point toward that final transcendent vision.

Chapter 13

The Enchantment of the Tomb in John Keats's 'Eve of St. Agnes'

The building of church funereal monuments has been called "a peculiarly British art form" (Penny 1). By the Romantic period, Britain's interest in the tomb sculpture that decorated her churches was documented by the publication of scholarly volumes on the subject, notably Richard Gough's volumes titled *The Sepulchral Monuments in Great Britain,* which appeared between 1786 and 1796, and Charles Alfred Sothard's *Monumental Effigies of Great Britain,* which was published posthumously in 1832.

This period also marks a resurgence of interest in the gothic style. Iconography suggestive of the Middle Ages appealed at once to the senses of the picturesque and of the sublime; gothic ornament mingled with the rococo served as decorative embellishment while it simultaneously recalled the "Dark Ages" of tyranny, superstition, and blind faith (Penny 113-114).

John Keats's narrative poem "The Eve of Saint Agnes" reflects this medievalism in Romantic Britain's visual arts. The tableau vivant Madeline stages in her chamber re-creates the aesthetic motifs of late medieval tomb architecture and of sepulchral representations of the dead. In order to maintain the integrity of her own artistic, imaginative vision, Madeline kills herself into art. She does this by enacting rituals of life and art that are themselves designed to procure divine 'visionary' intervention.

Just as young women fulfill the traditions of St. Agnes's

holy day so that they may see their future husband in their dreams, tomb sculpture is designed to petition God for the deceased's place in Heaven. The ritualized performance of the female body in Madeline's tableau implicitly invites Porphyro's participatory gaze in order to criticize that same scopophilic desire that would have her killed into an object of art; she anticipates his possessive, objectifying gaze with a fixed vision of her own.

Madeline stages her own death and thus asserts her authority over the text of her body. She thwarts Porphyro's challenge to her self-possession by drawing him into her sepulchral vision. Porphyro succeeds in penning his own script on Madeline's body only after he succumbs to the mandate of her imagination. In contrast to the masculinocentric trend of previous critics, which posits Porphyro as the primary actor in the narrative, I offer a reading centered on the authority of Madeline, the over determined yet self-realized "object" of male desire in the "Eve of St. Agnes."

Keats begins his narrative in the chill and darkness of an abandoned chapel, void of life save for the self-flagellating Beadsman whose wasted form figures the tolling of his death knell, already rung. On the tombs of the chapel, "The sculptured dead, on each side, seem to freeze,/ Emprison'd in black, purgatorial rails." The knights and ladies of these family monuments have been carved as *priant* figures, "praying in dumb orat'ries." (In Medieval tomb sculpture, the *priant* represents the deceased in postures of religious devotion, kneeling, with hands folded in prayer).

As Wendy Steiner points out, "the pun on 'frieze' and 'freeze' parallels the sculptures themselves, which are doubly dead, because they are statues and because they are statues of the dead - the dead figures of romance knights and ladies, in fact, depicted in the act of prayer. Their dreary chill makes the Beadsman's prayers seem even more a failure of vital spirituality, again a double death - the mere static image of the deluded act of prayer 'in the dumb orat'ries' " (Steiner 69). When Madeline later stages her own funereal "frieze," she rehearses through her aesthetic "death in life" her own eventual *priant* figure and thus revitalizes the potential for creative expression in such static images of deluded prayer as the *priants* that decorate the family chapel.

The most notable feature of Madeline's private chamber clearly echoes the architectural structure and sculptural motifs of the medieval funeral monuments in the family chapel below. The scene of Madeline's tableau vivant is framed by "A casement high and triple-arch'd..../ All garlanded with carven imag'ries/ Of fruits, and flowers, and bunches of knot-grass/ ....And in the midst, 'mong thousand heraldries,/ And twilight saints, and dim emblazonings,/ A shielded scutcheon blush'd with blood of queens and kings." Kathleen Cohen notes that carvings of fruits and flowers often adorned tombs of this period as symbols of regeneration and, by extension, resurrection. Family mottoes and emblems of genealogy graced the elaborate arches and casements that contained the sculpted representations of the deceased in order to announce the heritage and status of the family.

As Madeline kneels in prayer in front of this window she constructs herself as a *priant* figure, encased within the architectural design of the tomb: "Full on this casement shone the wintry moon,/ As down she knelt for heaven's grace and boon;/ Rose-bloom fell on her hands, together prest,/ And on her silver cross soft amethyst...." Aesthetic trappings of death distort natural phenomena as well; even the moonlight that floods the room is colored and shaped to illuminate Madeline's tableau of death in life. When Madeline lays herself in her bed, in shroud-like "blanched linen, smooth and lavender'd," she recreates yet another sepulchral figure, that of the *transi*, the representation of the deceased after death, usually depicted recumbent, wrapped in only a shroud, in varying stages of decomposition.

The *transi* is usually placed on the lowest level of the tomb, clearly figuring the interment of the deceased. While in this position, sound asleep, Madeline most suggestively articulates death. As Keats writes in his "Sonnet to Sleep," sleep is the "soft embalmer" of the night that seals the "hushed casket" of the soul. Interestingly, her passivity and stillness encourage

Porphyro to extend his possessive gaze to a grasp; he materializes his visual consumption of her body in the feast he spreads before the bed.

On this night, Madeline's bed is at once a site for sex and for death, a marital bower and a death-bed or tomb. Porphyro sets the table for a lavish feast at the same level where Madeline's death-like figure rests. The consumption of these delicacies, then, figures both a necrophilic desire to possess, and a narcissistic cannibalism that involves the total absorption of the beloved into the self. The terms of sexual consummation, however, are ultimately set by Madeline herself, by the fixity of a gaze that overpowers Porphyro, despite his own well demonstrated command of a voyeuristic stare.

Porphyro hides in the "close secrecy" of Madeline's closet, an architectural feature which contains all the darkness and anonymity of a closed coffin. In the closet, "embower'd from the light," Porphyro prepares for "gazing on that bed," a gaze which anticipates his sexual encounter with Madeline. Angela, for one, equates his gaze with a sexual act, telling Porphyro that having seen Madeline undressed, preparing for bed, he "must need[s] the lady wed." Interestingly, it isn't Madeline's naked figure that captures Porphyro's fancy: he blazons instead the accouterments of her femininity, her clothes and her jewelry.

Peter Brooks writes that because to achieve the goal of one's desire would result in the "death of desiring," and thus the silencing of the text (Brooks 20), "the object of attention and desire—most obviously, the person of the beloved—is not detailed in its nakedness but rather approached by way of its phenomenal presence in the world, which means by way of the clothing and accessories that adorn and mask the body. The approach to the body of the beloved may strive toward unveiling....but it also tends to become waylaid in the process of this unveiling, more interested in the lifting of the veils than in what is finally unveiled. An interest in the way, rather than simply the endpoint, is indeed virtually a definition of narrative" (Brooks 19).

Accordingly, Keats suspends his text in silence when

Madeline steps out of the foam of her "rich attire" and walks to her bed; we learn only that "soon, trembling in her soft and chilly nest,/....perplex'd she lay," and Porphyro is left gazing "upon her empty dress." Keats figures Porphyro's sexual "little death" in veiled language; he "melts" into Madeline's dream, killed into art so that she might make a place for him in her aesthetically realized vision of love and sexuality.

The tension of this scene lies in a doubled act of unveiling. Porphyro's leering, which is the ocular vehicle for Keats's narrative, undresses Madeline. The woman herself is little more than the sum of her accessories. Madeline's design, however, in staging this theatrical ritual, is to undress language, to lift the veil and expose the gap between aestheticized femininity and the identity this image conceals. Madeline's tableau vivant performs what Mary Ann Doane describes as "masquerade," which, "in flaunting femininity, holds it at a distance.

Womanliness is a mask which can be worn or removed. The masquerade's resistance to patriarchal positioning....lie[s] in its denial of the production of femininity as closeness, as presence-to-itself, as, precisely, imagistic. Masquerade .... involves a realignment of femininity, the recovery, or more accurately, simulation, of the missing gap or distance. To masquerade is to manufacture a lack in the form of a certain distance between oneself and one's image....By destabilizing the image, the masquerade confounds [the] masculine structure of the look. It effects a defamiliarization of female iconography" (Doane 25-6).

Madeline's performance, then, positions her as a critic, rather than a victim, of a masculine scopophilic economy. Hers is a harsh indictment: Madeline's masquerade incorporates a death mask and evokes the funerary aesthetics of a tomb. In order to maintain the integrity of her imaginative vision, Madeline stages an aesthetic allegory of speaking death. Elizabeth Bronfen writes that "staging disembodiment as a form of escaping personal and social constraints serves to criticize those cultural attitudes that reduce the feminine body to the position of dependency and passivity, to the vulnerable object of sexual incursions" (Bronfen 142). By killing herself into art, Madeline adheres to the visions of her dreams. When Porphyro wakes her, Madeline's wide eyes cause him to sink to his knees, "pale as a smooth-sculptured stone." Madeline draws the astonished (turned to stone) Porphyro into her tableau, into the frozen state of her de-realized world, a condition of inanimation that Keats himself longed for. In a letter to Fanny Brawne, the poet writes: "I have two luxuries to brood over in my walks, your loveliness and the hour of my death.

O that I could have possession of them both in the same minute" (Bush 291). Keats's longing to "possess" both Fanny and death suggests his sexualized relationship to a feminized death. This conflation of femininity and death also reveals an almost necrophilic narcissism; the poet is "half in love" with his own "easeful death" as he engenders a "lovely" female body with the universal condition of mortality. As Bronfen asserts, "part of the equation between femininity and death resides precisely in the fact that Woman as man's object of desire....is on the side of death....because she so often serves as a non-reciprocal 'dead' figure of imaginary projection, given that, in Lacan's terms, 'the whole of [man's] realization in the sexual relation comes down to fantasy' " (Bronfen 63).

Madeline, as an object of art, becomes a figure of Porphyro's "imaginary projection." With her tableau, Madeline ultimately undermines the scopophilic projection of an unwitting Porphyro. She remains, however, at the mercy of the poet's narrative. With Madeline as a self-inscribed figure of art, "The Eve of St. Agnes" can be read as an ekphrastic poem.

James Heffernan proposes a model of ekphrastic poetry that accounts for the authority that Madeline invests in her aesthetic self-representation, and the ambivalent way in which the male poet engages with a feminized object of art. Heffernan writes that ekphrasis "evokes the power of the silent image even as it subjects that power to the rival authority of language," and that "the contest it stages is often powerfully gendered: the expression of a duel between male and female gazes, the voice of male speech striving to control a female image that is both alluring and threatening, of male narrative trying to overcome the fixating impact of beauty poised in space" (Heffernan 1). In "The Eve of St. Agnes," this contest plays out on a number of levels, both within the text, between Madeline and Porphyro, and extra-textually, between Madeline and Keats, the poet/narrator.

The image Madeline creates "excites both 'ekphrastic hope'—the desire for union—and the 'ekphrastic fear' of being silenced, petrified, and thus unmanned by the Medusan 'other' " (Heffernan 108). Madeline is Medusan in that her gaze represents a female power to freeze/frieze the enthralled male and "enchant, subvert, or threaten" his voice (Heffernan 108). When Porphyro awakens the sleeping Madeline, or resurrects her from her death-like stillness, the "vision of her sleep," inspired by religious meditation, remains before her eyes. Madeline's gaze, fixed on Porphyro, causes him to sink to his knees, "pale as smooth sculptured stone."

Her stare astonishes Porphyro, who remains kneeling, "with joined hands and piteous eye,/ Fearing to move or speak, she look'd so dreamingly." Pained that, in reality, Porphyro's eyes aren't "spiritual and clear," his looks no longer "immortal," as they were in her vision, Madeline asks him not to leave her in the "eternal woe" of her awakened consciousness. Thus Madeline allows Porphyro to melt into her dream, to worship, like a pilgrim, at the "silver shrine" of her beauty, achieving an "ekphrastic union" on her own terms that simultaneously betrays Porphyro's voyeuristic obsessions by objectifying him as a piece of stone.

The male narrator's, or Keats's, act of engendering dialogue with a female art object reveals a violent impulse. The trajectory of the poem "repeatedly threatens to rape the fixed beauty of visual art [Madeline's tableau] with the language of narrative" (Heffernan 114). But where Porphyro, and by extension, Keats himself, read Madeline as a hieroglyph, the image as the woman, Madeline's frieze is an act of authorship, of self-realization; her reading of herself plays on the distance she establishes between "tableau" and "vivant," between the artistic representation and the life itself. She is not a "fixed beauty"; through her image and her voice Madeline articulates her resistance to the threat Porphyro poses within the text and the threat Keats poses extra-textually.

Her speech comes at the moment of her awakening, and with her voice she further "hoodwinks" Porphyro, playing on his voyeuristic fantasies of consumption, in order to write her own ending to the story her sepulchral image embodies. Madeline's words point to her betrayal, her deception at the hands of Porphyro, whose leering eyes in life are anything but "spiritual and clear," as they were in her vision. "No dream, alas! alas! and woe is mine!" Madeline cries, "thou forsakest a deceived thing."

Through speech, the act of reading her own image, Madeline crosses the line between visual and verbal representation. In this transgressive act Madeline's voice "preempts the interrogating, narrating voice of the male speaker"(Heffernan 115). Madeline's last line in the poem expresses, at best, a sense of resignation about her fate with Porphyro. In her awakened state, Madeline likens herself to "a dove forlorn and lost with sick unpruned wing." Although Porphyro succeeds in robbing Madeline's nest of her "sweet self," clearly the achievement of his iconophilic desire results in the death of his desiring.

Keats's narrative loses its erotic tension, and the poem moves to a close in the atmosphere of Madeline's sepulchral allegory. The two "glide like phantoms" through the dark, silent house, while the Baron and his guests have nightmares of coffin-worms. The end of the poem is ambiguous, and clearly doesn't bode well for the couple. Keats writes "and they are gone: ay, ages long ago/ These lovers fled away into the storm." The poem ends where it began, with the neglected Beadsman praying in "his ashes cold," and as a result the sense of closure is one of entombment. The resolution of the narrative hermetically seals the poem in a "hushed casket."

Porphyro's misinterpretation of Madeline's sepulchral tableau, his mis-recognition of the female visionary as merely a vision, points to Keats's misplaced trust in the "eternal present of pure being" that a feminine aesthetic suggests (Heffernan 114). "The Eve of Saint Agnes" points to the bankruptcy of an aesthetic vision that would reduce the feminine to the status of icon, and thus deny women artistic and authorial agency.

Madeline's tableau vivant recalls Michelangelo's allegorical figure of Night in the Medici chapel, and the words he attributes to her: "It is sweet to sleep but even sweeter to be of stone. While evil and dishonor last, it is my blessing not to see, not to feel. Therefore, do not awaken me. Hush! speak softly" (Hagstrum 74).

Chapter 14

Negative Fictions in Keats's Lamia, The Eve of St. Agnes, and Isabella

Romantic revisionist practices testified to the movement's revival of the romance world, populated with brave chivalric heroes, youthful paramours, cruel tyrants, wizards and fairies, living out their existences amongst elfin grottoes, the leafy vales of Arcady, and blissful Spenserian bowers. Romanticism's return to the romance genre recognised it as a literary mode already accustomed to political, social and aesthetic controversy since its adoption by John Bunyan, John Milton and Edward Spenser.

Although the Romantic movement reworked the aesthetic, social, and political allegories of romance, in response to both the outcome of the French Revolution and domestic political affairs, the essential quest motif and the dual conception of reality were retained by Romanticism. Romantic poets unearthed in, and affirmed through the romance mode, their own belief in the pivotal dualities of innocence and experience, life and death, surface and depth, and the ideal and the real.

Keats's romances often portray these complex relations as an auto-erotic journey that points towards the inherent dangers of confusing fiction and fact. Keats translates the absence at the heart of these visionary quests into a negative poetic fiction in which nature is no longer construed as a mediator of the transcendental and eternal, but as a constant reminder of human mutability and the inevitability of death; what Coleridge's 'Dejection: An Ode' terms '[r]eality's dark dream'. After his rejection of Wordsworthian consolation,

Keats discovers in romance a literary terrain rich with potential that permits a reorientation to an aesthetic which embraces tragedy through a series of negating images. From the outset of *Endymion,* Keats is alert to the possibility that the 'bower' of romance can all too readily surrender its idyll back to the 'o'er-darkened ways' (I, 4; 10-11) of the world of human existence.

His early romance depicts a conflict between fictions of the ideal and the harsh circumstances of the ordinary and real, between the heightened sense of self-knowledge attained through visionary modes of consciousness and the self-deception of the illusory. Keats ensures his narrative's close witnesses the revealed Cynthia united with Endymion, her lover, and his sister, Peona. Having achieved communion with the transcendental, Endymion abandons the web of human relations and the 'gloomy wood' to which Peona returns.

Though Keats's poetic sleight of hand asserts a metaphysical fiction, his poetry points to Peona's very real desertion. The youthful Endymion's 'spiritualiz'd' apotheosis is not a transcendental escape from the mutability of his 'mortal state' (IV, 991-3), as the world he abandons is left much darker for his absence. Ultimately, Endymion's encounter with Cynthia discloses her fictive nature as an idealised woman and is a reminder that even idealising fictions conceal as much as they reveal. The reader, like Peona is torn between a fiction of transcendence and a negative awareness of reality's darkness.

More fully implicated in the imaginative workings of his later romances, *Endymion*'s uncertain ending anticipates Keats's mature poetic preoccupation with a process of disclosure and deceit. Keats's negative poetic fictions question the consolatory aspect of Wordsworthian poetics through their sensitivity to interplay between the idealised dream mode and the tragedy of waking reality. Keats's 'La Belle Dame Sans Merci' adopts this technique of negative fiction to present the complex relation between dreaming and waking, transcendental sublimity and the transient world of ordinary experience. Enchanted by a 'fairy's child' whose 'eyes were wild', Keats's 'knight at arms' (14; 16; 1) is apparently united with the otherworldly and yet his union is not the joyous one claimed for Endymion.

Once enthralled by the wiles of a 'fairy's child', Keats's knight hovers between an indistinct mode of existence - caught between dreaming and waking - as a 'woe-begone' figure (2; 6) in a landscape characterised by negativity and absence. He can never be reunited with the fairy creature and nature cannot provide him with a reassuring myth of consolation. Nature withdraws from the scene abandoning the knight to his plight, unable to comfort him, it reflects only his desolation as 'the sedge is wither'd from the lake, / And no birds sing' (47-8). Negation and absence pervade even the knight's description of the 'fairy's child' as her magical, fleeting, beauty is only glimpsed through a retrospective account of her fading memory (13-16). The knight recounts how, enticed by her gentle 'fairy's song' and 'language strange' (24; 27), he was led to the familiar romance motif of the visionary bower; in this case, an enchanted creature's 'elfin grot'.

Like the many bowers encountered in *Endymion* this 'elfin grot' is where the protagonist experiences a dream-vision, although the knight's vision is strikingly different from those in Keats's earlier romance: 'And there she lulled me asleep, / And there I dream'd - Ah! woe betide! / The latest dream I ever dream'd / On the cold hill's side'. No solace is derived from this dream-visionary experience. Rather than encouraging belief in an otherworldly sphere, the dream marks a transition from an enchanted 'elfin grot' to the reality of a 'cold hill's side'.

This dream-vision reinforces the horror of mundane reality, stressing its absences and shortcomings, instead of elevating the dreamer to a higher plane, or mode of consciousness. No consolation is discovered by the dreaming knight for the irrecoverable loss of the beautiful lady, because the emptiness of his story's climactic dream episode underlines the vacancy at the heart of his retrospective narration which in turn is indicative of his own vacant and abandoned existence. Death and absence characterise all the other noble men who have fallen under the sway of this fairy creature.

Deceived by what they, too, thought would lead to fulfilment and union with a higher reality, they become a synecdoche of impoverished 'starv'd lips in the gloam'. Despite the knight's claim that 'I awoke and found me here', Keats's ballad never distinguishes clearly between waking and dreaming, recollection and invention, or even in the knight's case, life and death. The anguish of Keats's knight leaves him '[a]lone and palely loitering' in an apparently wakeful state, similar to the condition of the 'death pale' noble men who inhabit his dream. Even the fairy creature herself exists only as a product of mental recollection.

The blurring of these distinct modes of consciousness and existence rehearses a problem to which Keats persistently returns in his poetic career, centred on the question of 'was it a vision, or a waking dream? Do I wake or sleep?' ('Ode to a Nightingale', 79-80). In trying to formulate an adequate response, 'La Belle Dame Sans Merci' queries the nature of its own modes of consciousness and the fictive framework it employs to interpret the phenomenal universe. Keats's knight, like Peona, is unable to create a Wordsworthian fiction of consolation to soothe his abandonment.

Instead he produces a negative fiction that can only disclose the ambiguous nature of his tragic predicament, but never transform his existing state. Keats's fascination with an alluring fairy creature reveals that his aspiration toward these imaginatively created symbols of the otherworldly were more often than not inter-woven with an awareness of reality's darkness; in *Endymion*'s terms these imaginative encounters trigger a bewildering 'journey homeward to habitual self' (II, 276), troubled that the wondrous fairy creature of imagination may conceal the mischievous nature of the 'fog-born' elf (II, 277). Keats's romances create this ontological confusion by diagnosing the fictional status of both idealised and tragic interpretations of reality.

Lamia's narrative questions how difficult it is to interpret the experiential world and discloses the fictional status of two apparently distinct interpretative modes. Lycius's encounter with the elfin Lamia exposes a much harsher reality concealed by, on one hand, a mask of sensual illusion and, on the other, an illusory sense of order in the form of a philosophical system. What endangers Lamia's enchanted existence is Apollonius's desire to contain and define her nature within his philosophical 'catalogue of common things' (II, 233).

In spite of Lycius's love for the fairy creature he cannot entirely shed his mentor's 'philosophic gown' (I, 364) and persists in trying to restrict Lamia's identity to a single name: "Hast any mortal name, / Fit appellation to this dazzling frame?" (II, 88-9). Such an impulse to 'catalogue' existence will inevitably fail to categorise Lamia's elfin nature (a colourful blend of human and animal, lover and demon, mortal and immortal), which outwardly appears as a series of dissolving 'silver moons', eclipsed by shades of 'vermilion-spotted, golden, green and blue' (I, 48; 50; 52-65). Both Apollonius's and Lycius's final naming of Lamia as "[a] serpent!" reduces her to an inhuman 'frightful scream' (II, 305-6). The fairy creature's carefully woven illusion is undone by the 'cold philosophy' (II, 230) of mentor and student alike.

Naming Lamia, ironically, exposes Apollonius's false claim that language truly represents the world, because Lamia's loss of illusion produces a 'gordian shape' (I, 47) not of her former majesty, but a reptilian creature with impassive 'orbs' for eyes and a 'horrid presence' (II, 267). Apollonius's 'cold philosophy' does not give Lamia back her fairy form, but instead constructs his own empirically based vision of her as a serpent. Apollonius and Lamia are not diametrically opposed; rather they are two distinct aspects of the same illusory mode. Apollonius represents an impulse towards self-knowledge and Lamia is aligned with the illusory dream of an idealised mode of being.

Neither Apollonius nor Lamia are willing to confront the fictional status of the order they impose upon the world. Apollonius becomes a treacherous weaver of wizardry, entangling Lamia in his own illusory spell of philosophy, to conjure her up as a hideous parody of her former self and denounce her as a "foul dream" (II, 271). Lycius's initial response recreates Apollonius as a demonic trickster: "[L]ook upon that gray-beard wretch! / Mark how, possess'd his lashless eyelids stretch / Around his demon eyes!" (II, 287-9). Lamia's 'purple-lined palace of sweet sin' (II, 31) is another illusory retreat from reality.

An elaborate product of an idealised fiction of order and being, it is as suffocating as Apollonius's restrictive philosophical education of Lycius:'[F]rom every ill / Of life I have preserv'd thee to this day!' (II, 297-8). Lamia's palace, for all its apparent abundance, is ultimately sterile and imitative, characterised by an artificial 'pervading brilliance and perfume' (II, 174) and its 'mimicking...[of]...a glade / Of palm' (II, 125-6). Even Lycius's journey - or rather magicking away 'by a spell' (I, 345) - to Lamia's haunt suggests a state of sleep-walking which blurs distinctions between waking and dreaming, knowing and doing: 'They pass'd the city gates, he knew not how, / So noiseless, and he never thought to know' (I, 348-9).

At first glance, Corinth appearing to Lycius '[a]s men talk in a dream' (I, 350) might suggest he is embarking upon a transcendental voyage, when actually, he is receding from reality into a superficial bower of sensual bliss. Lamia does not escape her 'wreathed tomb' (I, 38), exchanging incarceration within a serpentine body for imprisonment within her self-constructed palace, held hostage by Corinthian society. Lamia's blessing and curse is to live out her existence within her illusory private realm. To recognise Lamia's fictional status is to unravel her own mode of existence, disclosing a very real awareness of individual terror and tragedy hidden previously by her enchanting illusions.

Lycius links these two kinds of illusory modes in *Lamia,* fulfilling both the role of philosophic apprentice to the cerebral Apollonius and passionate lover to the sensual Lamia. The youth dies disillusioned, forced to acknowledge that Lamia and Apollonius are two different kinds of 'deceiving elf' ('Ode to a Nightingale', 74). His death at the close of the poem is a macabre representation of the illusory dream mode disclosing its realistic counterpart. A public ceremony of marriage should have united the lovers, but instead it separates them forever, as the act of matrimony leads only to the preparation of Lycius's funeral, symbolised by his 'marriage robe' becoming his death shroud (II, 311).

The stifling and exclusive fictions of Apollonius and Lamia are translated into actual tragedy. Not even Lamia's exquisite illusory dream mode can elide the reality of death, which bursts in upon her secluded palace when the Corinthian wedding guests arrive (a reminder of human reality beyond Lamia's enchanted circle). Lamia cannot exist isolated forever from Corinth in an illusory dream, because to possess a 'body fit for life' (I, 39) demands an acceptance of human tragedy and death.

The lovers' retreat into an artificial romance bower is violated by external social pressures, symbolic of darker forces repressed by Lamia's magical existence. Unlike Porphyro and Madeline, in *The Eve of St. Agnes*, who apparently elude a tragic encounter with social pressures by eloping (not undertaking a public ceremony of marriage) and escaping undetected from a castle's hostile society. Such a positive reading of the lovers' elopement suggests that their escape be from the dark reality of the castle's interior to an ideal existence beyond the confinement of its walls.

But the castle is only a set for the narrative's dramatic action, intended to enhance *The Eve of St. Agnes*'s fairy-tale atmosphere. The interior of the castle is not entirely dark, because its inhabitants and structure conspire with Madeline and Porphyro. Their escape is aided by a benign beldame, a drunken Porter, an ineffectual 'bloodhound', 'bolts [which] full easy slide' and 'chains that lie silent on the foot worn stone' (363-9).

Keats's lovers do not retreat from dark reality into an illusory dream mode, even if their story is absorbed into legend's ideal and immutable realm. Instead Porphyro and Madeline flee from a magical castle - itself a product of ideal illusion - into a troubled 'storm' of tragic reality. The treachery of their flight into a dawn storm can be gauged from Porphyro's optimistic description of it as an "elfin-storm from faery land" which, recalling *Endymion*'s perilous 'fog-born elf'

(II, 276), anticipates a return to a 'habitual self' (II, 277) and reality's darkness.

The youthful lovers fail to transcend the perils of human existence, because whether they remain within or without the castle their fate is predicted by the beldame and Beadsman; the first '[d]ied palsy-twitch'd' and the other 'unsought for slept among his ashes cold'. In spite of the lovers' vibrance their untold future is blighted by the prospect of death, as the passage of time will inevitably consign them to a similar deathly state. Narrative emphasis is placed on loss and unfulfilment, as central to *The Eve of St. Agnes* is Madeline's unrealised dream and sexual encounter with Porphyro.

Even the castle's austerely gothic interior does not predict a hoped for regeneration, instead it depicts a series of fixed inarticulate 'carven imag'ries' of the 'sculptur'd dead'. This interior marks out Keats's fairy-tale castle as 'old romance['s]' last bastion and final tomb, existing without a regenerative voice to ensure either a rejuvenation of the lovers or the world of romance. Porphyro's expression of love for Madeline verbally re-enacts a courtly legend captured in 'an ancient ditty, long since mute'.

Equally, Madeline performing her rite of 'St. Agnes' Eve' seeks to voice the romance of what 'she had heard old dames full many times declare' meaningfully into the present. These efforts to translate the 'dumb oratories' of 'old romance' into articulate active love are surrounded by the castle's suppression of sound: 'The kettle-drum, and far-heard clarinet, / Affray his ears, though but in dying tone: - / The hall door shuts again, and all the noise is gone'. Madeline also lapses into silence, as her attempt to re-enact courtly tradition leads to her being 'hoodwink'd with faery fancy' and incapable of one 'uttered syllable'.

Even after she awakes from her enchanted sleep she is only able 'to moan forth witless words with many a sigh'. Despite being within the castle's safe haven, Madeline's dream is not a consolatory ideal illusion, rather a disclosure of 'old romance['s]' fictional status. This dream experience discloses an awareness of absence, desertion and unfulfilment, reflecting the illusory mode's adoption of a tragic language of negative fiction.

Madeline's new found speech - echoing Keats's abandoned knight - desires an idealised 'old romance', preferring her own imaginatively created Porphyro over his actual presence: "how chang'd thou art! how pallid, chill, and drear! / 'Give me that voice again, my Porphyro, / 'Those looks immortal, those complainings dear!". When Madeline does speak her desire is not the present voice of Porphyro, instead she longs after her own forever absent dream-representation of his voice and identity.

Just as Porphyro's recitation of "La Belle Dame Sans Merci" reduces him to a silent form, who fears 'to move or speak' and resembles the stonework figures decoratively carved on the castle's walls: 'Upon his knees he sank, pale as smooth-sculptured stone'. Such a resemblance intimates that Porphyro and Madeline will be absorbed into a tradition of courtly legend. Porphyro will be absorbed into a tradition of heroic lovers when his actions are consistent with being a voyeur, skulking in a 'closet', and appearing to Madeline's eyes as "pallid, chill and drear".

Not even in this fairy-tale world is Porphyro ascribed a role of handsome prince and legitimate suitor. Instead, he is an inexperienced paramour who makes 'jellies soother than the creamy curd' rather than love. Porphyro only serves Madeline with luxuriant and exotic dishes in an attempt to overwhelm her pervading sense of absence with sheer abundance. Yet Madeline's realisation that life is "eternal woe" cannot be avoided. The lovers' sexual encounter is framed between Madeline fearing for Porphyro's death and Porphyro hearing the "iced gusts" of an "elfin-storm': 'At these voluptuous accents, he arose, / Ethereal, flush'd, and like a throbbing star / Seen mid the sapphire heaven's deep repose; / Into her dream he melted...'.

Keats's portrayal of their love-making, as an idealistic union between Madeline's dream of Porphyro and his actual presence is an act of supplementation, which points towards a deathly absence, represented by those darker forces lurking beyond the walls of Keats's fairy-tale castle. *The Eve of St. Agnes*'s portrayal of an idealised romance and dream threatens at every narrative instance to unravel itself, laying bare those elements of reality banished from Keats's enchanted castle.

Silence and death remain a constantly deferred threat to the lovers, even after they have 'fled away into the storm'. The narrative projects their escape into the past of immortal legend to preserve them against the ravages of time, represented by the beldame and Beadsman. *The Eve of St. Agnes* moves full circle from the lifeless existence of a beldame and Beadsman to the hopeful fulfilment of youthful love - or the recovery of idealised 'old romance' - to return only to the inevitable social reality of death. A retelling of Porphyro's and Madeline's legend will once again conjure up and break the castle's charmed circle, exposing its own tentative existence - undoing the spell of its enchanted spot - to disclose what tragedy its illusory mode struggles to conceal.

In retelling Boccaccio's medieval romance, Keats ironically discloses this precarious existence of the idealising visionary mode, as *Isabella*'s modern narrator establishes a direct relation between the tragic love affair of the poem's two lovers and the active retelling of their story. Readers are forced to share not simply in the initial delight of the lovers, but in the responsibility of the discovery of their secret by Isabella's brothers, because the narrator reveals their secret meeting place to them.

Lorenzo's demise emanates from his social illegitimacy, as in the eyes of Isabella's brothers; he is a lowly and unsuitable suitor. The romantic 'bower of hyacinth and musk', for all its atmosphere of closed secrecy and concealment in the half-light 'before the dusk', is to be engulfed in the darkness of a tragic 'woe'. The reader is implicated in this 'woe' through those 'idle ears' that will share and have shared in the 'many doleful stories'. Keats's narrator ensures this bower of illusion is explicitly aware of its own fictional attempt to conceal the tragic mode, so the modern and gothic nature of *Isabella*'s narrative is forced to disclose itself. Similarly, the lovers' secrecy, or the secrecy of the brothers' 'jealous conference' to murder Lorenzo, or Isabella's secret re-planting of her lover's head in the basil-pot (*stanza* 52), are also disclosed through a retelling of Boccaccio's tale. Boccaccio's original story becomes, for Keats, a symbol of fast-fading traditional romance (145-7; 149-52), which is about to be displaced by his own darker, ironical and often, black-humoured account of the ill-fated love affair of Isabella and Lorenzo.

Lorenzo returns (from beyond the grave) to pay a midnightly visitation to Isabella, appearing as a spectre to divulge the secret of his murder. The ghostly Lorenzo hovers on the edge of human existence as a 'pale shadow', who enacts a gothic death-in-life state, with 'cold doom / Upon his lips', a 'lorn voice' and a 'miry channel for his tears' (277-8; 279; 280). Keats's description of Lorenzo's words as a 'strange sound' accompanied by a 'ghostly under-song', ensures the voice synecdoche displaces the description of his physical state, so that the *his* of Lorenzo's earthly semblance can be substituted for the supernatural and neuter form of '[*i*]*ts* eyes, though wild, were still all dewy bright' (*my italic,* 289).

Enthralled by a pair of eyes, rather like Keats's knight, Isabella does not produce a consoling fiction of the illusory dream mode. Lorenzo's visitation reveals her brothers' dark deeds, his own dishevelled appearance, and withdraws to leave 'atom darkness in a slow turmoil'. Despite the tragedy and horror of the situation, conscious bathos pervades *Isabella*'s narrative tone, so that Lorenzo's account of his own under-handed death appears as, on 'the sodden turfed dell / Where, without any word, from stabs he fell', or his love's grief and exhaustion amounts to, '[*i*]*t* made sad Isabella's eyelids ache' (*my italics*, 327). Such bathetic comments prepare the way for Isabella's transfixed gaze into Lorenzo's eyes to pass into her later fixation with a basil-pot, containing her lover's recovered head and the plant weaned on tears.

Isabella's dotage on the 'fast mouldering head' dramatises the predicament of the illusory visionary mode, persistently blighted by an awareness of the pain and mutability of human existence, which it claims to elide. Lorenzo's decaying head and the growing basil plant become Isabella's only source of focus and consolation, acting as a grotesque parody of the life-sustaining and life-perfecting ideal sought out by the questor of romance. Nurturing the basil plant with 'the continual shower / From her dead eyes' may drain Isabella's 'drooping' body (452-3; 458), but there is little doubt that, without the preserving solace she derives from its 'magic touch', 'sweet Isabel...will die'.

For Isabella the secret of Lorenzo's concealed head is important, because it substitutes, rather perversely, the secret love she once shared with him. Naturally, when this secret - like that of their love - is discovered and taken by her brothers to a 'secret place' Isabella is beside herself with grief. The brothers' appropriation of Isabella's final secret condemns their sister to misery, because she has lost even the decayed and tattered remnant of her secret and private exchanges with Lorenzo, whether earthly or supernatural. Worse still, Isabella's 'lone and incomplete' state is a product of what she cherishes most, an intimate secret, although one known only to her brothers, who have fled Florence.

Isabella is destined to spend the rest of her days in search of the 'secret place'. She never resorts to transcendental fictions of consolation, instead deriving comfort from what can be salvaged of Lorenzo's physical body, in this instance the re-discovery of the hidden basil-pot along with Lorenzo's decomposing head. Even as Isabella descends into insane obsession, black humour is still present in her 'lorn voice', characterised by a 'melodious chuckle in the strings'. The enchanting and ideal world of romance is forced by Keats's narrator to unpick the fabric of its own illusory fictions, reducing itself to the chant, heard by 'idle ears' and passed onto others, "O cruelty, / To steal my basil-pot away from me!'.

The lovers in Keats's narrative poems cannot remain within the interior safety of their own illusory and private fictions, as they must legitimise their identities and existence in the exterior public sphere, if their love is not to become sterile and suffocating. Such lovers' illusory strongholds against mutability are constantly tested by tragic realisations and the, often, suffocating infertility that their self-imposed isolation produces. Retelling their love affairs involves a suspension of the lovers between the illusory and tragic modes, enabling a re-enactment of their youthful amorous encounters and ensuring their place amongst the established canon of romance. Consequently, Keats's lovers remain forever on the verge of regeneration and unregenerated, eternally suspended like the unconsummated couple portrayed on the Grecian Urn or the 'sculptur'd dead' (*The Eve of St. Agnes*, 14) fashioned on the castle's walls.

Explorations of the alluring literary terrain of romance provided the younger Keats with a greater scope for his unpractised creative powers but the genre was never, for him, a straightforward retreat from the tensions and pressures of reality. Keats's poetry depicts visionary states that point towards a haunting of idealised fictions by the reality they feign to elude. This poetic anxiety emerges in Keats's world of romance as a succession of hauntings. Isabella is haunted by the loss of her murdered lover, the knight-at-arms is forever tormented by an encounter with a fairy creature, Endymion is troubled by the absence of Cynthia, Lycius's philosophic enquiry disrupted by Lamia's presence, and Madeline's waking hours unsettled by her dream.

Self-consciously modern, Keats's romances play out and critique existing anxieties and tensions integral to this literary genre. Keats understood that fictions of idealised dreams have the potential to disclose waking nightmares of reality. Out of the once safe haven of romance's brilliant illusory bowers, Keats successfully induces a birth of tragedy.

Chapter 15

Ode to a Nightingale

Ode to a Nightingale is a poem by John Keats. It was written in May 1819 in the garden of the Spaniards Inn, Hampstead, London. It was first published in *Annals of the Fine Arts* in July of the same year.

Referred to by critics of the time as "the longest and most personal of the odes," the poem describes Keats' journey into the state of Negative Capability. The poem explores the themes of nature, transience and mortality, the last-named being the most personal to Keats, making a direct reference to the death in 1818 of his brother, Tom. In the poem, Keats imagines the loss of the physical world and sees himself dead—he uses an abrupt, almost brutal word for it—as a "sod" over which the nightingale sings.

The contrast between the immortal nightingale and mortal man, sitting in his garden, is made all the more acute by an effort of the imagination. The presence of weather is noticeable in the poem, as spring came early in 1819, which brought nightingales all over the heath. According to Keats' friend, Charles Armitage Brown, a nightingale had built its nest near his home in the spring of 1819.

Out of Keats's six major odes of 1819, *Ode to Psyche* was probably written first with *To Autumn* written last. Somewhere between writing these two, Keats wrote *Ode to a Nightingale.* The actual date when Keats wrote the ode, along with *Ode on Indolence, Ode on Melancholy* and *Ode on a Grecian Urn* is unknown because he only dated the poems as being written during May 1819. However, he worked on the four poems together and they are united in both their stanza forms and their themes. The exact order of the poems is uncertain, but they form a sequence within their structures although the actual order of the poems within the sequence is unnecessary. While Keats was writing *Ode on a Grecian Urn* and the other poems, his friend Charles Brown was busy transcribing copies of the poems and then submitting them to Richard Woodhouse.

It is known that the *Ode to a Nightingale* only took a morning to composed, a feat that places the ode besides only a handful of other "great" English poems. We know of this feat because of how Brown described the composition of the poem: "In the spring of 1819 a nightingale had built her nest near my house. eats fellt a tranquil and continual joy in her song; and one morning he took his chair from the breakfast-table to the grass-plot under a plum-tree, where he sat for two or three hours. When he came into the house, I perceived he had some scraps of paper in his hand, and these he was quietly thrusting behind the books. On inquiry, I found those scraps, four or five in number, contained his poetic feelings on the song of our nightingale."

STRUCTURE

Ode to Nightingale was probably the first of the middle set of four odes that Keats wrote following *Ode to Psyche* as implied by Brown. There is further evidence in the structure of the poems because Keats combines two different types of lyrical in an experimental way: the odal hymn and the lyric of questioning voice that responds to the odal hymn. This combination of structures is similar to that in *Ode on a Grecian Urn*, and, in both oems, the dual form creates a sort of dramatic element within the poem. The stanza forms of the poem is a cmbination of elements from Pretrarchan sonnets and Shakespearean sonnets.

When it came to vowel forms, Keats incorporated pattern of alternating historically "short" and "long" vowel sounds in his ode. In particular, line 18 ("And purple-stained mouth") has the historical pattern of "short" followed by "long" followed by "short" and followed by "long". This alteration is continued in longer lines, including line 31 ("Away! away! for I will fly to thee") which has five pairs of alternations. However, other lines, such as line 3 ("Or emptied some dull opiate to the drains") rely on a pattern of five "short" vowels followed by "long" vowel and "short" vowel pairings until it ends with a "long" vowel.

These are not the only combination patterns present, and there are patterns of two "short" vowels followed by a "long" vowel in other lines, including 12, 22, and 59, which are repeated twice and then followed up with two sets of "short" vowel and then "long" vowel pairs. This reliance on vowel sounds is not unique to this ode, but is common to Keats's other 1819 odes and his *Eve of St. Agnes*.

The poem also incorporates a complex reliance on assonance. In many of Keats's poems, Keats incorporates the internal vowel sound reptition in a conscious pattern. Such a reliance on assonance found in very few English poems. Within *Ode to a Nightingale,* an example of this pattern can be found in line 35 ("Already with thee! tender is the night") where the "ea" of "Already" connects with the "e" of "tender" and the "i" of "with" connects with the "i" of "is". This same pattern is found again in line 41)"I cannot see what flowers are at my feet") with the "a" of "cannot" linking with the "a" of "at" and the "ee" of "see" linking with the "ee" of "feet". This system of assonance can be found in approximately a tenth of the lines of Keats's later poetry.

When it came to other sound patterns, Keats relied on double or triple caesuras within approximately 6% throughout the 1819 odes. An example from *Ode to a Nightingale* can be found within line 45 ("The grass, the thicket, and the fruit-tree wild") as the pauses after the commas are a "masculine" pause.

Furthermore, Keats began to reduce the amount of Latin based words and syntax that he relied on in his poetry, which in turn shortened the length of the words that dominate the poem. There is also an emphasis on words beginning with consonants, especially those that begin with "b", "p" or "v". These three consonants are relied on heavily in the first stanza, and they are used syzygically to add a musical tone within the poem.

METER

Keats relies on spondee throughout his 1819 odes. In particular, he relies on it in 8.3% of his lines, including line 12:

/ ¢ / / ¢ ¢ / / ¢ /

Cool'd a long age In the *deep delv* ed earth and line 25:

¢ / ¢ / ¢ / / / / /

Where pals y Shakes a few, *sad, last, gray hairs*

Walter Jackson Bate argues that the use of spondees appears in lines 31–34 to create a feeling of slow flight, and that "in the final stanza of the *Ode to a Nightingale*, the distinctive use of scattered spondees, together with initial inversion, lend an approximate phonetic suggestion of the peculiar spring and bounce of the bird in its flight."

POEM

The ode consists of eight stanzas, each containing ten lines. The rhyme scheme (*ababcdecde*) has a link to the sonnet form, with each stanza uniting a Shakespearian quatrain (*abab*) with a Petrarchan sextet (*cdecde*). This stanzaic prosody is characteristic of Keats's odes, and may well have evolved from his intensive work and theory on the sonnet form (see, for example, "If by Dull Rhymes our English Must be Chained").

The opening lines of the poem make use of heavy vowel sounds to slow them down (e.g. "heart," "aches," "drowsy," and "numbness"). The Hippocrene, referenced in the second stanza, is the legendary fountain of the muses, located on Mt. Helicon.

Keats' relationship with the bird clearly changes as the text progresses and his consciousness drifts into a dreaming, imaginative space. In the first stanza, Keats refers to it with awe, using phrases such as "Light-winged Dryad of the trees," but by the seventh stanza refers to it simply as "bird". Indeed, in the final stanza the speaker addresses the animal as "deceiving elf", implying irritation at the nightingale's hypnotic song for the effect it had on him. Similarly, his views about the nightingale's song change as the poem progresses, the description "high requiem" giving way to "plaintive anthem" in the final stanza.

The turn in the poem occurs when Keats repeats the word "Forlorn!" between the penultimate and final stanzas. He is wakened from his close reverie with the bird by the sound of the word "forlorn," and he finds the bird flying away from the poetic dreamspace that provided the atmosphere of most of the ode. Keats's confusion marks the closing lines of the poem, in which he asks: "Was it a vision, or a waking dream? Fled is that music:– Do I wake or sleep?"

THEMES

Ode to a Nightingale describes a series of conflicts between reality and the romantic ideal. In the words of Richard Fogle, "The principal stress of the poem is a struggle between ideal and actual: inclusive terms which, however, contain more particular antitheses of pleasure and pain, of imagination and commonsense reason, of fullness and privation, of permanence and change, of nature and the human, of art and life, freedom and bondage, waking and dream."

Of course, the nightingale's song is the dominant image and dominant "voice" within the ode. The nightingale is also the object of empathy and praise within the poem. However, the nightingale and the discussion of the nightingale is not simply about the bird or the song, but about human experience in general. This is not to say that the song is a simple metaphor, but it is a complex image that is formed through the interaction of the conflict voices of praise and questioning.

On this theme, David Perkins summarizes the way *Ode to a Nightingale* and *Ode on a Grecian Urn* perform this when he says, "we are dealing with a talent, indeed an entire approach to poetry, in which symbol, however necessary, may possibly not satisfy as the principal concern of poetry, any more than it could with Shakespeare, but is rather an element in the poetry and drama of human reactions". However, there is a difference between an urn and a nightingale in that the nightingale is not an eternal entity. Furthermore, in creating any aspect of the nightingale immortal during the poem the narrator separates any union that he can have with the nightingale.

The poem relies heavily on the process of sleeping and discusses both dreams and the act of awaking. Such uses are not unique to Keats's poery, and *Ode to a Nightingale* shares many of the same themes as Keats's *Sleep and Poetry* and *Eve of St. Agnes*. This further separates the image of the nightingale's song from its closest comparative image, the urn as represented in *Ode on a Grecian Urn*. The nightingale is distant and mysterious, and even disappears at the end of the poem. The dream image emphasizes the shadowness and elusiveness of the poem. These elements make it impossible for there to be a complete self identification with the nightingale, but it also allows for self-awareness to permeate throughout the poem, albeit in an altered state.

Midway through the poem, there is a split between the two actions of the poem: the first is an attempt to identify with the nightingale and its song, and the second is to discuss the convergence of the past with the future while experiencing the present. This second theme is reminiscent of Keats's view of human progression through the Mansion of Many Apartments and how man develops from experiencing and wanting only pleasure to understanding truth as a mixture of both pleasure and pain. The Elysian fields and the nightingale's song in the first half of the poem represent the pleasurable moments which overwhelm the individual like a drug. However, the experience does not last forever, and the body is left desiring it until the narrator fels helpless without the pleasure. Instead of embracing the coming truth, the narrator clings to poetry in order to hide from the loss of pleasure. Poetry does not bring about the pleasure that the narrator original asks for, but it does liberate him from his desire for only pleasure.

This emphasis on pleasure provoked Albert Guerard, Jr. to argue that within the poem is a "longing not for art but a free reverie of any kind. The form of the poem is that of progression by association, so that the movement of feeling is at the mercy of words evoked by chance, such words as *fade* and *forlorn,* the very words which like a bell tolls the dreamer back to his sole self." However, Fogle points out that the terms Guerard emphasizes are "associational translations" and that Guerard misunderstands Keats's aesthetic.

After all, the acceptance of the loss of pleasure by the end of the poem is an acceptance of life and, in turn, of death. Death was a constant theme that permeats aspects of Keats poetry because he was exposed to death of his family members throughout his life. Within the poem, there are many images of death. The nightingale experiences a sort of death and even the god Apollo experiences death, but his death reveals his own divine state. As Perkins explains, "But, of coure, the nightingale is not thought to be literally dying. The point is that the deity or the nightingale can sing without dying. But as the ode makes clear, man cannot, or, at least, not in a visionary way."

With this theme of a loss of pleasure and inevitable death, the poem, according to Claude Finney, describes "the inadequacy of the romantic escape from the world of reality to the world of ideal beauty". Earl Wasserman essentially agrees with Finney, but he extended his summation of the poem to incorporate the themes of Keats's Mansion of Many Apartments when he says, "the core of the poem is the search for the mystery, the unsuccessful quest for light within its darkness" and this "leads only to an increasing darkness, or a growing recognition of how impenetrable the mystery is to mortals." With these views in mind, the poem recalls Keats's earlier view of pleasure and an optimistic view of poetry found within his earlier poems, especially *Sleep and Poetry,* and rejects them.

This loss of pleasure and incorporation of death imagery lends the poem a dark air, which connects *Ode to a Nightingale* with Keats other poems that discuss the demonic nature of poetic imagination, including *Lamia.*

In the poem, Keats imagines the loss of the physical world and sees himself dead—he uses an abrupt, almost brutal word for it—as a "sod" over which the nightingale sings. The contrast between the immortal nightingale and mortal man, sitting in his garden, is made all the more acute by an effort of the imagination.

CRITICAL RECEPTION

During the early 20th century, F. R. Leavis wrote, "One remembers the poem both as recording, and as being for the reader, an indulgence." Fogle responds, "I find Mr. Leavis too austere, but he points out a quality which Keats plainly sought for. His profusion and prodigality is, however, modified by a principle of sobriety." Cleanth Brooks and Robert Penn Warren see the poem as "a very rich poem. It contains some complications which we must not gloss over if we are to appreciate the depth and significance of the issues engaged."

Bate believes that the speed and intensity with which *Ode to a Nightingale* was written places it among only small group of great English poems written with such speed. Furthermore, he writes, "We are free to doubt whether any poem in English of comparable length and quality has been composed so quickly." Perkins believes that "Although the *Ode to a Nightingale* ranges more widely than the *Ode on a Grecian Urn*, the poem can also be regarded as the exploration or testing out of a symbol, and, compared with the urn as a symbol, the nightingale would seem to have both limitations and advantages."

In "Two odes of Keats's". William C Wilkinson suggested that *Ode to a Nightingale* was deeply flawed because it contained too many "incoherent musings" that failed to supply a standard of logic that would allow the reader to understand the relationship between the poet and the bird.

The Poetry of John Keats - A Celebration of Beauty, Classicism and Romantic RichnessBeing an ardent lover of poetry, to be more specific, romantic poetry, I have always been fascinated with the sense of oneness I feel with the poets' world. Romantic poetry, for some of its major attributes like pictorial quality, imagery, mysticism, absorption in the beauty and life of nature, classical features and above all, celebration of beauty and aestheticism—has a huge amount of appeal to the highly refined and sophisticated readers of all times. And surprisingly, it is this pictorial quality, sensuous delight in nature, sheer artistic beauty and richness of imagery unfolded by romantic poets that continue to inspire us in some way even after so many years!

When we come to think of the Romantic poets, the name John Keats, the finest flower of the Romantic Movement-comes foremost on our minds. Deeply revered as one of the greatest word-painters in English poetry, his verses present subtle imagery and a fusion of different sensations that has time and again, produced musical effects, and in that, he was rather a conscious artist.

The age of Keats and the literary influence on Keats:

The Romantic era, as history says, was the time when almost the whole of Europe was intensely shaken by the ideas and ideologies of the French Revolution. Major poets of that period were greatly inspired by the personal and political liberty of the revolution, breaking the bonds of the artistic conventions of the 18th century. Those were the times when these ideas and ideals "awaked the youthful passion of Wordsworth, of Coleridge", "stirred the wrath of Scott" and "worked like yeast on Byron"... However, Keats was distinguished from his contemporary poets and literary figures in the fact that the excitement and the turmoil that gathered round the revolution was not directly represented in his poetry.

Thus saying, it is worth mentioning that some portions of 'Hyperion', 'Fall of Hyperion', and 'Endymion' do bear testimony to that fact that Keats was influenced by the political turmoil - but it's definitely not as pronounced as the works of Wordsworth, Coleridge, or Shelley. His poetry, on the other hand, was an embodiment of his vision of beauty that he sees everywhere in nature, in art, in human deeds of chivalry and in the fascinating tales of ancient Greece. This in fact, was the profoundest and the most innermost experience of Keats' soul, which he expresses most emphatically in his 'Ode on a Grecian Urn':

"Beauty is Truth, Truth Beauty', that is all/ Ye know on earth, and all ye need to know."

Tracing his poetic growth, researchers have found out that he was educated almost exclusively by the English poets. While in the early part of his career, the influence of Edmund Spenser, specially his 'Faerie Queene', was instrumental in awakening his imaginative genius; the brooding love of sensuous beauty, the luxuriance of fancy and the response to the charm of nature characteristic of Spenser's poems were to be re-echoed in Keats' poems.

In the later years, critics have cited the influence of Shakespeare, Milton, and even Wordsworth in his poems. While the influx of Shakespearean words, allusions find expression in the 1817 volume of his 'Endymion', he was also greatly influenced by the distinctive spirit and vocabulary of the old English poets, especially those of the Renaissance. Thus saying, it is worth mentioning that the influence of Milton's 'Paradise Lost' is highly visible in his 'Hyperion'. At the same breath, the classical influence on his poetry has also been a subject of intense research by scholars.

Critics today say that what makes the poetry of Keats the most distinguished among all romantic poets is the fact that his poetic genius blossomed under the romantic breeze, and matured under the sunshine of classicism. The genuine classicism of ancient Greece, which shows the characteristic classical restraint, is very much present in his poems. What more, it is harmoniously blended with the romantic ardor of his poetry, which results in a wonderful fusion of romantic impulse and classical severity.

This statement holds much truth when we take into account his more mature Odes, where we notice Keats' sense of form, purity and orderliness. His Odes have all the spontaneity and freedom of imagination that characterize the poetry of the Romantic era. For example, when in his 'Ode to a Nightingale', the poet describes the bird's song as the voice of eternity and expresses intense longing to die in the hope of merging with eternity, there is this romantic suggestiveness of sensual delight of the poet in these lines:

"The same that oft-time hath/Charmed magic casements, opening on the foam/Of perilous seas, in faery lands forlorn".

However, at once, the poet restrains himself with the lines:

"Forlorn! The very word is like a bell/To toll me back from thee to my sole self"...which is a perfect example of romantic passion fused with classical restraint. In all his mature Odes, including 'Ode to a Nightingale', Ode on a Grecian Urn', 'Ode to Melancholy' and 'Ode to Psyche', he is said to have cast aside his over-loaded diction of his earlier poems and come out with a romantic richness that is replete with the Hellenic clarity characterizing Greek literature.

The poetic alienation and the theme of melancholy:

While beauty and mutability are said to be the recurrent themes in Keats' mature Odes, critics have pointed out that he was somewhat "obsessed by the close juxtaposition of joy and grief, delight and pain". Some point out, that in his pursuit of beauty, he became an escapist, ignoring the realities of life. In his earlier poems, 'Isabella', 'Lamia', The Eve of St. Agnes' and others, his imagination certainly plays with the romance of love, with medieval elements, cruel, mysterious ladies, 'a faery's child', the spell and enchantment of the magical world.

However, all this is characterized by his sense of alienation as a creative thinker, which, assume a deeper tone and meaning in his later works, i.e., his Odes. Throughout his journey as a poet, he strived to harmonize what scholars today say 'the life of sensation with life of thought'. His earlier hankering for unreflecting enjoyment of sensuous delights, as seen in his 'Sleep and Poetry', is later replaced by a strong yearning to subject himself persistently and unflinchingly, to the joy and beauty of life, that is accompanied by the inevitable pain, hopelessness and despair of life. Hence, the lines:

"Joy whose hand is ever at his lips/Bidding adieu". Keats knew that joy and beauty on this earth is transient, and from this transience, the melancholy so very typical of his poems originate. Melancholy, he says, "dwells with beauty/Beauty that must die".

It is this triumph of the stoic acceptance of life over despair which he attains through a deep spiritual experience, as he expresses in his 'Ode on a Grecian Urn', "When old age shall this generation waste/Thou shall remain in midst of other woe than ours'... These lines can never come from the pen of an escapist. For me, he was purely a thinker profoundly concerned with the mystery of life which he deals as a poet, not as a political rebel or as a philosopher. Scholastic researches strive to bring out new perspectives of his poetry even today. As a reader, I would be content exploring the romantic fervor and richness of imagery of his poems for years to come!

Keats's first volume had been launched, to quote the words of Cowden Clarke, 'amid the cheers and fond anticipations of all his circle. Every one of us expected (and not unreasonably) that it would create a sensation in the literary world.' The magniloquent Haydon words these expectations after his manner:—'I have read your *Sleep and Poetry* —it is a flash of lightning that will rouse men from their occupations and keep them trembling for the crash of thunder that *will* follow.'

Sonnets poured in on the occasion, and not from intimates only. I have already quoted one which Reynolds, familiar with the contents of the forthcoming book, wrote a few days before its publication to welcome it and at the same time to congratulate Keats on his sonnet written in Clarke's copy of the *Floure and the Lefe* . Leigh Hunt, always delighted to repay compliment with compliment, replied effusively in kind to the sonnet in which Keats had dedicated the volume to him. Richard Woodhouse, of whom we shall soon hear more but who was as yet a stranger, in the closing lines of a sonnet addressed to Apollo, welcomed Keats as the last born son of that divinity and the herald of his return to lighten the poetic darkness of the land:—

Have these thy glories perish'd? or in scorn Of thankless man hath thy race ceased to quite? O no! thou hear'st! for lo! the beamèd morn Chases our night of song: and, from the lyre Waking long dormant sounds, Keats, thy last born, To the glad realm proclaims the coming of his sire.

Sonnets are not often addressed by publishers to their clients: but one has been found in the handwriting of Charles Ollier, and almost certainly composed by him, expressing admiration for Keats's work. The brothers Ollier, it will be remembered, were Shelley's publishers, and for a while also Leigh Hunt's and Lamb's, and Charles was the poetry-loving and enthusiastic brother of the two, and himself a writer of some accomplishment in prose and verse.

But in point of fact, outside the immediate Leigh Hunt circle, the volume made extremely little impression, and the public was as far as possible from being roused from its occupations or made tremble. 'Alas!' continues Cowden Clarke, 'the book might have emerged in *Timbuctoo* with far stronger chance of fame and appreciation. The whole community as if by compact, seemed determined to know nothing about it.'

Clarke here somewhat exaggerates the facts. Leigh Hunt kept his own review of the volume back for some three months, very likely with the just idea that praise from him might prejudice Keats rather than serve him. At length it appeared, in three successive numbers of the *Examiner* for July, the first number setting forth the aims and tendencies of the new movement in poetry with a conscious clearness such as to those taking part in a collective, three-parts instinctive effort of the kind comes usually in retrospect only and not in the thick of the struggle.

In the second and third notices Hunt speaks of the old graces of poetry reappearing, warns 'this young writer of genius' against disproportionate detail and a too revolutionary handling of metre, and after quotation winds up by calling the volume 'a little luxuriant heap of

Such sights as youthful poets dream On summer eves by haunted stream.'

Two at least of the established critical reviews noticed the book at length, Constable *Scots and Edinburgh Magazine,* and the *Eclectic Review,* the chief organ of lettered nonconformity, owned and edited by the busy dissenting poet and bookseller Josiah Conder. Both criticisms are of the preaching and admonishing kind then almost universally in fashion. The Scottish reviewer recognises in the new poet a not wholly unsuccessful disciple of Spenser, but warns him against 'the appalling doom which awaits the faults of mannerism or the ambition of a sickly refinement,' and with reference to his association with the person and ideas of Hazlitt and Hunt declares that 'if Mr Keats does not forthwith cast off the uncleanness of this school, he will never make his way to the truest strain of poetry in which, taking him by himself, it appears he might succeed.' The preachment of the *Eclectic* is still more pompous and superior.

There are mild words of praise for some of the sonnets, but none for that on Chapman's Homer. *Sleep and Poetry,* declares the critic, would seem to show of the writer that 'he is indeed far gone, beyond the reach of the efficacy of either praise or censure, in affectation and absurdity. Seriously, however, we regret that a young man of vivid imagination and fine talents should have fallen into so bad hands as to have been flattered into the resolution to publish verses, of which a few years hence he will be glad to escape from the remembrance.'

Notices such as this could not help a new writer to fame or his book to sale. But before they appeared Keats and his brothers, or they for him, had begun to fret at the failure of the volume and to impute it, as authors and their friends will, to some mishandling by the publishers. George in John's absence wrote to the Olliers taking them to task pretty roundly, and received the often-quoted reply drafted, let us hope, not by the sonneteer but by James Ollier, his business brother, and alleging of the work that—

By far the greater number of persons who have purchased it from us have found fault with it in such plain terms, that we have in many cases offered to take it back rather than be annoyed with the ridicule which has, time after time, been showered upon it. In fact, it was only on Saturday last that we were under the mortification of having our own opinion of its merits flatly contradicted by a gentleman, who told us he considered it 'no better than a take in.'

Meanwhile Keats had found other publishers ready to take up his next work, and destined to become his staunch and generous friends. These were Messrs Taylor and Hessey of 93 Fleet Street. John Taylor, the chief partner, was a man of high character and considerable attainments, who had come up from Nottinghamshire to open a business in London ten years earlier. He was already noted as an authority on Junius and was to be a little later the editor as well as publisher of the *London Magazine*, and the good friend and frequent entertainer (in the back parlour of the publishing house in Fleet Street) of his most distinguished contributors.

How and through whom Keats was introduced to his firm is not quite clear: probably through Benjamin Bailey, a new acquaintance whom we know to have been a friend of Taylor's. Bailey was an Oxford man five years older than Keats. He had been an undergraduate of Trinity and was now staying up at Magdalen Hall to read for orders. He was an ardent student of poetry and general literature as well as of theology, a devout worshipper of Milton, and scarcely less of Wordsworth, with whom he had some personal acquaintance. Of his appetite for books Keats wrote when they had come to know each other well: 'I should not like to be pages in your way; when in a tolerably hungry mood you have no mercy.

Your teeth are the Rock Tarpeian down which you capsize epic poems like mad. I would not for forty shillings be Coleridge's Lays [i.e. *Lay Sermons*] in your way.' Bailey was intimate with John Hamilton Reynolds and his family, and at this time a suitor for the hand of his sister Mariane. In the course of the winter 1816-17 Reynolds had written to him enthusiastically of Keats's poetical promise and personal charm. When at the beginning of March Keats's volume came out, Bailey was much struck, and on a visit to London called to make the new poet's acquaintance. Though it was not until a few months later that this acquaintance ripened into close friendship, it may well have been Bailey who recommended Keats and Taylor to each other.

Relations of business or friendship with Taylor necessarily involved relations with Richard Woodhouse, a lettered and accomplished young solicitor of twentynine who was an intimate friend of Taylor's and at this time apparently the regular reader and adviser to the firm. Woodhouse was sprung from an old landed stock in Herefordshire, some of whose members were now in the wine-trade (his father, it seems, was owner or part owner of the White Hart at Bath). He had been educated at Eton but not at the university: his extant correspondence, as well as notes and version-books in his hand, show him to have been a good linguist in Spanish and Italian and a man of remarkably fine literary taste and judgment. He afterwards held a high position as a solicitor and was one of the founders of the Law Life Insurance Society.

These three new friendships, with Benjamin Bailey, John Taylor, and Richard Woodhouse, formed during the six weeks between the publication of his book (March 3) and the mid-April following, turned out to be among the most valuable of Keats's life, and were the best immediate results the issue of his first volume brought him. During this interval he and his brothers were lodging at 17 Cheapside, having left their old quarters in the Poultry. Some time in March it was decided, partly on Haydon's urging, that John should for the sake of quiet and self-improvement go and spend some time by himself in the country, and try to get to work upon his great meditated *Endymion* poem. He writes as much to Reynolds, concluding with an adaptation from Falstaff expressive of anxiety for the health of some of those dear to him—probably his brother Tom and James Rice:—

My brothers are anxious that I should go by myself into the country—they have always been extremely fond of me, and now that Haydon has pointed out how necessary it is that I should be alone to improve myself, they give up the temporary pleasure of living with me continually for a great good which I hope will follow. So I shall soon be out of Town. You must soon bring all your present troubles to a close, and so must I, but we must, like the Fox, prepare for a fresh swarm of flies. Banish money —Banish sofas—Banish Wine—Banish Music; but right Jack Health, honest Jack Health, true Jack Health—Banish Health and banish all the world.

On the 14th of April Keats took the night mail for Southampton, whence he writes next day a lively letter to his brothers. By the 17th, having looked at Shanklin and decided against it, he was installed in a lodging at Carisbrooke. Writing to Reynolds he gives the reasons for his choice, mentioning at the same time that he is feeling rather nervous from want of sleep, and enclosing the admirable sonnet On the Sea which he has just composed—

It keeps eternal whisperings around Desolate shorn, etc.—

It was the intense haunting of the lines in the scene on Dover Cliff in King Lear beginning 'Do you not hear the sea,' which moved him, he says, to this effort. He was reading and re-reading his Shakespeare with passion, and phrases from the plays come up continually in his letters, not only, as in the following extract, in the form of set quotations, but currently, as though they were part of his own mind and being. Having found in the lodging-house passage an engraved head of Shakespeare which pleased him and hung it up in his room (his landlady afterwards made him a present of it), he bethinks him of the approaching anniversary, April 23:—

I'll tell you what—on the 23d was Shakespeare born. Now if I should receive a letter from you, and another from my Brothers on that day 'twould be a parlous good thing. Whenever you write say a word or two on some Passage in Shakespeare that may have come rather new to you, which must be continually happening, notwithstanding that we read the same Play forty times—for instance, the following from the Tempest never struck me so forcibly as at present,

Urchins

Shall, for the vast of night that they may work, All exercise on thee—

How can I help bringing to your mind the line—

In the dark backward and abysm of time.

I find I cannot exist without Poetry—without eternal Poetry-half the day will not do—the whole of it—I began with a little, but habit has made me a Leviathan. I had become all in a Tremble from not having written anything of late—the Sonnet over—leaf did me good. I slept the better last night for it—this Morning, however, I am nearly as bad again. Just now I opened Spenser, and the first Lines I saw were these—

The noble heart that harbours virtuous thought,
And is with child of glorious great intent,

Can never rest until it forth have brought
Th' eternal brood of glory excellent.

'I shall forthwith begin my *Endymion*,' he adds, and looks forward to reading some of it out, when his correspondent comes to visit him, in a nook near the castle which he has already marked for the purpose.

But Haydon's prescription of solitude turned out the worst Keats could well have followed in the then state of his mind, fermenting with a thousand restless thoughts and inchoate imaginations and with the feverish conflict between ambition and self-distrust. The result at any rate was that he passed the time, to use his own words, 'in continual burning of thought, as an only resource,' and what with that and lack of proper food felt himself after a week or ten days 'not over capable in his upper stories' and in need of change and companionship. He made straight for his last year's lodging at Margate and got Tom to join him there. Thence in the second week of May he writes a long letter to Hunt and another to Haydon.

To Hunt he criticises some points in the last number of the *Examiner*, and especially, in his kindhearted, well-conditioned way, deprecates a certain vicious allusion to grey hairs in an attack of Hazlitt upon Southey. Later on we shall have to tell of the critical savagery of *Blackwood* and the *Quarterly*, now long since branded and proverbial.

But it should be borne in mind, as it by no means always is, that the Tories were far from having the savagery to themselves. When Hazlitt, for one, chose to strike on the liberal side, he could match Gifford or Lockhart or Wilson or Maginn with their own weapons. To realise the controversial atmosphere of the time, here is a passage, and not the fiercest, from the Hazlitt article in which Keats found too venomous a sting. Southey's first love, rails Hazlitt, had been the Republic, his second was Legitimacy, 'her more fortunate and wealthy rival':—

He is becoming uxorious in his second matrimonial connection; and though his false Duessa has turned out a very witch, a murderess, a sorceress, perjured, and a harlot, drunk with insolence, mad with power, a griping rapacious wretch, bloody, luxurious, wanton, malicious, not sparing steel, or poison, or gold, to gain her ends—bringing famine, pestilence, and death in her train—infecting the air with her thoughts, killing the beholders with her looks, claiming mankind as her property, and using them as her slaves—driving everything before her, and playing the devil wherever she comes, Mr Southey sticks to her in spite of everything, and for very shame lays his head in her lap, paddles with the palms of her hands, inhales her hateful breath, leers in her eyes and whispers in her ears, calls her little fondling names, Religion, Morality, and Social Order, takes for his motto,

Be to her faults a little blind,
Be to her virtues very kind—

sticks close to his filthy bargain, and will not give her up, because she keeps him, and he is down in her will. Faugh!

It is fair to note that the mistress thus depicted as Southey's is an allegorical being, while the *Blackwood* scurrilities were often directly personal.

After asking how Hunt own new poem, *The Nymphs,* is getting on, Keats tells how he has been writing some of *Endymion* every day the last fortnight, except travelling days, and how thoughts of the greatness of his ambition and the uncertainty of his powers have thrown him into a fit of gloom; hinting at such moods of bleak and blank despondency as we shall find now and again figuratively described in the text of *Endymion* itself.

I have asked myself so often why I should be a poet more than other men, seeing how great a thing it is,... that at last the idea has grown so monstrously beyond my seeming power of attainment that the other day I nearly consented with myself to drop into a Phaeton ... I see nothing but continual uphill journeying. Now is there anything more unpleasant than to be so journeying and to miss the goal at last? But I intend to whistle all those cogitations into the sea, where I hope they will breed storms enough to block up all exit from Russia. Does Shelley go on telling strange stories of the deaths of kings? Tell him there are strange stories of the deaths of poets. Some have died before they were conceived. The same evening Keats begins to answer a letter of encouragement and advice he had just had from Haydon. This is the letter of Haydon's from which I have already quoted the passage about the efficacy of prayer as Haydon had experienced it. Perfectly sincere and genuinely moved, he can never for a minute continuously steer clear of rant and fustian and self-praise at another's expense.

Never despair, he goes on, while the path is open to you. By habitual exercise you will have habitual intercourse and constant companionship; and at every want turn to the Great Star of your hopes with a delightful confidence that will never be disappointed. I love you like my own brother: Beware, for God's sake, of the delusions and sophistications that are ripping up the talents and morality of our friend.

He will go out of the world the victim of his own weakness and the dupe of his own self-delusions, with the contempt of his enemies and the sorrow of his friends, and the cause he undertook to support injured by his own neglect of character. I wish you would come up to town for a day or two that I may put your head in my picture. I have rubbed in Wordsworth's, and advanced the whole. God bless you, my dear Keats! do not despair; collect incident, study character, read Shakespeare, and trust in Providence, and you will do, you must.

Keats in answer quotes the opening speech of the King in *Love's Labour's Lost,*—

Let Fame, that all pant after in their lives
Live registered upon our brazen tombs, etc.,

saying that he could not bear to think he had not the right to couple his own name with Haydon's in such a forecast, and acknowledging the occasional moods of depression which have put him into such a state of mind as to read over his own lines and hate them, though he has picked up heart again when he found some from Pope's Homer which Tom read out to him seem 'like Mice' to his own. He takes encouragement also from the notion that has visited him lately of some good genius—can it be Shakespeare?—presiding over him. Continuing the next day, he is downhearted again at hearing from George of money difficulties actual and prospective. 'You tell me never to despair—I wish it was as easy for me to deserve the saying—truth is I have a horrid morbidity of Temperament which has shown itself at intervals it is I have no doubt the greatest Enemy and stumbling block I have to fear—I may even say it is likely to be the cause of my disappointment.'

Then referring to Haydon's warning in regard to Hunt, he goes half way in agreement and declares he would die rather than be deceived about his own achievements as Hunt is. 'There is no greater sin after the seven deadly,' he says, 'than to flatter oneself into the idea of being a great poet: the comfort is, such a crime must bring its own penalty, and if one is a self-deluder indeed accounts must one day be balanced.'

In the same week, moved no doubt by the difficulties George had mentioned about touching the funds due from their grandmother's estate, Keats writes to Taylor and Hessey, in a lively and familiar strain showing the terms of confidence on which he already stood with them, asking them to advance him an instalment of the agreed price for *Endymion*. He mentions in this letter that he is tired of Margate (he had already to another correspondent called it a 'treeless affair') and means to move to Canterbury. At this point there occurs an unlucky gap in Keats's correspondence. We know that he and Tom went to Canterbury from Margate as planned, but we do not know exactly when, nor how long he stayed there, nor what work he did (except that he was certainly going on with the first book of *Endymion*), nor what impressions he received.

It was his first visit to a cathedral city, and few in the world, none in England, are more fitted to impress. Chichester and Winchester he came afterwards to know, Winchester well and with affection; but it was with thoughts of Canterbury in his mind that he planned, some two years later, first a serious and then a frivolous verse romance having an English cathedral town for scene (The Eve of St Mark, The Cap and Bells). The heroine of both was to have been a maiden of Canterbury called Bertha; not, of course, the historic Frankish princess Bertha, daughter of Haribert and wife of Ethelbert king of Kent, who converted her husband and prepared his people for Christianity before the landing of Saint Augustin, and who sleeps in the ancient church of Saint Martin outside the walls: not she, but some damsel of the city, named after her in later days, whom Keats had heard or read of or invented,—I would fain know which; but I have found no external evidence of his studies or doings during this spring stay at Canterbury, and his correspondence is, as I have said, a blank.

Some time in June he returned and the three brothers were together again: not now in City lodgings but in new quarters to which they had migrated in Well Walk, Hampstead. Their landlord was one Bentley the postman, with whom they seem to have got on well except that Keats occasionally complains of the 'young carrots,' his children, now for making a 'horrid row,' now for smelling of damp worsted stockings. The lack of letters continues through these first summer months at Hampstead. The only exception is a laughingly apologetic appeal to his new publishers for a further advance of money, dated June 10th and ending with the words,-'I am sure you are confident of my responsibility, and of the sense of squareness that is always in me.'

For the rest, indirect evidence allows us to picture Keats in these months as working regularly at *Endymion*, having now reached the second book, and as living socially, not without a certain amount of convivial claret-drinking and racket, in the company of his brothers and of his friends and theirs. Leigh Hunt was still close by in the Vale of Health, and both in his circle and in Haydon's London studio Keats was as welcome as ever. Reynolds and Rice were still his close intimates, and Reynolds's sisters in Lamb's Conduit Street almost like sisters of his own.

He was scarcely less at home in the family of his sister-in-law that was to be, Georgiana Wylie. The faithful Severn and the faithful Haslam came up eagerly whenever they could to join the Hampstead party. An acquaintance he had already formed at Hunt's with the Charles Dilkes and their friend

Charles Brown, who lived as next-door neighbours at Wentworth Place, a double block of houses of their own building in a garden at the foot of the Heath, now ripened into friendship: that with Dilke rapidly, that with Brown, a Scotsman who by his own account held cannily aloof from Keats at first for fear of being thought to push, more slowly.

Charles Wentworth Dilke, by profession a clerk in the Navy Pay Office, by predilection a keen and painstaking literary critic and antiquary, had been stimulated by the charm of Lamb's famous volume of *Specimens* to work at the old English dramatic poets, and had recently (being now twenty-seven) brought out a set of volumes in continuation of Dodsley *Old Plays*. In matters political and social he was something of a radical doctrinaire and 'Godwin-perfectibility man' (the label is Keats's), loving decision and positiveness in all things and being therein the very opposite of Keats, who by rooted instinct as well as choice allowed his mind to cherish uncertainties and to be a thoroughfare for all thoughts (the phrase is again his own).

There were many but always friendly discussions between Keats and Dilke, and their mutual regard never failed. Charles Brown, Dilke's contemporary, schoolfellow, and close friend, was a man of Scottish descent born in Lambeth, who had in early youth joined a business set up by an elder brother in Petersburg. The business quickly failing, he had returned to London and after some years of struggle inherited a modest competence from another brother. A lively, cultivated, moderately successful amateur in literature, journalism, and drama, he was in person bald and spectacled, and portly beyond his years though active and robust; in habits much of a trencher-man ('a huge eater' according to the abstemious Trelawny) and something of a *viveur* within his means; exactly strict in money matters, but otherwise far from a precisian in life or conversation; an ardent friend and genial companion, though cherishing some fixed unreasonable aversions: in a word, a truly Scottish blend of glowing warm-heartedness and 'thrawn' prejudice, of frank joviality and cautious dealing.

It was in these same weeks of June or July 1817, soon after

the beginning of the Oxford vacation, that Benjamin Bailey again came to town and sought after and learned to delight in Keats's company.

He meant to go back and read at Oxford for the latter part of the vacation, and invited Keats to spend some weeks with him there. Keats accepted, and the visit, lasting from soon after mid August until the end of September, proved a happiness alike to host and guest. At this point our dearth of documents ceases.

Bailey's memoranda, though not put on paper till thirty years later, are vivid and informing, and Keats's own correspondence during the visit is fairly full. I will take Bailey's recollections first, and give them in his own words, seeing that they paint the writer almost as well as his subject; omitting only passages that seem to drag or interrupt. First comes the impression Keats made on him at the time of their introduction in the spring, and then his account of the days they spent together in Oxford.

I was delighted with the naturalness and simplicity of his character, and was at once drawn to him by his winning and indeed affectionate manner towards those with whom he was himself pleased. Nor was his personal appearance the least charm of a first acquaintance with the young poet. He bore, along with the strong impress of genius, much beauty of feature and countenance. His hair was beautiful—a fine brown, rather than auburn, I think, and if you placed your hand upon his head, the silken curls felt like the rich plumage of a bird.

The eye was full and fine, and softened into tenderness, or beamed with a fiery brightness, according to the current of his thoughts and conversation. Indeed the form of his head was like that of a fine Greek statue:—and he realized to my mind the youthful Apollo, more than any head of a living man whom I have known.

At the commencement of the long vacation I was again in London, on my way to another part of the country: and it was my intention to return to Oxford early in the vacation for the purpose of reading. I saw much of Keats. And I invited him to return with me to Oxford, and spend as much time as he could afford with me in the silence and solitude of that beautiful place during the absence of the numerous members and students of the University.

He accepted my offer, and we returned together. I think in August 1817. It was during this visit, and in my room, that he wrote the third book of *Endymion*.... His mode of composition is best described by recounting our habits of study for one day during the month he visited me at Oxford. He wrote, and I read, sometimes at the same table, and sometimes at separate desks or tables, from breakfast to the time of our going out for exercise,—generally two or three o'clock.

He sat down to his task,—which was about 50 lines a day,—with his paper before him, and wrote with as much regularity, and apparently as much ease, as he wrote his letters.... Sometimes he fell short of his allotted task, but not often: and he would make it up another day. But he never forced himself. When he had finished his writing for the day, he usually read it over to me: and he read or wrote letters until we went for a walk. This was our habit day by day. The rough manuscript was written off daily, and with few erasures.

I remember very distinctly, though at this distance of time, his reading of a few passages; and I almost think I hear his voice, and see his countenance. Most vivid is my recollection of the following passage of the finest affecting story of the old man, Glaucus, which he read to me immediately after its composition:—

The old man raised his hoary head and saw
The wildered stranger—seeming not to see,
The features were so lifeless. Suddenly
He woke as from a trance; his snow white brows
Went arching up, and like two magic ploughs
Furrowed deep wrinkles in his forehead large,
Which kept as fixedly as rocky marge,
Till round his withered lips had gone a smile.

The lines I have italicised, are those which then forcibly struck me as peculiarly fine, and to my memory have 'kept as fixedly as rocky marge.' I remember his upward look when he read of the 'magic ploughs,' which in his hands have turned up so much of the rich soil of Fairyland. When we had finished our studies for the day we took our walk, and sometimes boated on the Isis.... Once we took a longer excursion of a day or two, to Stratford upon Avon, to visit the birthplace of Shakespeare. We went of course to the house visited by so many thousands of all nations of Europe, and inscribed our names in addition to the 'numbers numberless' of those which literally blackened the walls. We also visited the Church, and were pestered with a commonplace showman of the place.... He was struck, I remember, with the simple statue there, which, though rudely executed, we agreed was most probably the best likeness of the many extant, but none very authentic, of Shakespeare.

His enjoyment was of that genuine, quiet kind which was a part of his gentle nature; deeply feeling what he truly enjoyed, but saying little. On our return to Oxford we renewed our quiet mode of life, until he finished the third Book of *Endymion*, and the time came that we must part; and I never parted with one whom I had known so short a time, with so much real regret and personal affection, as I did with John Keats, when he left Oxford for London at the end of September or the beginning of October 1817.

Living as we did for a month or six weeks together (for I do not remember exactly how long) I knew him at that period of his life, perhaps as well as any one of his friends. There was no reserve of any kind between us.... His brother George says of him that to his brothers his temper was uncertain; and he himself confirms this judgment of him in a beautiful passage of a letter to myself. But with his friends, a sweeter tempered man I never knew. Gentleness was indeed his proper characteristic, without one particle of dullness, or insipidity, or want of spirit. Quite the contrary. 'He was gentle but not fearful,' in the chivalric and moral sense of the term 'gentle.' He was pleased with every thing that occurred in the ordinary mode of life, and a cloud never passed over his face, except of indignation at the wrongs of others.

His conversation was very engaging. He had a sweet toned voice, 'an excellent thing' in *man* as well as 'in woman...

.' In his letters he talks of *suspecting* everybody. It appeared not in his conversation. On the contrary, he was uniformly the apologist for poor, frail human nature, and allowed for people's faults more than any man I ever knew, especially for the faults of his friends. But if any act of wrong or oppression, of fraud or falsehood, was the topic, he rose into sudden and animated indignation. He had a truly poetic feeling for women; and he often spoke to me of his sister, who was somehow withholden from him, with great delicacy and tenderness of affection. He had a soul of noble integrity: and his common sense was a conspicuous part of his character. Indeed his character was in the best sense manly.

Our conversation rarely or never flagged, during our walks, or boatings, or in the evening. And I have retained a few of his opinions on Literature and criticism which I will detail. The following passage from Wordsworth *Ode on Immortality* was deeply felt by Keats, who however at this time seemed to me to value this great Poet rather in particular passages than in the full-length portrait, as it were, of the great imaginative and philosophic Christian Poet, which he really is, and which Keats obviously, not long afterwards, felt him to be.

Not for these I raise
The song of thanks and praise;
But for those obstinate questionings
Of sense and outward things,
Failings from us, vanishings;
Blank misgivings of a creature

Moving about in worlds not realized, *High instincts, before which our mortal nature* Did tremble like a guilty thing surprized.

The last lines he thought were quite awful in their application to a guilty finite creature, like man, in the appalling nature of the feeling which they suggested to a thoughtful mind. Again, we often talked of that noble passage in the lines on *Tintern Abbey:—*

That blessed mood,
In which the burthen of the mystery,

In which the heavy and the weary weight
Of all this unintelligible world
Is lightened.

And his references to this passage are frequent in his letters. But in those exquisite stanzas,

She dwelt among the untrodden ways,
Beside the springs of Dove.
ending,—
She lived unknown and few could know
When Lucy ceased to be;
But she is in her grave, and oh,
The difference to me.

The simplicity of the last line he declared to be the most perfect pathos.

Among the qualities of high poetic promise in Keats was, even at this time, his correct taste. I remember to have been struck with this by his remarks on that well known and often quoted passage of the *Excursion* upon the Greek Mythology-where it is said that

Fancy fetched
Even from the blazing chariot of the Sun
A beardless youth who touched a golden lute,
And filled the illumined groves with ravishment.

Keats said this description of Apollo should have ended at the 'golden lute,' and have left it to the imagination to complete the picture, how he 'filled the illumined groves.' I think every man of taste will feel the justice of the remark.

Every one now knows what was then known to his friends that Keats was an ardent admirer of Chatterton. The melody of the verses of the marvellous Boy who perished in his pride, enchanted the author of *Endymion*. Methinks I now hear him recite, or *chant*, in his peculiar manner, the following stanza of the Roundelay sung by the minstrels of Ella:—

Come with acorn cup and thorn
Drain my hertys blood away;
Life and all its good I scorn;
Dance by night or feast by day.

The first line to his ear possessed the great charm. Indeed

his sense of melody was quite exquisite, as is apparent in his own verses; and in none more than in numerous passages of his *Endymion*.

Another object of his enthusiastic admiration was the Homeric character of Achilles—especially when he is described as 'shouting in the trenches.' One of his favourite topics of discourse was the principle of melody in verse, upon which he had his own notions, particularly in the management of open and close vowels. I think I have seen a somewhat similar theory attributed to Mr Wordsworth. But I do not remember his laying it down in writing. Be this as it may, Keats's theory was worked out by himself. It was, that the vowels should be so managed as not to clash one with another, so as to hear the melody,—and yet that they should be interchanged, like differing notes of music to prevent monotony....

Bailey here tries to reconstruct and illustrate from memory Keats's theory of vowel sounds, but his attempt falters and breaks down.

Keats's own first account of himself from Oxford is in a letter of September 5th to the Reynolds sisters, then on holiday at Littlehampton: a piece of mere lively foolery and rattle meant to amuse, in a taste which is not that of to-day. Five days later he writes the first of that series of letters to his young sister Fanny which acquaints us with perhaps the most loveable and admirable parts of his character. She was now just fourteen, and living under the close guardianship of the Abbeys, who had put her to a boarding school at Walthamstow. Keats shows a tender and considerate elder-brotherly anxiety to get into touch with her and know her feelings and likings:—

Let us now begin a regular question and answer—a little pro and con; letting it interfere as a pleasant method of my coming at your favourite little wants and enjoyments, that I may meet them in a way befitting a brother.

We have been so little together since you have been able to reflect on things that I know not whether you prefer the *History of King Pepin* to Bunyan *Pilgrim's Progress*—or *Cinderella* and her glass slipper to Moor *Almanack*. However in a few

Letters I hope I shall be able to come at that and adapt my scribblings to your Pleasure. You must tell me about all you read if it be only six Pages in a Week and this transmitted to me every now and then will procure full sheets of Writing from me pretty frequently.

This I feel as a necessity for we ought to become intimately acquainted, in order that I may not only, as you grow up love you as my only Sister, but confide in you as my dearest friend. When I saw you last I told you of my intention of going to Oxford and 'tis now a Week since I disembark'd from his Whipship's Coach the Defiance in this place. I am living in Magdalen Hall on a visit to a young Man with whom I have not been long acquainted, but whom I like very much—we lead very industrious lives—he in general Studies and I in proceeding at a pretty good rate with a Poem which I hope you will see early in the next year.

Perhaps you might like to know what I am writing about. I will tell you. Many Years ago there was a young handsome Shepherd who fed his flocks on a Mountain's Side called Latmus he was a very contemplative sort of a Person and lived solitary among the trees and Plains little thinking that such a beautiful Creature as the Moon was growing mad in Love with him. However so it was; and when he was asleep on the Grass she used to come down from heaven and admire him excessively for a long time; and at last could not refrain from carrying him away in her arms to the top of that high Mountain Latmus while he was a dreaming—but I dare say you have read this and all the other beautiful Tales which have come down from the ancient times of that beautiful Greece.

If you have not let me know and I will tell you more at large of others quite as delightful. This Oxford I have no doubt is the finest City in the world—it is full of old Gothic buildings—Spires—towers—Quadrangles-Cloisters—Groves etc and is surrounded with more clear streams than ever I saw together. I take a Walk by the Side of one of them every Evening and, thank God, we have not had a drop of rain these days.

He goes on to tell her (herein echoing Hunt's opinion) how

much better it would be if Italian instead of French were taught everywhere in schools, and winds up:—

Now Fanny you must write soon—and write all you think about, never mind what—only let me have a good deal of your writing. You need not do it all at once—be two or three or four days about it, and let it be a diary of your Life. You will preserve all my Letters and I will secure yours—and thus in the course of time we shall each of us have a good Bundle—which, hereafter, when things may have strangely altered and God knows what happened, we may read over together and look with pleasure on times past—that now are to come.

Next follows another letter to Jane Reynolds; partly making fun, much better fun than in the last, about Dilke's shooting and about the rare havoc he would like to make in Mrs Dilke's garden were he at Hampstead: partly grave in the high style into which he is apt at any moment to change from nonsense:—

Now let us turn to the sea-shore. Believe me, my dear Jane, it is a great happiness to see that you are, in this finest part of the year, winning a little enjoyment from the hard world. In truth, the great Elements we know of, are no mean comforters: the open sky sits upon our senses like a sapphire crown—the Air is our robe of state—the Earth is our throne and the Sea a mighty minstrel playing before it—able, like David's harp, to make such a one as you forget almost the tempest cares of life. I have found in the ocean's music,—varying (tho' self-same) more than the passion of Timotheus, an enjoyment not to be put into words; and, 'though inland far I be,' I now hear the voice most audibly while pleasing myself in the idea of your sensations.

To Reynolds Keats writes on September the 21st:—

For these last five or six days, we have had regularly a Boat on the Isis, and explored all the streams about, which are more in number than your eye-lashes. We sometimes skim into a Bed of rushes, and there become naturalized river-folks,—there is one particularly nice nest, which we have christened ' Reynolds's *Cove*,' in which we have read Wordsworth, and talked as may be; I think I see you and Hunt meeting in the

Pit.-What a very pleasant fellow he is, if he would give up the sovereignty of a room pro bono. What evenings we might pass with him, could we have him from Mrs H. Failings I am always rather rejoiced to find in a man than sorry for; they bring us to a level.

Then follows a diatribe against the literary and intellectual pretensions of certain sets of ladies, from which he has felt an agreeable relief in some verses he has found on taking down from Bailey's shelves the poems of Katherine Phillips, 'the matchless *Orinda.*' The verses which pleased him, truly of her best, are those *To M. A. at parting*, and Keats goes on to copy them in full. Had Orinda been a contemporary, he might not, indeed, have failed to recognise in her a true woman of letters: but would he not also have found something to laugh and chafe at in the poses of that high-flying coterie of mutual-admirers, Silvander and Poliarchus, Lucasia and Rosania and Palæmon, of which she was the centre? This is one of the very few instances to be found in Keats's work or correspondence of interest in the poetry of the Caroline age.

Quite in the last days of his visit Keats, whose mind and critical power had been growing while he worked upon *Endymion*, and whom moreover the long effort of composition was clearly beginning to fatigue, confides to Haydon his dissatisfaction with what he has done:-'You will be glad to hear that within these last three weeks I have written 1000 lines—which are the third Book of my Poem. My Ideas with respect to it I assure you are very low—and I would write the subject thoroughly again—but I am tired of it and think the time would be better spent in writing a new Romance which I have in my eye for next summer—Rome was not built in a day—and all the good I expect from my employment this summer is the fruit of Experience which I hope to gather in my next Poem.'

Coming back in the first week of October to Hampstead, whither his brothers had by this time also returned from a trip to Paris, Keats was presently made uncomfortable by evidences of discord among his friends and reports of what seemed like disloyalty on the part of one of them, Leigh Hunt, to himself. Haydon had now left the studio in Great Marlborough Street for one in Lisson Grove, and the Hunts, having come away from Hampstead and paid a long late-summer visit to the Shelleys at Marlow, were lodging near him in the same street.

'Everybody seems at loggerheads,' Keats writes to Bailey. 'There's Hunt infatuated—there's Haydon's picture in statu quo—There's Hunt walks up and down his painting-room—criticising every head most unmercifully.' Both Haydon and Reynolds, he goes on, keep telling him tales of Hunt: How Hunt has been talking flippantly and patronisingly of *Endymion,* saying that if it is four thousand lines long now it would have been seven thousand but for him, and giving the impression that Keats stood to him in the relation of a pupil needing and taking advice. He declares in consequence that he is quite disgusted with literary men and will never know another except Wordsworth; and then, more coolly and sensibly, 'now, is not this a most paltry thing to think about?... This is, to be sure, the vexation of a day, nor would I say so many words about it to any but those whom I know to have my welfare and reputation at heart.'

During the six or seven autumn weeks spent at Hampstead after his return from Oxford Keats was getting on, a little flaggingly, with the fourth book of *Endymion,* besides writing an occasional lyric or two.

Fresh from the steadying and sympathetic companionship of Bailey, he keeps up their intimacy by affectionate letters in which he discloses much of that which lay deepest and was best in him. Writing in the first days of November he congratulates Bailey on having got a curacy in Cumberland and promises some day to visit him there; says he is in a fair way to have finished *Endymion* in three weeks; mentions an idea he has of shipping his brother Tom, who has been looking worse, off to Lisbon for the winter and perhaps going with him; and gets in by a side wind a masterly criticism of Wordsworth's poem *The Gipsies* and also of Hazlitt's criticism of it in the *Round Table.*

A fragment of another letter, dated November the 5th,

alludes with annoyance, not for the first time, to some failure of Haydon's to keep his word or take trouble about a young man from Oxford named Cripps whom he had promised to receive as pupil and in whom Bailey and Keats were interested. The same fragment records the appearance in *Blackwood* (the *Endinburgh Magazine,* as Keats calls it) of the famous first article of the Cockney School series, attacking Hunt with a virulence far beyond even the accustomed licence of the time, and seeming by the motto prefixed to it (verses of Cornelius Webb coupling the names of Hunt and Keats) to threaten a similar handling of Keats later on.

'I don't mind the thing much,' says Keats, 'but if he should go to such lengths with me as he has done with Hunt, I must infallibly call him to an Account if he be a human being, and appears in Squares and Theatres, where we might possibly meet—I don't relish his abuse.'

Some time about mid-November Keats, his health and strength being steadier than in the spring, felt himself in the mood for a few weeks of solitude and went to spend them at Burford Bridge Inn, in the beautiful vale of Mickleham between Leatherhead and Dorking. The outing, he wrote, was intended 'to change the scene-change the air—and give me a spur to wind up my poem, of which there are wanting 500 lines.' Keats dearly loved a valley: he loved even the sound of the names denoting one. In his marginal notes to a copy of *Paradise Lost* he gave a friend we find the following:—

'Or have ye chosen this place
After the toil of battle to repose
Your wearied virtue, for the ease you find
To slumber here, as in the vales of Heaven?'

There is cool pleasure in the very sound of vale. The English word is of the happiest chance. Milton has put vales in heaven and hell with the very utter affection and yearning of a great Poet. It is a sort of Delphic Abstraction—a beautiful thing made more beautiful by being reflected and put in a Mist. The next mention of Vale is one of the most pathetic in the whole range of Poetry:—

'Others, more mild, Retreated in a silent valley, sing With notes

angelical to many a harp Their own heroic deeds and hapless fall By doom of battle.'

How much of the charm is in the valley!

There, from his inmost self, speaks a poet of another poet, and as if to and for poets, deep calling unto deep. But in his every-day vein of speech or writing Keats was always reticent in regard to the scenery of places he visited, disliking nothing more than the glib ecstasies of the tourist in search of the picturesque. When he has looked round him in his new quarters at Burford Bridge he says simply, writing to Reynolds on November the 22nd, 'I like this place very much.

There is Hill and Dale and a little river. I went up Box Hill this evening after the moon—"you a' seen the Moon"-came down and wrote some lines.' 'Whenever I am separated from you,' he continues, 'and not engaged in a continuous Poem, every letter shall bring you a lyric-but I am too anxious for you to enjoy the whole to send you a particle:' the whole, that is, of *Endymion*. The sequel shows him to be just as deep and ardent in the study of Shakespeare as when he was beginning his poem at Carisbrooke in the spring. 'I never found so many beauties in the Sonnets—they seem to be full of fine things said unintentionally—in the intensity of working out conceits:' and he goes on to quote passages and phrases both from them and from *Venus and Adonis*. Next, with a sudden change of mind about letting Reynolds see a sample of *Endymion*, 'By the Whim-King! I'll give you a stanza, because it is not material in connexion, and when I wrote it I wanted you to give your vote, pro or con.'—The stanza he gives is from the song of the Constellations in the fourth book, certainly one of the weakest things in the poem: pity Reynolds had not been there indeed, to give his vote *contra*.

On the same day, November 22, Keats writes to Bailey a letter even richer in contents and more self-revealing than this to Reynolds. It gives the indispensable key both to much in his own character and much of the deeper speculative and symbolic meanings underlying his work, from *Endymion* to the *Ode on a Grecian Urn*. Beginning with a wise and tolerant reference to the Haydon trouble, and throwing out a passing hint of the distinction between men of Genius, who have not, and men of Power, who have, a proper individual self or determined character of their own, Keats passes at the close to an illuminating self-confession which is also a contrast between himself and his correspondent:—

You perhaps at one time thought there was such a thing as worldly happiness to be arrived at, at certain periods of time marked out,—you have of necessity from your disposition been thus led away—I scarcely remember counting upon any happiness —I look not for it if it be not in the present hour,—nothing startles me beyond the moment. The Setting Sun will always set me to rights, or if a Sparrow come before my Window, I take part in its existence and pick about the gravel. The first thing that strikes me on hearing a misfortune having befallen another is this—'Well, it cannot be helped: he will have the pleasure of trying the resources of his Spirit'—and I beg now, my dear Bailey, that hereafter should you observe anything cold in me not to put it to the account of heartlessness, but abstraction-for I assure you I sometimes feel not the influence of a passion or affection during a whole Week—and so long this sometimes continues, I begin to suspect myself, and the genuineness of my feelings at other times—thinking them a few barren Tragedy Tears.

Readers of *Endymion* will recognize a symbolic embodiment of a mood akin to this in the Cave of Quietude in the fourth book. But the great value of the letter, especially great as a help to the study of *Endymion* in general, is in the long central passage setting forth his speculations as to the relation of imagination to truth, meaning truth ultimate or transcendental. He finds his clue in the eighth book of *Paradise Lost*, where Adam, recounting to Raphael his first experiences as newcreated man, tells how twice over he fell into a dream and awoke to find it true: his first dream thus confirmed in the result being how 'One of shape divine' took him by the hand and led him into the garden of Paradise: his second, how the same glorious shape came to him and opened his side and from his rib fashioned a creature:

Manlike, but different sex, so lovely fair,

That what seem'd fair in all the World, seem'd now
Mean, or in her sum'd up, in her contain'd
And in her looks, which from that time infus'd
Sweetness into my heart, unfelt before,
And into all things from her Air inspir'd
The spirit of love and amorous delight.
She disappear'd, and left me dark, I wak'd
To find her, or for ever to deplore
Her loss, and other pleasures all abjure:
When out of hope, behold her, not far off,
Such as I saw her in my dream, adorn'd
With what all Earth or Heaven could bestow
To make her amiable.

It was no doubt this second of Adam's dreams that was chiefly in Keats's mind. His way of explaining his speculations to his friend is quite unstudied and inconsecutive; he is, as he says, 'continually running away from the subject,' or shall we say letting the stream of his ideas branch out into side channels from which he finds it difficult to come back? But yet their main current and purport will be found not difficult to follow, if only the reader will bear one thing well in mind: that when Keats in this and similar passages speaks of 'Sensations' as opposed to 'Thoughts' he does not limit the word to sensations of the body, of what intensity or exquisiteness soever or howsoever instantaneously transforming themselves from sensation into emotion: what he means are intuitions of the mind and spirit as immediate as these, as thrillingly convincing and indisputable, as independent of all consecutive stages and formal processes of thinking: almost the same things, indeed, as in a later passage of the same letter he calls 'ethereal musings.' And now let the poet speak for himself:—

O! I wish I was as certain of the end of all your troubles as that of your momentary start about the authenticity of the Imagination. I am certain of nothing but of the holiness of the Heart's affections, and the truth of Imagination. What the Imagination seizes as Beauty must be Truth—whether it existed before or not,—for I have the same idea of all our passions as of Love: they are all, in their sublime, creative of essential Beauty. In a Word you may know my favourite speculation by my first Book, and the little Song I sent in my last, which is a representation from the fancy of the probable mode of operating in these Matters. The Imagination may be compared to Adam's dream, he awoke and found it truth:—I am more zealous in this affair, because I have never yet been able to perceive how anything can be known for truth by consecutive reasoning-and yet it must be. Can it be that even the greatest Philosopher ever arrived at his Goal without putting aside numerous objections?

However it may be, O for a life of Sensations rather than of Thoughts! It is 'a Vision in the form of Youth,' a shadow of reality to come—and this consideration has further convinced me,—for it has come as auxiliary to another favourite speculation of mine,—that we shall enjoy ourselves hereafter by having what we called happiness on Earth repeated in a finer tone. And yet such a fate can only befall those who delight in Sensation, rather than hunger as you do after Truth. Adam's dream will do here, and seems to be a Conviction that Imagination and its empyreal reflexion, is the same as human life and its spiritual repetition.

But, as I was saying, the simple imaginative Mind may have its rewards in the repetition of its own silent Working coming continually on the Spirit with a fine Suddenness. To compare great things with small, have you never, by being surprised with an old Melody, in a delicious place by a delicious voice, *felt* over again your very speculations and surmises at the time it first operated on your soul? Do you not remember forming to yourself the Singer's face—more beautiful than it was possible, and yet, with the elevation of the Moment, you did not think so? Even then you were mounted on the Wings of Imagination, so high that the prototype must be hereafter—that delicious face you will see.

There is one sentence in the above which gives us special matter for regret. Keats speaks of 'the little Song I sent in my last, which is a representation from the fancy of the probable mode of operating in these matters.' Such a song, if we had it, would doubtless put forth clearly and melodiously in concrete imagery the ideas which Keats in his letter tries to expound in the abstract language of which he is by nature so much less a master. Of 'my last,' that is of his preceding letter to Bailey, unhappily but a fragment is preserved, and the song must have been lost with the sheet or sheets which went astray, seeing that none of Keats's preserved lyrics can be held to answer to his account of this one.

His words have a further interest as proving that now in these days of approaching winter, with his long poem almost finished, he allowed himself to digress into some lyric experiments, as in its earlier stages he had not done. External testimony and reasonable inference enable us to identify some of these experiments. Two or three lightish love-lyrics, whether impersonal or inspired by passing adventures of his own, are among the number. That beginning 'Think not of it, sweet one, so,' dates definitely from November 11, before he left Hampstead.

To nearly about the same time belongs almost certainly the very daintily finished stanzas 'Unfelt, unheard, unseen, which one at least of Keats's subtlest critics considers (I cannot agree with her) the first of his technically faultless achievements. So also, I am convinced, does that much less happily wrought thing, the little love-plaint discovered only two years ago and beginning—

You say you love, but with a voice
Chaster than a nun's who singeth
The soft vespers to herself
When the chime-bell ringeth—
O love me truly!
You say you love; but with a smile
Cold as sunrise in September,
As you were St Cupid's nun,
And kept his week of Ember.
O love me truly!—

and so forth. Here again, it seems evident, we have an instance of an echo from one of the old Elizabethan poets (this time an anonymous song-writer) lingering like a chime in Keats's memory. Listen to the first three stanzas of *A Proper*

Wooing Song, written to the tune of the *Merchant's Daughter* and printed in Clement Robinson *Handful of Pleasant Delites,* 1584:—

Maide will ye loue me yea or no?
tell me the trothe and let me go.
It can be no lesse than a sinful deed,
trust me truly,
To linger a Louer that lookes to speede,
in due time duly.
You maides that thinke yourselves as fine,
as Venus and all the Muses nine:
The Father Himselfe when He first made man,
trust me truly,
Made you for his helpe when the world began,
in due time duly.
Then sith God's will was even so
why should you disdaine your Louer tho?
But rather with a willing heart,
loue him truly;
For in so doing you do your part
let reason rule ye.

The metrical form of Keats's verses is not, indeed, the same as that of the Elizabethan song, but I think he must certainly have had the cadence of its refrains more or less consciously in his mind's ear.

A definite and dated case of a lyrical experiment suggested to Keats at this time by an older model is the famous little 'drear-nighted December' song in which he re-embodies, with new and seasonable imagery, the ancient moral of the misery added to misery by the remembrance of past happiness. This was composed, as Woodhouse on the express testimony of Jane Reynolds informs us, in the beginning of this same December, 1817) when Keats was finishing *Endymion* at Burford Bridge.

Any reader familiar with the aspect of the spot at that season, when the overhanging trees have shed their last gold, and spars of ice have begun to fringe the sluggish meanderings of the Mole, will realise how deeply the sentiment of the scene and season has sunk into Keats's verse. Well as the piece is known, I shall quote it entire, not in the form in which it is printed in the editions, but in that in which alone it exists in his own hand-writing and in the transcripts by his friends Woodhouse and Brown:—

In drear-nighted December,
Too happy, happy tree,
Thy branches ne'er remember
Their green felicity:
The north cannot undo them,
With a sleety whistle through them;
Nor frozen thawings glue them
From budding at the prime.
In drear-nighted December,
Too happy, happy brook,
Thy bubblings ne'er remember
Apollo's summer look;
But with a sweet forgetting,
They stay their crystal fretting,
Never, never petting
About the frozen time.
Ah! would 'twere so with many
A gentle girl and boy!
But were there ever any
Writh'd not at passed joy?
The feel of not to feel it,
When there is none to heal it,
Nor numbed sense to steel it,
Was never said in rhyme.

Do readers recall what the greatest of metrical magicians, who would be so very great a poet if metrical magic were the whole of poetry, or if the body of thought and imagination in his work had commonly half as much vitality as the verbal music which is its vesture, —do readers recall what Mr Swinburne made of this same measure when he took it up half a century later in the *Garden of Proserpine*?

But in attending to these incidental lyrics we risk losing sight of what was Keats's main business in these weeks, namely the bringing to a close his eight months' task upon *Endymion*. In finishing the poem he was only a little behind the date he had fixed when he wrote its opening lines at Carisbrooke:—

Many and many a verse I hope to write,
Before the daisies, vermeil rimm'd and white,
Hide in deep herbage; and ere yet the bees
Hum about globes of clover and sweet peas,
I must be near the middle of my story.
O may no wintry season, bare and hoary,
See it half finish'd: but let Autumn bold,
With universal tinge of sobre gold,
Be all about me when I make an end.

The gold had almost all fallen: in the passage in which Keats makes Endymion bid what he supposes to be his last farewell to his mortal love it is the season itself, the season and the autumnal scene, which speak, just as they spoke in the 'drear-nighted December' lyric:—

The Carian
No word return'd: both lovelorn, silent, wan,
Into the vallies green together went.
Far wandering, they were perforce content
To sit beneath a fair lone beechen tree;
Nor at each other gaz'd, but heavily
Por'd on its hazle cirque of shedded leaves.

and again:—

At this he press'd
His hands against his face, and then did rest
His head upon a mossy hillock green,
And so remain'd as he a corpse had been
All the long day; save when he scantly lifted
His eyes abroad, to see how shadows shifted
With the slow move of time,—sluggish and weary
Until the poplar tops, in journey dreary,
Had reach'd the river's brim. Then up he rose,
And slowly as that very river flows,
Walk'd towards the temple grove with this lament:
'Why such a golden eve? The breeze is sent

Careful and soft, that not a leaf may fall
Before the serene father of them all
Bows down his summer head below the west.
Now am I of breath, speech, and speed possest,
But at the setting I must bid adieu
To her for the last time. Night will strew
On the damp grass myriads of lingering leaves,
And with them shall I die; nor much it grieves
To die, when summer dies on the cold sward.'

That point about making, as it were, a dial-hand of a certain group of poplars with their moving shadows would have a special local interest if one could find the place which suggested it. The sun sets early in this valley in the winter. I know not if there is any group of trees still standing that could be watched thus lengthening out its afternoon shadow to the river's edge.

Opposite the last line in the manuscript of *Endymion* Keats wrote the date November 28, whence it would appear that it had taken him some ten days at most to complete the required five hundred lines. He did not immediately leave Burford Bridge, but stayed on through the first week or ten days of December, setting to work at once, it would appear, on the revision of his long poem, and composing, we know, the 'drear-nighted December' lyric, and perhaps one or two others, before he returned to the fraternal lodgings at Hampstead.

The scheme of a winter flight to Lisbon for the suffering Tom had been given up, and it had been arranged instead that George should take him to spend some months at Teignmouth. They were to be there by Christmas, and Keats timed his return so as to be with them for a week or two at Hampstead before they started. *Endymion* was not published until the following April, but inasmuch as with its completion there ends the first, the uncertain, experimental, now rapturously and now despondently expectant phase of Keats's mind and art, let us make this our opportunity for studying it.

Chapter 16

Cloudy Trophies

In July, 1820, John Keats published his third and final book, "Lamia, Isabella, The Eve of St. Agnes and Other Poems." He had no reason to expect that it would be a success, with either the public or the critics: in his short career, the twenty-four-year-old poet had known nothing but rejection on both fronts. After his first book, "Poems," appeared, in 1817, his publishers, the brothers Charles and James Ollier, refused to have anything more to do with him.

In a letter to the poet's brother George, they wrote, "We regret that your brother ever requested us to publish his book, or that our opinion of its talent should have led us to acquiesce in undertaking it." They went on, "By far the greater number of persons who have purchased it from us have found fault with it in such plain terms, that we have in many cases offered to take the book back rather than be annoyed with the ridicule which has, time after time, been showered upon it."

When Keats's long poem "Endymion" came out, the following year, from a different firm, the ridicule was even worse, and far more public. The leading Tory magazines of the day published savagely satirical reviews, linking the poem's undisciplined exuberance with its author's working-class origins. Keats was the son of a stable-keeper, and he had trained as an apothecary: no wonder, the critics smirked, that he had fallen in with the sentimental "Cockney School" of poets, led by the radical journalist Leigh Hunt. Keats's class and his liberal politics were enough to damn him sight unseen, as the *Quarterly Review* made clear when its critic admitted that he had not bothered to read "Endymion" to the end: "If any one should be bold enough to purchase this 'Poetic Romance,' and so much more patient, than ourselves, as to get beyond the first book, and so much more fortunate as to find a meaning, we entreat him to make us acquainted with his success." *Blackwood's Magazine* said, "It is a better and a wiser thing to be a starved apothecary than a starved poet; so back to the shop Mr John, back to 'plasters, pills, and ointment boxes.'"

After all this, Keats could hardly have been optimistic about his third volume. He grumbled in a letter to George that he ought to give up writing and become a doctor—it couldn't be any "worse than writing poems, & hanging them up to be fly-blown on the Review shambles." But he must have been particularly unsettled by a review in the *Literary Chronicle and Weekly Review*. The book was not mocked; the anonymous critic simply said, more in sorrow than in anger, that it was not much good. "We confess this volume has disappointed us; from Mr Keats's former productions, we had augured better things," the paper opined. "We are confident he can do better."

To Keats, this would have been the bitterest verdict of all, for by the summer of 1820 he knew that he would not live to publish another book. Tuberculosis was slowly choking him to death, leaving him without the will or the energy to work: he had written almost no poetry since late the preceding year, and would write no more before he died, in Rome, in February, 1821. Keats continued to believe that, with time and study, he would have become a great poet, but he was starting to agree with the critics that nothing he had written could prove it. A year before his death, he wrote that he was reconciled to failure: " 'If I should die,' said I to myself, 'I have left no immortal work behind me—nothing to make my friends proud of my memory—but I have lov'd the principle of beauty in all things, and if I had had time I would have made myself remember'd.' "

Of all the piteous elements in Keats's story, none is more distressing than the idea that he went to his grave convinced of his failure. For Keats's last book, in addition to the three masterpieces named in its title, included a series of odes—"Ode to a Nightingale," "Ode on a Grecian Urn," "Ode to Psyche," "Ode on Melancholy," and "To Autumn"—that are now universally regarded as among the greatest poems in the English language. If any single book ever earned its author immortality, it was this one. And, as Stanley Plumly points out in "Posthumous Keats", his moving new study of the poet's work and legend, "one could form a considerable collection from what was left out of this last book." Some of Keats's best poems, including "La Belle Dame Sans Merci," were never collected in his lifetime.

Did Keats really believe that, having written such poems, he was a failure? The question is more urgent in his case than in any other poet's, for no writer ever yearned for fame more ardently than Keats. His ambition was all the more remarkable considering that he started life with none of the advantages of the noble Byron or the wealthy Shelley. Born in 1795, the eldest child of a prosperous working-class family, he soon learned how precarious his fortunes really were. His father, Thomas, died in a riding accident when Keats was eight years old, a blow made worse by the remarriage of his mother, Frances, just a couple of months later. The hasty marriage was brief, and when it collapsed Frances disappeared in a cloud of scandalous rumors, leaving her children in the care of their grandmother. When she came back home, a few years later, it was to die. John nursed her through the final stages of consumption, as he was to do with his youngest brother, Tom, in 1818.

Keats, orphaned at the age of fourteen, was not entirely without resources. A small legacy paid for his apprenticeship to a surgeon, after which he went on to medical school, leaving in 1816 with a license to practice as an apothecary—the lowest, most menial kind of medical man. But by then he had decided that poetry, not medicine, was his calling. In the time remaining to him—less than five years—he lived off the remains of his inheritance in order to devote himself to greatness.

From his first mature poem, the sonnet "On First Looking Into Chapman's Homer," written just before his twenty-first birthday, to his last—the dreamlike fragment "The Fall of Hyperion," which he abandoned just before his twenty-fourth—this ambition was Keats's major theme.

. In that first poem, written in the early-morning hours after a night spent reading Homer with friends, Keats evokes his dawning sense of the immense realm of poetry—"like stout Cortez when with eagle eyes / He stared at the Pacific"—and of the heroic effort required to carve out for himself one of the "goodly states and kingdoms" which "bards in fealty to Apollo hold." In the last, he records a hallucinatory encounter with the goddess Moneta, who tells him that his quest has failed, that he is not a poet but a mere dreamer:

The poet and the dreamer are distinct,
Diverse, sheer opposite, antipodes.
The one pours out a balm upon the world,
The other vexes it.

Keats offered an apparently unambiguous assessment of his short career when he told his friend Joseph Severn—a young painter who volunteered to accompany him to Rome, and nursed him through his last months—that he did not want his name to appear on his tombstone. Instead, he instructed, it should simply read, "Here lies one whose name was writ in* water."

Yet Plumly, an award-winning poet, is deeply attuned to the subtleties of poetic ambition, and he points out that the famous epitaph is not quite as resigned as it seems. "The fact that Keats did not want his name to appear on the tombstone adds only interest to the mystery of who might be buried so anonymously," Plumly writes.

"The unnamed is, after all, written in stone, not water." It is the epitaph not of a man accepting oblivion but of a poet cultivating his legend from beyond the grave. Plumly quotes Keats's publisher John Taylor, who approved of the anonymous gravestone because he foresaw "that it will be as clear an indication to posterity as the plainest, everyday inscription that one may find in Westminster Abbey."

Such moments of canny sympathy justify the unusual approach that Plumly takes in "Posthumous Keats." Instead of simply recounting the life and analyzing the poems, Plumly pursues his intuitions through a series of linked essays, all of them concerned with aspects of the poet's death and afterlife. He explores the "drawings, paintings, engravings, and sculptings" of Keats's face "by some forty separate artists," showing how he was turned into the Victorians' archetypal poet, "perfected and abstracted" into unrecognizability. He narrates Keats's last days in Rome, evoking the eerie contrast between the sensual city and the increasingly incorporeal sufferer. He shows us Keats running into Coleridge on Hampstead Heath, and quotes the older poet's prophecy: "When I shook him by the hand there was death!"

Through this interweaving of themes and episodes—a "walk around in Keats's life and art, not simply through them"—Plumly emphasizes, as a more conventional biography never could, the fatal, fated quality of Keats's career. He shows how Keats, in a way that feels unique even among the doomed Romantics, became posthumous while he was still alive. In one sense, this is because he knew that he was dying long before death arrived. Thanks to his medical training, and to his experiences nursing his mother and his brother, Keats was well acquainted with the symptoms of tuberculosis. On February 3, 1820, when he fell into a coughing fit and brought up blood on the sheets, he had no doubt what was in store. "I know the colour of that blood. It's arterial blood," his friend Charles Brown remembered Keats saying. "That blood is my death-warrant. I must die."

For the next year, Keats went along with his doctors' various treatments—bloodletting, starvation diets, complete avoidance of excitement. He agreed to leave England, on the slight chance that Italian air would cure him. But he could never trick himself into believing that his first, fatal diagnosis was mistaken. In November, 1820, in the last letter Keats wrote, he told Brown, "I have an habitual feeling of my real life having past, and that I am leading a posthumous existence."

Keats is hardly the only nineteenth-century writer to have died a lingering, consumptive death; what sets him apart is that his art, from the beginning, was connected with the imagination of death, especially his own. Like Socrates, he could have said that his life was a long preparation for death, so often had he written about it in poems and letters. Keats's "posthumous existence," one might say, began at the moment he became a poet.

That is why, after he died, so many of his lines began to look eerily like premonitions. In "Sleep and Poetry," an early attempt at a long poem, Keats was already bargaining for time to complete his work: "O for ten years, that I may overwhelm / Myself in poesy; so I may do the deed / That my own soul has to itself decreed." By the age of twenty-one, he was imagining what it would be like to lie in his grave:

If I do fall, at least I will be laid
Beneath the silence of a poplar shade;
And over me the grass shall be smooth shaven;
And there shall be a kind memorial graven.

The union of poetry and death, in Keats's work, only became more intimate as his powers grew. In March, 1817, shortly after the Parthenon marbles taken from Greece by Lord Elgin had been put on display at the British Museum, the painter Benjamin Robert Haydon took Keats to see them. A day or two later, Keats recorded his impressions in a sonnet that invokes death in its very first line:

My spirit is too weak—mortality
Weighs heavily on me like unwilling sleep,
And each imagined pinnacle and steep
Of godlike hardship, tells me I must die.

Why should the sublimity of these images immediately have reminded Keats that he must die? One might as well ask why he exclaimed, in another poem, "Verse, Fame, and Beauty are intense indeed, / But Death intenser." Or why, in one of his last poems, a love sonnet, he yearned "Still, still to hear her tender-taken breath, / And so live ever—or else swoon to death."

It would be easy to explain Keats's preoccupation with death by assigning it a straightforward biographical cause. Many biographers and critics have pointed to the early loss of his father, and to his bedside view of his mother's and brother's slow deaths. Then, there was his experience as a student at Guy's Hospital, in London, where he attended gruesome surgeries and dissections. To an extent unusual even by the grim standards of his time, Keats was constantly surrounded by death and dying. It was only rational for him to wonder if he, too, would die young. This was, in fact, the subject of one of his most moving sonnets—the one that begins, "When I have fears that I may cease to be / Before my pen has gleaned my teeming brain."

Plumly unsparingly relates the bodily reality of Keats's sickness and death. His description of the poet's last days is as clinical as anything Keats might have observed while walking the wards:

First the coughing of "a fawn coloured mixture" of blood and phlegm, then diarrhea, then laxity and gripping of the bowels, then food—warm milk and pudding—then the cycle starting over again, with the sweats lasting usually until dawn. The waste itself was mucus, nothing solid, though in the struggle not to go under, the expectorations seemed to thicken and boil in the throat.

After all this, it might seem insane to assert, with Wallace Stevens, that "death is the mother of beauty." Yet Stevens was the most Keatsian of twentieth-century poets, and his famous line is absolutely faithful to Keats's belief. To understand why Keats meditated so constantly on death, it is not necessary to look to his biography; one need only listen to his writing.

When it first dawned on him that he might be a poet, Keats—well aware of his class disadvantages and his limited education—was almost frightened by his audacity. "I have asked myself so often," he wrote to Leigh Hunt in May, 1817, "why I should be a Poet more than other Men,—seeing how great a thing it is." But it did not take long for Keats to sense that his gifts were equal to his ambition. Bad reviews in the quarterlies, he once told George, were "a mere matter of the moment—I think I shall be among the English Poets after my death."

But Keats was not content to wallow in visions of glory. Once he took fame as his destiny, he began to question its value and purpose. This is a kind of self-questioning that comes to most poets only in middle age, if it comes at all. To Keats, who compressed the experience of a lifetime into a career of five years, it came in his early twenties. And it led him inevitably to the paradox of posthumousness, the way that immortality is gained only at the price of mortality.

"There is an awful warmth about my heart like a load of Immortality," Keats once declared. Yet he recognized that no dead poet, however famous, can actually enjoy his fame, as he acknowledged in a bitter sonnet to Robert Burns: "Yet can I gulp a bumper to thy name— / O smile among the shades, for this is fame!".

For art to deserve the supreme value that Keats assigned it, it must mean something more than the glorification of the artist. Beauty must be a good in its own right, even a metaphysical principle. In serving beauty, Keats came to believe, he was in some obscure way serving the divine, not just his own ambitions. Finally, he decided, "I should write from the mere yearning and fondness I have for the Beautiful even if my night's labours should be burnt every morning and no eye ever shine upon them."

This worship of the beautiful has often appeared, to Keats's detractors, as crass sensuality. A critical trope connecting Keats's luxuriant language with his low origins has been remarkably durable. In Matthew Arnold's view, Keats's love letters displayed "the entire want of tone, the abandonment of all reticence and all dignity, of the merely sensuous man, of the man who 'is passion's slave.' ... One is tempted to say that Keats's love-letter is the love-letter of a surgeon's apprentice." In the same vein, W. B. Yeats wrote, "I see a schoolboy when I think of him, / With face and nose pressed to a sweet-shop window," a boy "poor, ailing and ignorant, / Shut out from all the luxury of the world, / The coarse-bred son of a livery-stable keeper."

Yeats was thinking of passages like the one from "The Eve of St. Agnes," in which Keats conjures up "a heap / Of candied apple, quince, and plum, and gourd, / With jellies soother than the creamy curd, / And lucent syrups, tinct with cinnamon."

So sternly does the literary superego command the sublimation of these childish pleasures that, even today, Plumly sounds suspicious of the "luxury, drapery, weft, and rich weave" of Keats's romances. Such lusciousness strikes him as "middle-brow" and "enabling," the side of Keats that the Victorians loved—tendencies that "reinforce rather than resist convention."

There is no such enabling to be found, however, in the great odes. Written between April and September of 1819, these five poems represent the apex of Keats's achievement, because they heighten almost beyond endurance the tension between beauty and death.

Keats is not content to give either of these competing drives a simple victory. He does not say that beauty is defeated by the inevitability of death, or that death is an illusion that beauty's radiance can dispel. Instead, the poems are a series of sustained balances: in the "Grecian Urn," between "heard melodies" and those "unheard," the "sensual ear" and the "spirit"; in the "Nightingale," between "the weariness, the fever, and the fret" of human life and the "ecstasy" of song. In the last stanza of the "Ode on Melancholy," these opposites join in a mysterious avowal:

Ay, in the very temple of Delight
Veiled Melancholy has her sovran shrine,
Though seen of none save him whose strenuous tongue
Can burst Joy's grape against his palate fine;
His soul shall taste the sadness of her might,
And be among her cloudy trophies hung.

To be defeated by sorrow, in this poem, is to triumph over it. The poet's reward is no longer to collect a trophy from posterity but to become a trophy himself—as though his suffering and his pleasure were an offering to the gods.

Yet the consolations of poetry, as "Posthumous Keats" reminds us, last only as long as the poem lasts. The sublimity of the odes did not stop Keats from suffering in body and mind, or from cursing the fate that allowed him to taste the pleasures of life and art so intensely, only to snatch them away. "Keats, of all poets, cannot be divided between the artist and the man," Plumly writes. But in a sense it is precisely the violent sundering of the artist and the man that is Keats's tragedy.

The poet saw autumn as fulfillment, the season that "set budding more, / And still more, later flowers for the bees, / Until they think warm days will never cease." The man died in winter, in a foreign country, certain that his work had not kept the promises his imagination made. "Is there another Life? Shall I awake and find all this a dream?" he asked in one of his last letters home. "There must be," he decided. "We cannot be created for this sort of suffering."

Chapter 17

Ode on a Grecian Urn

Ode on a Grecian Urn is a poem by John Keats written in 1819 and first published in January 1820. It was one of Keats's "Five Great Odes of 1819" which also included Ode on Indolence, Ode on Melancholy, Ode to a Nightingale, and To Autumn. Its inspiration is partly considered to be a visit by Keats to the exhibition of the Elgin Marbles and partly related to Keats's experience with the aesthetic theories of Benjamin Haydon, Keats's friend and painter, and his collection of Grecian prints.

The lyric poem is divided into five stanzas, each with ten lines, and reflects upon the images on an ancient Grecian urn with images of Ancient Greeks to whom the narrator addresses his discourse. The poem transitions from a scene depicting a lover eternally pursuing a beloved without fulfillment to a scene that describes a village in which its people ventured off to perform a sacrifice. The final lines of the poem declare that "Beauty is truth, truth beauty," -that is all/ Ye know on earth, and all ye need to know", a line which has provoked critical consideration.

Ode on a Grecian Urn was composed at a leisurely pace. The actual date when Keats wrote the ode, along with *Ode on Indolence, Ode on Melancholy* and *Ode to a Nightingale* is unknown because he only dated the poems as being written during May 1819. However, he worked on the four poems together and they are united in both their stanza forms and their themes. The exact order of the poems is uncertain, but they form a sequence within their structures although the actual order of the poems within the sequence is unnecessary.

While Keats was writing *Ode on a Grecian Urn* and the other poems, his friend Charles Brown was busy transcribing copies of the poems and then submitting them to Richard Woodhouse.

The creation of the ode could not have happened until after Benjamin Haydon's articles on in the *Examiner* on 2 May and 9 May 1819, because both articles influence the theme of the poem. In the first article, Haydon's influence is found in his description of Greek sacrifices and worships along with an emphasis on a boy who is "wholly absorbed in the harmony of his own music" and that "all classes were crowding to sacrifice". The second article contrasts Raphael and Michelangelo, and Michelangelo's art "look as if they were above the influence of time; they seem as if they would never grow old, and had never been young". Later in the article, he described how medieval sculptures had an "immoveable stillness a look as if the figures were above the troubles of life, and saw through the imbecillity of appetite or passion". When the *Examiner* published Keats's ode, the articles by Haydon were also reprinted.

The relationship between Haydon and Keats proved as a strong influence on Keats's poems, and it was at Haydon's office that Keats was able to see various collections of prints that contained imaged Greek artwork including urns. One such work was an engraving by Henry Moses, which Keats most certainly knew. This experience recalled in Keats's mind his early experience with the Elgin Marbles: the exhibition of Greek artifacts on display at the British Museum, which was also the inspiration for his sonnet titled "On Seeing the Elgin Marbles". Keats's inspiration was not limited to simply Haydon or his first hand experience of the Elgin Marbles, but to many other contemporary sources.

STRUCTURE

The ode is an ancient form originally written for musical accompaniment. In general, the ode of the Romantic genre is a poem of 30 to 200 lines that meditates progressively upon or directly addresses a single object or condition. *Ode on a*

Grecian Urn follows a strict structural pattern with each stanza containing 10 lines with ten syllables. The complex rhyme scheme of the poem shows a high level of complexity common among odes of Keats' time.

Line Groupings

- The first four lines of every stanza have a structure of ABAB
- The remaining 6 lines of the First and Last stanza follow a pattern of CDEDCE
- The Third and Fourth stanzas end with a structure of CDECDE
- The Second stanza ends CDECED

The first four lines of each stanza are a Shakespearian based quatrain and the last six lines are a Miltonic based sestet.

The word "ode" itself is of Greek origin, meaning "sung." While ode-writers from antiquity adhered to rigid patterns of strophe, antistrophe, and epode, the form by Keats's time had undergone enough transformation that it really represented a manner rather than a set method for writing a certain type of lyric poetry. Keats' odes seek to find a "Classical balance" between two extremes, and in the structure of *Ode on a Grecian Urn*, these extremes are the symmetrical structure of Classical Literature and the asymmetry of Romantic Poetry. The use of the ABAB structure in the beginning lines of each stanza represents a clear example of structure found in Classic literature, and the remaining six lines appear to break free of the traditional poetic styles of Greek and Roman odes.

POEM

In the first and last stanza of *Ode to a Grecian Urn* the poet addresses the urn itself from an outward perspective, allowing the narrator to speak directly to the object and to the reader at once. In the middle three stanzas, the poem focuses on the individuals painted on the urn and the relationship between the individual and art. The narrator silences the urn by describing it as the "bride of quietness", which allows him to speak for it using his own impressions. The narrator addresses the urn by saying:

Thou still unravished bride of quietness!
Thou foster-child of silence and slow time (lines 1-2)

because it is born from stone and made by the hand of an artist who does not communicate through words. As stone, it is able to slow time and become an eternal piece of artwork. As eternal, the urn is capable of producing a story that is outside of time, and that "sylvan historian" expresses

A flow'ry tale more sweetly than our rhyme:
What leaf-fringed legend haunts about thy shape
Of deities or mortals, or of both,
In Tempe or the dales of Arcady?
What men or gods are these? What maidens loth?
What mad pursuit? What struggle to escape?
What pipes and timbrels? What wild ecstasy? (lines 4-10)

The questions are too ambiguous to create a definite scene, but elements of it are revealed. There is a pursuit and a strong sexual element.

The melody accompanying the pursuit is intensified in the second stanza:

Heard melodies are sweet, but those unheard
Are sweeter; therefore, ye soft pipes, play on;
Not to the sensual ear, but, more endeared,
Pipe to the spirit ditties of no tone: (lines 11-14)

There is a hint of a paradox in which indulging causes someone to only want more and a soundless music is desired by the soul. There is also a stasis that prohibits the characters on the urn from ever being fulfilled:

Bold Lover, never, never canst thou kiss,
Though winning near the goal -yet, do not grieve;
She cannot fade, though thou hast not thy bliss,
For ever wilt thou love, and she be fair! (lines 17-20)

In the third stanza, the narrator begins by speaking to a tree, which will ever hold its leaves and will not "bid the Spring adieu." The paradox of life versus lifelessness extends beyond the lover and the fair lady and takes a more temporal shape as three of the ten lines begin with the word "forever." J. W. Myns Carr describes this phenomenon in "The Artistic Spirit of Modern Poetry"

Men and women perfect in the flesh, with their feet on perfect flowers, move across his fancy as in twilight. The poet has reached to their perfection, and returns laden with rich memories of the senses, but, being of his time, he could not cast of the somber uncertain cloud that hid the sun.

The unheard song never ages and the pipes are able to play forever, which leads to the lovers, nature, and all involved to be

For ever panting and for ever young;
All breathing human passion far above,
That leaves a heart high-sorrowful and cloyed,
A burning forehead, and a parching tongue. (lines 28-30)

A new paradox arises in these lines because, according to Harold Bloom, "A mouth that has no moisture and no breath may be able to summon breathless mouths, but it can as easily be called death-in-life as life-in-death".

In order to overcome this merged life and death paradox, the poem shifts to a new scene with a new perspective: The fourth stanza opens with the sacrifice of a virgin cow, an image that appeared in the Elgin Marbles, and Douglas Bush suggests that Keats could be drawing this image from the "lowing heifer" in the marbles, from Claud's *Sacrifice to Apollo,* or Raphael's cartoon "The Sacrifice at Lystra", which was also on display at the British Galery in the spring of 1819.

Who are these coming to the sacrifice?
To what green altar, O mysterious priest,
Lead'st thou that heifer lowing at the skies,
And all her silken flanks with garlands drest?
What little town by river or sea-shore,
Or mountain-built with peaceful citadel,
Is emptied of its folk, this pious morn?
And, little town, thy streets for evermore
Will silent be; and not a soul to tell
Why thou art desolate, can e'er return.(lines 31-40)

All that exists in the scene is a procession of individuals, and the narrator conjectures on the rest. The alter and town exist are part of a world outside of art, and the poem challenges the limitations of art through describing their possible existence. The questions are unanswered because there is no one who can ever know the true answers as the locations are not real.

With the final stanza, according to Bloom, "Keats begins... by reminding himself that it is only the artifice of eternity before him" when he says:

O Attic shape! Fair attitude! with brede
Of marble men and maidens overwrought,
With forest branches and the trodden weed;
Thou, silent form, dost tease us out of thought
As doth eternity: Cold pastoral! (lines 41-45)

There is a limit within the audience to comprehend the eternal scene, but the silent urn is still able to speak. The story it tells is both cold and passionate, and it is able to help mankind:

When old age shall this generation waste,
Thou shalt remain, in midst of other woe
Than ours, a friend to man, to whom thou sayst,
"Beauty is truth, truth beauty," -that is all
Ye know on earth, and all ye need to know. (lines 45-50)

Although the poem does not include the subjective involvement of the poet, the urn within the poem requires a human observer, as Walter Jackson Bate puts it: "the very origin of the urn presupposed the hope that it would be rescued into full existence by some later 'greeting of the Spirit." The poem captures aspects of Keats's idea of "Negative Capability", as the reader does not know who the figures are on the urn, what they are doing, or where they are going. Instead, the speaker revels in this mystery, as he does in the final couplet, which does not make immediate, ascertainable sense but continues to have poetic significance nonetheless. The ode ultimately deals with the complexity of art's relationship with real life.

Throughout the poem, other paradoxes emerge as the narrator compares his world with that of the Ancient Grecians on the urn. In the opening line, he refers to the urn as a "bride of quietness", which causes Cleanth Brooks to argue that Keats contrasts the urn with the structure of the ode, which was originally intended to be sung. Likewise, he points to another paradox that arises when the narrator finds immortality on the side of an urn meant to carry the ashes of the dead.

In her study of *Ode on a Grecian Urn,* Lilia Melani lists five paradoxes that lead to the ending lines on truth and beauty:

- The discrepancy between the urn with its frozen images and the dynamic life portrayed on the urn
- The human and changeable versus the immortal and permanent,
- Participation versus observation
- Life versus art

As the ending couplet is in direct contrast to many of Keats' poems, for example "La Belle Dame Sans Merci" or "Lamia", in which a man is deceived by a woman's beauty, literary critics have begun interpreting it in a new way. Critics such as Sonia Sikka conclude that the narrator, representative of Keats, is criticizing the Urn as he says that all it will ever need to know is that beauty is truth and truth beauty. This reading of the text suggests levels of both jealousy and disdain as the narrator admires the simplicity of the world depicted by the urn but finds it incapable of providing deeper meaning.

CRITICAL RESPONSE

I.A. Richards relied on the final lines of the *Ode on a Grecian Urn* to discuss "pseudo-statements" in poetry, saying:

On the one hand there are very many people who, if they read any poetry at all, try to take all its statements seriously- and find them silly... This may seem an absurd mistake but, alas! it is none the less common. On the other hand there are those who succeed too well, who swallow 'Beauty is truth, truth beauty....,' as the quintessence of an aesthetic philosophy, not as the expression of a certain blend of feelings, and proceed into a complete stalemate of muddle-mindedness as a result of their linguistic naivety.

In response to Richards, T. S. Eliot argues that the final lines were a serious blemish on a beautiful poem, and the reason must be either that I fail to understand it, or that it is a statement which is untrue. And I suppose that Keats meant something by it, however remote his truth and his beauty may have been from these words in ordinary use. And I am sure that he would have repudiated any explanation of the line which called it a pseudo-statement... The statement of Keats seems to me meaningless: or perhaps the fact that it is grammatically meaningless conceals another meaning from me.

Arthur Quiller-Couch seemingly agrees, claiming that the lines were "a vague observation—to anyone whom life has taught to face facts... actually an *uneducated* conclusion, albeit most pardonable in one so young and ardent."

Hugh Kenner, in *The Pound Era* states that Keats "interrogates an urn, and answers for it, and its last answer, about Beauty and Truth, may seem almost intolerably enigmatic" to describe what he believes to be a shortfall in Keats's ability to create a proper dialogue between the poet and the audience. Kenner uses *Ode on a Grecian Urn* to describe the difference between the protagonists found in the poems of Keats and Wordsworth and those found in the novels of 20th Century Literature.

And a novelist born half a century after Keats was to give fiction its characteristic 20th-century turn, inventing a protagonist who knew how to interrogate bloodstains, walking sticks, footprints, "Clues". (What Great issues, Watson, may hang upon a bootlace!)

To Kenner, the problem with Keats's Beauty and Truth statement arises out of the reader's inability to distinguish between the poet, his reflections on the urn, and any possible statement made by the urn. He concludes that Keats fails to provide his poet with enough characterization to be able to speak for the urn, a flaw that he considers to be corrected by Sir Arthur Conan Doyle in his portrayal of Sherlock Holmes.

The narrative of the poem that Kenner discusses is adressed in the works of Helen Vendler and Andrew Bennett. Vendler asserted that the poems were a study in aesthetics through the medium of reception as the urn was examined by the poet then re-examined by the reader, and Bennett builds on this idea by saying that "the audience is always already figured by narrative, then the intrusion of the 'otherness' of narrative into the self-identical lyric form of the ode necessarily produces an audience-effect".

Rick Rylance, in "The New Criticism", poses questions about the final lines of the poem and the direction of the word "ye" in line 50. He maintains that the ambiguity of the recipient of the Truth/Beauty statement led the New Critics to a new understanding of the final lines that was lost on Cleanth Brooks and other critics. However, he also quotes René Wellek's assertion that reducing a poem to doctrinal statement " is disastrous to understanding the uniqueness of a work: it disintegrates its structure and imposes alien criteria of value" in an attempt to show the New Critics both found value in the dissection of a poem down to simple words such as "ye" and lost the overall meaning of the poem by focusing on small excerpts of poems such as *Ode on a Grecian Urn*.

Chapter 18

Clare and the Ghost of Keats

John Clare was fascinated by both literary success and by individual authors, notably John Keats and Robert Bloomfield, whom he considered unjustly neglected. He values Keats's poems for their abstract beauties, cherishes their choice phrases and linguistic turns; but, in letters to their mutual publisher, John Taylor, he describes Keats in obscure phrases which, in his autobiography and correspondence of 1821, he reapplies to his own life.

My account of the mediated, self-reflexive and misrepresented relationship between the poets, and the importance of Keats in Clare's developing sense of his own cultural position, centres on two composite texts: "To the Memory of John Keats" and "The Fate of Genius."

Early in 1821, Clare exchanged regular letters with Taylor while writing his life story for the preface to the second collection. Whatever the subject—Clare's drunkenness and mental wanderings, his frustrating writer's block or, frequently, the detail of proofs and revisions for his forthcoming second volume—the letters convey a constant, unstated anxiety. They are constructed over the ghostly frame of speculation about Keats in the uncertain weeks before March 18, when Taylor received confirmation of Keats's death in Rome on February 23. He told Clare eight days later.

Coincidentally, John Scott, the editor of the London Magazine, was killed on February 16, in a duel with John Christie, acting for John Lockhart, the editor of Blackwood's Edinburgh Magazine. The loss was both personal and commercial, the culmination of Scott's indignation against

Blackwood's, a coincidence that contributed to the myth of Keats's having been killed by reviews in the Scottish press. A third violent occurrence underscored the relevance of contemporary literary animosity to Clare's own writing career.

On February 24, he wrote to Taylor, " Is poor Scott gone—Drakard the Editor of the 'Stamford News' has been severly beaten this week in a rather cowardly way by a person coming in with the excuse of buying a book who while D. turnd to look [for] it cudgeld him with a stick & rid off the stranger had a footman with him & is some one no doubt that the Paper has provokingly abused but who it is or for what cause he has beaten him I know not".

John Drakard, who supplied Clare with paper and books, had run a circulating library in Stamford (the market town five miles from Clare's home) and in 1830 engaged Clare as a regular contributor to his second newspaper, the Stamford Champion, having employed John Scott as editor of his first, the Stamford News. Clare's letter to Taylor, on or around March 8, demonstrates both the force of the connection and intensity of his response: "Mr G[ilchrist] tells me of Scott's death but I know all about it & about it & am as sorry for it as he can be tho I knew nothing more of the man then by his actions which tells me he had more honesty and honour then his enemey Lockhardt is a d—d knave & a coward & my insignificant self woud tell him so to his teeth—but Mr G tells me to stick to a Cudgel when I quarrel".

Octavius Gilchrist—co-founder with Drakard of the Stamford News was involved in his own controversy with the Revd William Bowles, a dispute over Pope that drew in Byron, and Clare (Barton). Taylor's report of March 9 presumably crossed in the post: "O. Gilchrist came up to attend poor Scott's Funeral which took place this Day. We heard yesterday of Keats; he was still alive, though very weak—but calmer than he had been. It was not considered that he would last many Days longer. Probably at the Time Scott died he also died". Taylor's final announcement of Keats's death in a letter to Clare on March 26, is appended with an invitation to "produce some Lines to his Memory" and a warning that the pressures of the literary marketplace are ubiquitous: "One of the very few Poets of the Day is gone—let another beware of Stamford. I wish you may keep to your Resolution of Shunning that Place for it will do you immense Injury if you do not—you know what I would say—".

Taylor's linking of Keats with Clare is not simply another admonition against excessive drinking; he is here responding to Clare's involvement with the literary controversies of Stamford. Replying to Clare's letters of March 20 and 24, he even echoes Clare's conspiratorial phraseology. On March 20, Clare bad complained, "the friends round here begin to be d—d teazing I shall shake em off ere long whatevers the consequence but I shall talk to you when I get to London about it [...]—you know who I mean without naming them—" On March 24, Clare explained that he had declined an invitation from his former champion (and Taylor's cousin) Edward Drury the previous evening because he was in no rush to return to Stamford.

The terms in which he reported Drury's enquiry—"wether I had any thing to send up to London as his brother James is down"—indicate the overlap between sociability and the practicality of literary production. Clare had no objection to such an overlap in principle—his enjoyed the communitarian spirit of Taylor and his London milieu—but relations with Drury, and with his brother James, a London printer, were strained. That Clare's letter contained his first new poem after a period of ill health, may have sharpened Taylor's anxiety to prevent Drury from insinuating himself as intermediary.

Their correspondence around the time of Keats's death expresses their need to construct an appealing biography. Eight days after Taylor reports Keats's death, Clare sent Taylor Sketches in the Life of John Clare, Written by himself & addressed to his Friend John Taylor Esqr March 1821. Taylor was impressed by Clare's prose and used this lengthy autobiographical account in his "Introduction" to The Village Minstrel, while tactfully expressing his hope that "many a year more will elapse my dear Friend before I find it useful as it will doubtless be when the Recollections of dep[arted] Genius are called for by an enquiring World." Taylor also used part of Clare's letter of March 7, 1821, concentrating on a section in which he "laments the purposed destruction of two elm trees which overhang his little cottage, in language which would surprise a man whose blood is never above temperate; but the reflection of a wiser head instantly follows". The terms parallel Clare's attribution of responsibility for his sonnet "To the Memory of John Keats" to "heart" rather than to "head." Taylor, however, to reclaim Clare as a philosopher, emphasized the "head," drawing a parallel with Pope's luxurious attachment to an old post.

In so doing he misses—for commercially appreciable reasons—the complex array of emotions and fantasies surrounding Clare's impassioned account of the threat to the trees: "I heard of Poor Scotts death by the Stamford Mercurey—Lifes not much to be regretted when we loose her she is such a lump of trouble & deception that I my self care not how soon I am done with her & if there was not such a fence of pains & heart aches between this world & death I shoud at this moment certainly be trying to break the bounds for a break neck leap into that unriddled blank of fancys terrors & confusions—my two favourite Elm trees at the back of the hut are condemned to dye [...] I shall have the 'Sketches of my Life' ready for sending you in a fortnight at most I shall be very minute in Hensons & Drurys affairs that your judgment may decide—& what I shall say you may take for the truth for I shall not withold praise unworthily or spare censure where its nessesary—I am in that muddy mellancholy again my ideas keep swimming & shifting in sleepy drowsiness from one thing to another—this letter will denote the crazy crackd braind fellow it has left behind—I do think from my soul that this comical complaint will carry me off ere long".

The letter reprises some of Clare's more obscure compliments to Keats. On June 10, 1820, for example, he had written to Taylor: "Poor Keats as a brother wanderer in the rough road of life & as one whose eye picks now & then a wild flower to cheer his solitary way who looks with his wild vain & crackd braind friend to the rude break neck hill where sits the illustrious inspirer—fame—who looks with me—as carless of her anointed few—but who as he turns away cannot help with me but heave a sigh I judge colors by complexion & for his feelings his love of nature & his genius I heartily love him". This intriguing description envisions a Parnassus, a "break neck bill" of poetic fame which Clare, like Keats in his own correspondence, treats as the comic province of an "anointed few" rendered absurdly irrelevant by the letter-writer's breathless wordplay (cf. to B.R Haydon, May 10-11, 1817; to Mrs. Wylie, Aug. 6, 1818). By the following year the comedy has turned a few shades darker; with Keats presumed to have shared Scott's fate, Clare feels his own aspiration shifting, longing to transgress metaphysical rather than literary bounds—"a break neck leap into that unriddled blank of fancys terrors & confusions".

Yet Clare remains a "crazy crackd braind fellow" with a "comical complaint", fearing for his life yet cheerfully diligent in constructing an autobiography to settle controversial issues in the history of his literary career. Writing the Sketches restored a purpose to Clare, whose complaint of January 2, 1821, had been only partially attributable to his "morning headache" after a seasonal visit to Gilchrist: "Give my respects to Keats & tell him I am a half mad melancholly dog in this moozy misty country he has latly cast behind him but I feel somthing better at least I fancy which I believe to tell truth is the whole of my complaint which I am so fussy over bytimes".

Before his greeting to Keats, he asks Taylor for advice: "only tell me my faults in long poems of the Ways in a village you last got & I shall know how to escape Shipwreck for the future with your compass I cannot feel satisfied without leading strings yet tho I think I want them less then before". In the same letter reporting on Keats's death, Taylor describes his sense of their collaborative editing: "I fancy you are at my Elbow prompting every Thought when I am correcting, and in fact I merely hold the Pen—thus it is that what I do to the Proofs is so like what you would have done that when done it hits your Ideas exactly".

Although Clare's poem seems to be a spontaneous

response to Keats's death, it was premeditated in his long, anguished anticipation of the news. Clare enlists Taylor as an approachable, constructive representative of the literary establishment: "I send you my sorrows for poor Keats while his memory is warmly felt—they are just a few beats of the heart—the head has nothing to do with them—therefore they will stand no criticism—". Clare's description of the poem as "a few beats of the heart" either denies its textuality or avows its immediacy. In the sonnet itself a more constructive organic metaphor hints at continued growth and renewal, a self-regenerating poetic which will ensure Keats's continued reputation:

The world, its hopes, and fears, have pass'd away;
No more its trifling thou shalt feel or see;
Thy hopes are ripening in a brighter day,
While these left buds thy monument shall be.
When Rancour's aims have past in nought away,
Enlarging specks discern'd in more than thee,
And beauties 'minishing which few display,—When
these are past, true child of Poesy,
Thou shalt survive—Ah, while a being dwells,
With soul, in Nature's joys, to warm like thine,
With eye to view her fascinating spells,
And dream entranced o'er each form divine,
Thy worth, Enthusiast, shall be cherish'd here,—Thy
name with him shall linger, and be dear. (Village Minstrel, II. 207)

Taylor—whose amendments are included in this version of the text—had initially replied that Clare's original draft "has only the Fault which you saw in it, too much Compression to do Justice to the Thoughts". Yet the suggestion in the fourth line of an organic continuity, based on the potential growth and reproduction of some specific mementos—"these left. buds"—which might be assumed to be textual, constitutes a material challenge to any such dualism of thought and word. This refusal of the poem to surrender its meanings to its poet sets up an uncomfortable contest, as the natural regeneration of line four disappears under a repeated co-mingling of the natural and divine spheres. The future sympathizer is both material and ideal: "a being" who "dwells" "in Nature" and who enjoys the conventional form of physical vision, and yet whose "soul," exposed to "fascinating spells," prompts an "entranced" reverie of "divine" forms. The climactic "Enthusiast" confirms this co-mingling and claims for Keats the achievement of bridging that divide, of transcending the purely physical. And yet in the end the separation is reaffirmed in the location of memory "here" and in the insubstantiality of the poet's preserved "name." The problem is that in a textual sense the "left buds" show no sign of blooming.

Clare's relationship with Keats was purely potential, a "negative capability." Although they never met, Taylor passed messages and comments between them, the reliability of which might be questioned given his habit of discouraging adverse criticism. He appears to have expected Clare to disapprove of Keats. When Clare suggested that he might not return Endymion, Taylor added "think as you will I begin to like it much". Clare's compliments begin with a letter to Taylor after his first trip to London: "give my sincere Respects to Keats & tell him I had a great desire to see him & that I like his first vol of Poems much I coud point many beauties in my thinking if I had time.

This compliment demonstrates how Clare's early gestures towards poetic community often involve his use of other writers' texts as sourcebooks. At first his admiration is fixed on individually selected "beauties," such as a "description of woody glooms" from Endymion which he quotes to Taylor, April 19, 1820 (Letters, 51). Later, after skimming the Lamia volume, he selects and copies to Hessey seven "striking" quotations.

Although he finds the new volume "not so warm as 'Endymion'" (Letters, 82), his imaginative description of Keats's technique values its variety: "I began on our friend Keats new Vol:—find the same fine flowers spread if I can express myself in the wilderness of poetry—for he la[u]nches on the sea without compass—& mounts pegassus without saddle or bridle as usual & if those cursd critics could be shovd out of the fashion wi their rule & compass & cease from making readers believe a Sonnet cannot be a Sonnet unless it be precisly 14 lines & a long poem as such unless one first sits down to wiredraw out regular argument & then plod after it in a regular manner the same as a Taylor cuts out a coat for the carcass—I say then he may push off first rate—but he is a child of nature warm & wild" (Letters, 80).

Clare's positioning of an unequipped Keats on the ocean or on Pegasus is a characteristic gesture, both Romantic fantasy and literalistic recasting of geometrical tools onto a geographical stage. In a passage of "Sleep and Poetry," which some reviews singled out for comment, Keats had identified the pedantic self-delusion of Boileau's followers, who "sway'd about upon a rocking horse / And thought it Pegasus," while feeling nothing of the storms outside. Keats continues:

But ye were dead
To things ye knew not of,—were closely wed
To musty laws lined out with wretched rule
And compass vile: so that ye taught a school
Of dolts to smooth, inlay, and clip, and fit,
Till, like the certain wands of Jacob's wit,
Their verses tallied. (Keats, 73-74 (ll.193-99))

Clare finds in Keats at this stage a new counter-cultural inspiration; using the label "child of nature," which he had previously ascribed to the local poet Anna Adcock, he contrasts Keats to Campbell and Rogers—"the critics own childern nursd in the critics garden & prund by the fine polishing knifes of the critics" (Letters, 81). In the tribute sonnet, he repeats this natural identification with the "true child of Poesy," the poet's natural credentials ensuring his continued popularity.

Reviewing Mark Storey's edition of Clare's correspondence, David Groves regrets the brevity of Clare's critical comments and their lack of sophistication: they are "invariably disappointing [...] flat, unsubtle and unsubstantiated" (Groves, 410). He complains that "[i]n Keats's poems Clare discovers 'fine flowers spread ... in the wilderness of poetry,'" eliding both the metaphorical intricacies of Clare's remarks on Lamia and—importantly—his attention to Keats as a poet developing through a particular period of time and in a particular cultural context. Overlooking the subtleties of the mediated relationship between Taylor's two prodigies, some critics seize on the issue of descriptive accuracy as the centre of a (largely imagined) dispute. For evidence, they have Taylor's report of Keats's comment on "Solitude" that "the Description too much prevailed over the Sentiment," and Clare's later complaint that "Keats keeps up a constant alusion or illusion to the Grecian mythol[og]y & there I cannot follow".

Clare's remark in letter to Herbert Marsh, the son of the Bishop of Peterborough, which survives only in draft form, is expanded in an alternative version in the Tibbles' edition of Clare's Prose: "when he speaks of woods Dryads & Fawns are sure to follow & the brook looks alone without her naiads to his mind yet the frequency of such classical accompaniment make it wearisome to the reader where behind every rose bush he looks for a Venus & under every laurel a thrumming Appollo" (Prose, 223).

Yet the letter accompanied a gift copy of Endymion, which Clare had given Marsh in 1829, alter Marsh admitted that he admired the Shelley's poetry but had not read Keats's. It reads as a partially formulated defence of Keats against the familiar "Blackwood stigma of Cockneyism."

His attack on Lockhart, cited above, is clearly motivated primarily by the death of Scott, exacerbated by Lockhart's disparaging remarks about Clare's Poems Descriptive of Rural Life and Scenery (1820) and his denunciation of Endymion (1818). While Clare would use terms from the hostile criticism against Keats in his later sonnets to Bloomfield, he used them sooner to develop his lines on Keats, in particular to consider the kinds of readings and misreadings which combine to shape a literary reputation.

The most concise and conventional symbol for an alternative literary tradition is the epitaph on the tombstone of the neglected rural poet. Clare's "The Fate of Genius" is indebted to Gray's "Elegy," to Wordsworth's figure of the Pedlar, as Helen Boden has pointed out, and to the recent death of Keats. Although he told Taylor on November 6, 1821, that the poem would "soon be started," Clare had first proposed it in a letter of May 3, 1821, just over a mouth after the news of Keats's death had reached him (Letters, 219, 187). In fact, the poem adapts and enlarges several features of Clare's tribute sonnet to Keats, which both poet and publisher had considered too condensed. The obscure reference in the sonnet to critics' accentuating Keats's faults and to minimizing his accomplishments ("Enlarging specks discern'd in more than thee, / And beauties 'minishing which few display") is echoed in "The Fate of Genius" by some obscurely personified figures:

The sexton's report that the poet's "learned friends" suspected that "malice killd him" (ll. 109-110) certainly alludes to the bitter recriminations over Keats's critical treatment. But the following lines, which address the suspicions of the general reader, begin to suggest the power of language to intervene in the familiar world. Clare recognizes the propensity of readers to literalize the poet's imagined landscapes:

'Else folks less learnd to different causes led
'Who read his books & marveld as they read
'Were he so free of ghost & fairey talks
'They thought he found them on his lonley walks
'& that some secret which he faild to keep
'Brought on their anger & his endless sleep (ll. 111-116)

This naive reading of the poet's death—as a murder perpetrated by the supernatural creatures from his own writing—is paralleled in two forms of sentimental commemoration by posthumous admirers: the daisies which grow on his grave each spring are often stolen and replanted "in garden scenes" in his memory, while the verses of his epitaph are reproduced by visitors who seek out his tombstone. Through such processes the poet's texts develop a continuing organic identity, reproducing themselves through the interest and intervention of a series of readers. Such an organic and textual afterlife might compensate for the neglect during the writer's lifetime, as Clare recognizes keenly in relation to Keats.

In their correspondence of early 1821, Clare and Taylor were in the uncomfortable position of discussing Keats's chosen epitaph—"Here lies one whose Name was writ on Water"—before they knew of his death. Both commented favourably, and the sentiment is reworked as the epitaph of genius which closes the poem:

'Here sleeps the hopes of one whose glowing birth
'Was found too warm for this unfeeling earth
'That frownd & witherd—yet the fruitfull stem
'Hides here & buds with others warm as them
'Waiting that sun to warm their bloom to smile
'& welcome heaven as their native soil (ll. 127-132)

The first two and a half lines echo Keats's recognition of a mutable world which quickly erases the record of the poet's life, but they infer that his works will indeed survive in a natural resurrection, a hybrid "heaven" which, with its sun and familiar flora, resembles "native soil."

The more concise tribute sonnet also juxtaposes trust in posterity with a celebration of the poet's earthly monuments, although there, as I have argued, the "left buds" remain textual.

Shortly after composing the sonnet, Clare wrote to Taylor of his irritation at hearing his first volume complimented as "pretty poems" (Letters, 185). He did not take offence, however, dismissing that publication as a childish plaything, and imagining the progression of his future volumes from this bud through blossom to crimson berries.

Significantly, again, the models are of organic regeneration and posthumous recognition: "in the last admiration shall let fall her muscles into reverence—like one reading a monument & with sacred enthuseasm between a smile & a tear—in pity & supprise pronounc em best of all".

This blend of pathos and rapture—which an embarrassed Clare immediately describes as "very foolish stuff" although allowing it to stand in the letter—fantasizes his own career in the mould he cast from his contemporaries, chiefly Keats. His self-description as "a crackd-braind aspiring hopfull & harmless son of the muses" recalls his earlier references to Keats, his more celebrated but less successful contemporary.

As in many of his accounts of the origins and development

of rural poets, Clare constructs and positions himself culturally, with considerable artifice, in relation to an imagined social interaction with writers whom he admired; and, just as when writing lines in honour of Keats and later, in 1823, of Robert Bloomfield, both while attempting to collect biographical tributes, he immerses himself in the language of poetic memory, focusing his awareness of reception and his developing interest in posterity through an obsessive fascination with the words of others.

Bibliography

F. Scott Fitzgerald refers to a line in *"Ode to a Nightingale"* in the title of his novel *Tender Is The Night*.

Arthur Ransome uses two references from *"On First Looking into Chapman's Homer"* in his children's books, the *Swallows and Amazons* series.

P.G. Wodehouse in his review of the first Flashman novel that came to his attention used a phrase from *"On First Looking into Chapman's Homer"*: *"Now I understand what that 'when a new planet swims into his ken' excitement is all about."*

J. D. Salinger, in his novella *Seymour: An Introduction*, introduces the reader to a certain haiku, the authorship of which he attributes to his most complex fictional creation, Seymour Glass.

The haiku reads as follows: *"John Keats/ John Keats/ John/ Please put your scarf on."* (Tuberculosis is a condition aggravated by cold weather.)

In allusion to Keat's complaint to Sir Isaac Newton for destroying the beauty of the rainbow, Richard Dawkins names his book *"Unweaving the rainbow"*

Dan Simmons's science-fiction novels of the *Hyperion Cantos* feature two characters with the cloned body of John Keats, as well as his personality (reconstructed and programmed into an AI). Some of the main themes of these novels, as well as their names, draw upon *"Hyperion"* and *"Endymion"*.

A quote from Keats appears in Phillip Pullman's novel *The Subtle Knife*, *"...capable of being in uncertainties, mysteries, doubts, without any irritable reaching after fact and reason"* (from a 21 Dec. 1817 letter by Keats on his theory of negative capability).

The popular teen series *Gossip Girl* mention Keats throughout the novels as the male protagonist Daniel Humphrey's poetic hero and is referenced numerous times by the character.

Robert Frost, in his poem *Choose Something Like a Star,* alludes to John Keats' poem Bright Star. The eighteenth line reads as follows: "*And steadfast as Keats' Eremite.*"

In 1977 author Anthony Burgess ("*A Clockwork Orange*", "*Napoleon Symphony*") recreated Keats' last days in Rome in a book entitled "ABBA ABBA".

Ann Brashares named one of her chapters in The Sisterhood of the Traveling Pants "*Heard melodies are sweet, but those unheard are sweeter; therefore, ye soft pipes, play on,*" from Ode to a Grecian Urn

In the introduction to Literary Theory, Terry Eagleton writes, "*If you approach me at a bus stop and murmur 'Thou still unravished bride of quietness,' then I am instantly aware that I am in the presence of the literary.*" What is murmured by the hypothetical bus rider is the first line of Keats' "*Ode to a Grecian Urn*".

In The Bear by William Faulkner, McCaslin Edmonds reads some lines of Ode on a Grecian Urn to Isaac McCaslin : "*She cannot fade,though thou hast not thy bliss/ Forever will thou love and she be fair!*"

Keats was mentioned in The Smiths' song "*Cemetry Gates*": "*Keats and Yeats are on your side\while Wilde is on mine*".

In pop singer Natasha Bedingfield's 2005 single "*These Words*", Keats is mentioned along with Byron and Shelley.

Keats in Hampstead, a play written and directed by James Veitch and based on the poet's time at Wentworth Place, premiered in the garden of Keats House in July 2007.

A radio play *The Mask Of Death* on the final days of John Keats in Rome written by the Indian English poet Gopi Kottoor captures the last days of the young poet as revealed through his circle of friends (Severn), his poetry and letters.

Hammersmith rock band Tellison adapt J.D. Salinger's haiku in their song "*Architects*", with the lyric "*John Keats, John*

Keats, John Keats, John, John Keats, John, Please put a scarf on".

On their 2005 album *The Runners Four*, the band Deerhoof included a song titled *"Spirit Ditties Of No Tone,"* referencing a line in Keats' poem, *"Ode on a Grecian Urn"*.

Two films about Keats's life are in pre-production as of July 2007:

A period drama about Keats's romance with Fanny Brawne titled *Bright Star*, set for release in 2008, is directed by Jane Campion and stars Ben Whishaw and Abbie Cornish in the lead roles.

A mockumentary 'grunge' musical based on Keats's letters and set in Seattle at the beginning of the 1990s, titled *Negative Capability*, directed by Daniel Gildark.

Dawson Leery from Dawson's Creek quotes Keats's poem *"Ode on A Grecian Urn"- "beauty is truth, truth beauty"* in Season 2, Episode *"The All-Nighter"*. The same Ode is quoted by Pacey in another episode of the same season, *"To Be or Not to Be..."*.

Keats's line from Book 1 of Endymion is referenced in the film *White Men Can't Jump* (1992) when a character admires a shot and says *"A thing of beauty is a joy forever. My man John Keats said that"*.

When I have fears that I may cease to be is mentioned in the film *Brief Encounter* (1945).

To Autumn is mentioned in the films *The Prime of Miss Jean Brodie* (1969) and *Bridget Jones's Diary* (2001).